Praise for *Stolen*

"This is a meticulous and finely written account of Dina Gold's struggle to seek belated justice for her mother, with all the twists and turns one would expect from a fictional detective story—but it is all true."

—E. Randol Schoenberg, attorney (*Woman in Gold*)

"Alongside *The Woman in Gold* now stands the building at Krausenstrasse 17/18 as a story of a legacy reclaimed by the tenacity of a woman determined to find justice for her relatives who suffered the horrors of the Holocaust."

—J. Edward Wright, Professor of Judaic Studies, University of Arizona.

"Dina Gold has written a crisp, page-turning nonfiction whodunit and proves herself to be an unyielding sleuth in the pursuit of justice for her family. At the same time, it is meticulously researched journalism that provides a fresh perspective on history."

—Nadine Epstein, editor and publisher, *Moment* magazine

"Her property becomes in a way the reader's property and we follow with great interest and intensity her efforts to recover not only a material legacy but the entire history of her family."

—Serge Klarsfeld, lawyer and Nazi hunter

"Dina Gold tells the fascinating story of the uphill attempts of one family—her own—to regain the property that had been stolen from them by the Nazis. It is an amazing story."

—Walter Laqueur, historian, political commentator, and author

"The Holocaust was an immense act of murder. But it was also an immense act of theft. The stolen property was seized and passed on, first by the Nazis and then by governments that followed. This is the story of a single such property."
—Walter Reich, Yitzhak Rabin Chair,
George Washington University, former Director of the
United States Holocaust Memorial Museum

"[H]er narrative is a personal one, similar to the book *The Lady in Gold* and the well-received movie *Woman in Gold*."
—*The Federal Lawyer*

"Gold's measured, compassionate prose makes it clear that it's not a tale of financial gain but one of justice and the survival of a persecuted people."
—Kirkus

"Gold's description of the veneer of legality that the Nazis used is important."
—*Los Angeles Review of Books*

"A granddaughter's grit, her investigative journalist skills, serendipity, the Germans' propensity for keeping records all combine to make a true historic adventure."
—The Jewish Press

". . . riveting, humane, and politically important."
—*Standpoint*

"[T]he story behind Dina Gold's book has not ended."
—*Jewish Chronicle*

"One is full of admiration for the author's persistence and courage in pursuing this complex claim..."
—Association of Jewish Refugees

STOLEN LEGACY

STOLEN LEGACY

NAZI THEFT AND THE QUEST FOR JUSTICE AT KRAUSENSTRASSE 17/18, BERLIN

DINA GOLD

Cover design by Tahiti Spears/ABA Design.
Interior design by Betsy Kulak/ABA Design.

The materials contained herein represent the opinions of the authors and/or the editors, and should not be construed to be the views or opinions of the law firms or companies with whom such persons are in partnership with, associated with, or employed by, nor of the American Bar Association unless adopted pursuant to the bylaws of the Association.

Nothing contained in this book is to be considered as the rendering of legal advice for specific cases, and readers are responsible for obtaining such advice from their own legal counsel. This book is intended for educational and informational purposes only.

We have made every effort to locate all copyright holders. Any errors or omissions will be corrected in subsequent editions.

Printed in the United States of America.

20 19 18 17 16   5 4 3 2 1

Library of Congress Cataloging-in-Publication Data

ISBN: 978-1-63425-427-4

Discounts are available for books ordered in bulk. Special consideration is given to state bars, CLE programs, and other bar-related organizations. Inquire at Book Publishing, ABA Publishing, American Bar Association, 321 N. Clark Street, Chicago, Illinois 60654-7598.

www.ShopABA.org

To the Memory of My Indomitable Mother,
Aviva Gold (née Annemarie Wolff)

KONRAD ADENAUER, CHANCELLOR OF THE FEDERAL REPUBLIC OF GERMANY (WEST GERMANY)

Bundestag, September 27, 1951

> *Im Namen des deutschen Volkes sind aber unsagbare Verbrechen begangen worden, die zur moralischen und materiellen Wiedergutmachung verpflichten, sowohl hinsichtlich der individuellen Schäden, die Juden erlitten haben, als auch des jüdischen Eigentums . . .*

In the name of the German people, unspeakable crimes were perpetrated which impose upon them the obligation to make moral and material amends, both as regards to the individual damage that Jews have suffered and as regards to Jewish property . . .

CONTENTS

FOREWORD

AMBASSADOR STUART E. EIZENSTAT
WASHINGTON, D.C.

As someone who has been deeply involved in Holocaust justice issues decades after the end of World War II in both the Clinton and Obama Administrations, as well as in private life, I am inspired by Dina Gold's compelling and beautifully written book about her quest to recover her family's grand six story building just yards from Checkpoint Charlie in what had been, before the fall of the Wall, East Berlin.

Her determination to fulfill what seemed the forlorn wish of her grandmother to get back the family's large property if the Berlin Wall ever fell, led her on an improbable and impressive search to become an expert in German inheritance law, find documents to prove ownership, make frequent trips to Berlin, and overcome bureaucratic obstacles.

This book is the first about a property claim in the former East Germany, and tells us much about how difficult property restitution is even today. Her family's fortune became a victim of the double-tragedy of 20th century Central and Eastern Europe: Nazism followed by Communism. The Wolff family property was forcibly sold by the Nazis and then, because it was in the Russian zone of East Berlin, was nationalized by the Communist German Democratic Republic, a misnomer if ever there were one.

There are several important lessons we discover from this impressive book. First, we learn of the lifestyle of her wealthy family in pre-

Hitler Germany, how integrated they were into the fabric of German economic life and how dramatically that changed.

Second, it demonstrates how difficult private property restitution is. It takes enormous effort, grit, determination, time and energy to pursue justice. In all the negotiations I have conducted, private property restitution and compensation has been the most difficult. I led the U.S. government's efforts during the Clinton Administration to obtain over $8 billion for Holocaust survivors or the families of victims of Nazi aggression, Jewish and non-Jewish, from Swiss and French banks for Holocaust-era accounts they never divulged; German and Austrian slave and forced labor companies who brutally employed millions of people in the service of the Third Reich, for which they had never been compensated; payments of tens of thousands of dollars to beneficiaries of insurance policies that had not been paid, often because of non-payment of premiums when the owners were in concentration camps; recovery of hundreds of Nazi-looted art pieces under the Washington Principles on Art; and the restitution or compensation for communally-owned buildings (synagogues, schools, community centers, even cemeteries). But the kind of restitution Dina Gold sought is rare. Only in the January 2001 agreement I negotiated with Austria, was there a process established for the compensation of Nazi-confiscated property, and in limited circumstances, restitution. The Austrians agreed to establish a $200 million fund and in an efficient and transparent process, almost 20,000 claims were honored. But this was the exception.

In the 2009 Terezín Declaration, where I led the U.S. delegation, and the 2010 Best Practices and Guidelines for Immovable (Real) Property Confiscated by the Nazis or Their Collaborators From 1933-1945, when I served as Special Representative of Secretary of State Clinton on Holocaust-Era Issues, we finally got over 40 nations to agree to make private property restitution more of a priority. But the pledges were not legally binding, and with few exceptions the results have been disappointing.

The reason why private property compensation and recovery has been so difficult is the irrational concern that Jews will try to get back their homes and buildings that private parties have occupied for decades. We made clear in the Best Practices and Guidelines that this is not the case. In almost all cases, the government can pay a modest percentage of the fair market value of the property. Those seeking actual restitution, as was the case for Krausenstrasse 17/18, would only be called for when the government held the building. An example of this fear is Poland, where the greatest amount of Nazi-looted property remains. I worked during the Clinton Administration with then Polish President Kwasniewski, who was genuinely committed to achieve justice in this area, but could not get the Polish parliament to pass an acceptable bill allowing claims for those living abroad, even though we emphasized this should cover not only Jewish property confiscated by the Nazis, but non-Jewish Polish property nationalized after the War. Their representative participated in every stage of the negotiation of the 2010 Best Practices agreement, but then they disavowed it months later, saying their name had been affixed to the document in error. For sure, the Polish people, Jews and non-Jews suffered grievous losses during World War II, perhaps 3.5 million Polish Jews and 3 million non-Jewish Poles. Also, it is possible for individual cases to succeed on occasion in recovering property. But the legal and cost barriers are almost insurmountable.

I remain hopeful that with new leadership in the Czech-based European Shoah Legacy Institute (ESLI), which we created in the 2009 Terezín Declaration, progress can be made. The European Union should actively encourage its member states to implement the 2010 Best Practices.

The other lesson from Dina Gold's splendid book is how now, 70 years after the Shoah, we are able to unearth new findings and discoveries, including the Gurlitt Munich art collection, and continue to seek belated justice, as in the negotiations with the French government for the deportation of Jews on the SNCF railway, who moved from France after the War. Following decades of relative neglect after the end of World War II, with the focus on the Cold War, the Holocaust remains more topical than ever, as does the sense of urgency to find creative ways to recover what was so grievously lost in the past before it is too late. In this sense, Dina Gold's remarkable work gives hope that it is never too late. Her story is a testament to the human spirit.

CAST OF CHARACTERS

MY FAMILY IN THE UK
Aviva Gold (née Annemarie Wolff), my mother
Dan Gold, my father
Adam Gold, my brother

MY FAMILY IN THE U.S.
Simon Henderson, my husband

MY FAMILY IN ISRAEL
Heinz Wolff, my mother's brother
Marion Wolff, my mother's sister
Micky Wolff, my mother's half-brother
Leor Wolff, my cousin, the eldest son of Micky Wolff

MY ANCESTORS
Heimann Wolff, my maternal great-great grandfather and founder of
   the fur business, H. Wolff
Victor Wolff, Heimann's son, my great grandfather
Lucie Wolff (née David), Victor's wife
Herbert Wolff, son of Victor and Lucie; my mother's father; my
   maternal grandfather
Nellie Wolff (née Danziger), my mother's mother; my maternal
   grandmother
Henrietta Danziger, Nellie's mother; my maternal great-grandmother
Fritz Wolff, son of Victor and Lucie, Herbert's brother
Charlotte Wolff (née Schwarz), Fritz's wife

MY MOTHER'S LEGAL TEAM IN THE UK
Hans Marcus
Dr. Sybille Steiner
Dr. Karsten Kühne

THE LAWYERS IN BERLIN FOR THE ISRAELI SIDE OF THE FAMILY
Barbara Erdmann
Suzanne Kossack

GERMAN OFFICIALS
**Representative of the German Finance Ministry in Berlin, the
Oberfinanzdirektion, Berlin**
Herr Bernt-Joachim Giese
**German Assets Compensation Agency, known as the
Vermögensamt (AROV)**
Frau Mirus
Herr Stephan Giessen
Herr Schnurbusch
Herr Moisich

U.S. OFFICIAL
Dr. David Marwell, director of the Berlin Document Center until
1994. He served as director of the Museum of Jewish Heritage in
New York City from 2000 to 2015

THE WOLFF FAMILY LEGAL TEAM IN 1930S BERLIN
Ludwig Salomon, the lawyer acting as executor of Lucie Wolff's will
(*Nachlassverwalter*)
Dr. Hans Fritz Abraham, the Wolff family lawyer (*Rechtsanwalt*)
Max Michaelis, Attorney at the Superior Court specializing in
foreclosure cases

OTHER
Dr. Kurt Hamann, chairman of the Victoria *Versicherung*
(Insurance Company)
Dr. Emil Herzfelder, Dr. Hamann's Jewish predecessor as chairman
of the Victoria.

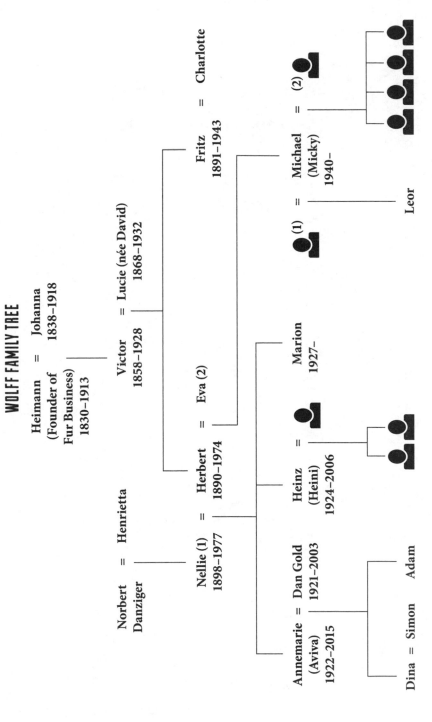

WOLFF FAMILY TREE

GLOSSARY

AMTSGERICHT
District Court (The Amtsgericht in Charlottenburg, a suburb of Berlin, was where we found many of the wills and inheritance certificates.)

ANFERTIGUNG FEINER PELZWAREN
Products made from fine fur (This is how the firm of H. Wolff described its business.)

AROV (AMT ZUR REGELUNG OFFENER VERMÖGENSFRAGEN)
Federal Office for the Settlement of Property Issues (It is usually referred to as *Vermögensamt*, or assets compensation agency, in this book.)

BUNDESMINISTERIUM FÜR VERKEHR—AUSSENSTELLE BERLIN
The Berlin Office of the Minister of the Transport (This was the name on the brass plate on the building when the ministry itself was still located in Bonn.)

BESCHEID
Decision

BUNDESARCHIV
The German National Archives
  (abbreviated as BArch in footnotes)

BUNDESMINISTERIUM
Federal Ministry

BUNDESREPUBLIK DEUTSCHLAND
Federal Republic of Germany, the full name of modern-day Germany. (Before unification in 1990 with East Germany, it was the proper name for West Germany.)

DEUTSCHE AUSRÜSTUNGSWERKE (DAW)
German Equipment Works (the SS-owned manufacturing company which used forced labor at several concentration camps)

DEUTSCHE DEMOKRATISCHE REPUBLIK (DDR)
The German Democratic Republic, a.k.a. East Germany

EINHEITSWERT
Tax value

ENTJUDUNG
Nazi term meaning "removal of Jews from the German economy"

ERBSCHEIN
Certificate of legal heirship/inheritance certificate

FINANZMINISTERIUM
Finance Ministry

GEDENKBUCH
Post-war "Book of Memory" (A West German government publication listing those German Jews killed in the Holocaust, including where and when they had been murdered.)

GESCHÄFTSHAUS
Business headquarters (The building at Krausenstrasse 17/18 was the *Geschäftshaus* of the firm of H. Wolff.)

GRUNDBUCH
Land registry document

GRUNDSTÜCK
Plot of land

HAUS DER DEUTSCHEN KUNST
House of German Art (Hitler established the organization in Munich to glorify Nazi art and denigrate modern and contemporary art, especially the work of Jewish artists.)

KOMMERZIENRAT
Honorary title for a prominent businessman (translated as "counselor of commerce")

NACHLASSVERWALTER
Executor of wills and specialist in inheritance matters (In the 1930s, Ludwig Salomon undertook this role for the Wolff family.)

OBERFINANZDIREKTION BERLIN
Regional office of the Finance Ministry

RECHTSANWALT
Lawyer (During the 1930s, the lawyer for the Wolff family was Hans Fritz Abraham.)

REICH
The German nation, also with a connotation of "German empire." (Hitler's Germany was known as the "Third Reich," and, because of this historical connection, the term is no longer used in contemporary discourse about modern-day Germany.)

DEUTSCHE REICHSBAHN, OR REICHSBAHN
German national railways. (In 1949, the German railways, which had been under the control of the Allies for four years, were returned to German national control. In West Germany, the railways were renamed

the *Deutsche Bahn*. In the Soviet area of control, which became East Germany, the railways continued to operate under the name of the *Deutsche Reichsbahn*. In 1994, after reunification, the two railway systems merged to form today's *Deutsche Bahn*.)

REICHSEISENBAHN
Literally, State Iron Road, i.e., German national railways

REICHSWIRTSCHAFTSMINISTERIUM
The Nazi-era Ministry of Economic Affairs

SCHUTZSTAFFEL (SS)
Literally, Protection Squadrons (the elite paramilitary organization of the Nazi Party, responsible for running the concentration and extermination camps).

STOLPERSTEIN (PLURAL STOLPERSTEINE)
Literally, stumbling stone (a concrete block bearing a brass memorial plaque on top placed in sidewalk outside last known address of a victim of Nazism).

STRASSE
Street

TREUHANDANSTALT
Trust agency (The state authority, which privatized the East German public sector on reunification in 1990. Created by the East German parliament before its own dissolution, the agency oversaw the restructuring and selling of about 8,500 firms with initially more than 4 million employees. For a time, it was the world's largest industrial enterprise. Property sold off included 2.4 million hectares of agricultural land and forests; the land and buildings of the former secret police, the *Stasi*; large parts of the property of the former East German military; large amounts of public housing; and such businesses as the state pharmacy network. It also took over ownership and sold property of East German political parties and state-run organizations.)

TREUHANDSTELLE
Trust authority (The East German government body, which theoretically owned property and land whose ownership could not be finally determined after the Second World War.)

VERKEHRSMINISTERIUM
Ministry of Transport

VERMÖGEN
Assets (including land, buildings, money, jewelry)

VERMÖGENSFRAGEN
Property issues; questions about assets

VERMÖGENSGESETZ
Assets Compensation Agency, the German government department, which administered, confiscated, or seized real estate and verified legal ownership. (At the time of the claim, Stephan Giessen was the deputy head. Later, the person our lawyers dealt with most often was Frau Mirus.) See AROV.

VERMÖGENGESETZ
Assets compensation law

VERSICHERUNG
Insurance

VOLLMACHT
Power of attorney

ZWANGSVERSTEIGERUNGSSACHE
Case of forced sale

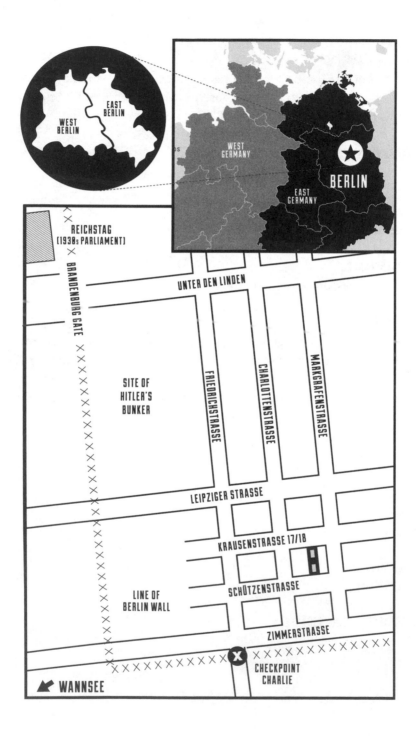

WEST BERLIN

EAST BERLIN

WEST GERMANY

BERLIN

EAST GERMANY

REICHSTAG
(1930s PARLIAMENT)

BRANDENBURG GATE

UNTER DEN LINDEN

SITE OF
HITLER'S
BUNKER

FRIEDRICHSTRASSE

CHARLOTTENSTRASSE

MARKGRAFENSTRASSE

LEIPZIGER STRASSE

KRAUSENSTRASSE 17/18

SCHÜTZENSTRASSE

LINE OF
BERLIN WALL

ZIMMERSTRASSE

CHECKPOINT
CHARLIE

WANNSEE

THE BUILDING

Krausenstrasse (Krausen Street) lies in the center of Berlin. Three streets essentially define the city: two run east-west—Leipziger Strasse (Leipzig Street) and, one-half mile to the north, the boulevard Unter den Linden (literally, under the linden trees). Running across the two, north-south, is Friedrichstrasse (Frederick Street). They are all part of *Mitte* (middle), the central borough of Germany's capital city. Krausenstrasse crosses Friedrichstrasse, just south of Leipziger Strasse.

Five hundred yards from where Friedrichstrasse intersects Unter den Linden, past the Adlon Hotel (now, as in Hitler's time, one of the most luxurious hotels in the city), stands the Brandenburg Gate. To one side of the gate is the U.S. embassy. To the south is the area where Hitler's bunker was once located. Close to it is an open space where 2,711 concrete slabs form the stark monument known as the Memorial to the Murdered Jews of Europe.

South on Friedrichstrasse, 100 hundred yards from where it crosses Krausenstrasse, is Checkpoint Charlie. Now it's just a museum and a coffee shop but, during the Cold War, when Berlin was divided between the East (the Soviet bloc) and the West (the United States and its Allies), it was the major crossing point between the two halves of the city. New buildings cover what was once stark open ground divided by barbed wire, and guarded by grim-faced soldiers and police. When international tensions grew, tanks from both the U.S. and the Soviet armies pointed their guns at each other at a range of just a few yards.

To the east, along Krausenstrasse, stands the building numbered 17/18, a combined number typical of the way properties are sometimes designated in Germany. In spoken and written German, the number comes after the name of the street, Krausenstrasse 17/18.

The building was constructed in 1908–1909, designed by the renowned architect Friedrich Kristeller, who had been commissioned by a prosperous Jewish fur trader, Victor Wolff, my great-grandfather. It was to be Victor's *Geschäftshaus* (business headquarters), the company's offices, storerooms, and sales floors. Six stories high, the building stretches back a whole block to the next street, Schützenstrasse. The rear entrance, originally numbered as Schützenstrasse 65/66 (but renumbered as 64), is almost as grand as the front. (Another block to the south, just 80 yards farther, lies Zimmerstrasse along which, during the Cold War, ran the Berlin Wall.)

Outside the front of the building on Krausenstrasse fly both the German and the European Union flags. It is now a government ministry where, immediately after German reunification in 1990, the Transport Minister had his office. Although modernized, much of the original stone facade remains, betraying its solid, architectural design. Indeed, in 1910, Krausenstrasse 17/18 featured in Volume 38 of the London publication "Academy Architecture and Architectural Review."[1] The edition devoted to German architecture contains a photograph with "H. Wolff" prominently positioned to one side of the main front entrance. (Victor's father, Heimann, my great-great-grandfather, established the firm in his name.) But this is what I know now. Back when this story all began, I knew nothing. Other than my grandmother's anecdotes, absolutely nothing. . . .

---

1. https://archive.org/details/academyarchitect38londuoft

PROLOGUE

When I was a child, my grandmother, Nellie Wolff, used to take me to a patisserie opposite Harrods department store in London and reminisce over coffee and cakes, which she could scarcely afford, about her life in prewar Germany. Often she would say, "Dina, when the Wall comes down, and we get back our building in Berlin, we'll be rich!"

I had no idea what she was talking about.

Her story of an enormous, immensely valuable, building that was rightfully ours was like a fairy tale. She might as well have been telling me about Jack and the Beanstalk or Sleeping Beauty.

I couldn't imagine that there really was such a building or that when I grew up, I would fight for years to try to win it back for our family.

PART
ONE

1

I'VE COME TO CLAIM MY FAMILY'S BUILDING

O n the afternoon of December 4, 1990, after a night in a small hotel in what was then West Berlin, I hailed a cab and gave the driver the address of a building I had never seen, Krausenstrasse 17/18. As we left the prosperity of the western sector, the apartment blocks and offices—even the people—became grayer and grimmer, like a scene from a Cold War spy movie.

We passed the remnants of the Berlin Wall, battered and covered in graffiti. Checkpoint Charlie was to my right as we drove into what had been, until only a year earlier, Communist East Berlin. Off to one side was the area where Hitler's bunker once was located. The cab turned a corner in the opposite direction and there, ahead of me, loomed a huge edifice. It looked even bigger because there was a vacant plot beside it, the remains of one of the many buildings reduced to rubble by Allied bombing during World War II. We stopped near the German flag flying at the front of the building, and I climbed out.

Several large, gold plaques were on display at the main entrance. One plaque, in German, declared the address to be the Berlin outpost of the

Federal Ministry of Transport which, at the time, was still headquartered in Bonn.

The afternoon was bitterly cold. Flurries of snow swirled about and left a light dusting on the Trabants, the East German-made cars, parked outside. It was 4:00 P.M. and daylight was fading. Workers were emerging from their offices and hurrying home.

Wrapped up in a red duffle coat with a hood and a wool hat, perhaps I didn't look like someone about to claim ownership of a vast and valuable government building. But, by then I was an investigative reporter with the BBC and, since the Wall had come down, there was talk of the new, united Germany returning property stolen from thousands of Jews in East Berlin and East Germany. I had resolved to win back my family's property, even though almost everyone close to me thought I was wasting my time.

I forced back my fears and told myself, "I'm here and I have nothing to lose." I marched through the double doors, across the marble entrance hall, and up to the receptionist—a heavy, middle-aged woman knitting inside a glass booth. I asked, in my imperfect German, if she spoke English. She looked back at me blankly and picked up the phone.

A few minutes later, a portly man in an ill-fitting brown suit appeared; he introduced himself as Herr Münch and asked what I wanted. I guessed the worst that could happen now was he would call the police and charge me with trespassing.

"I've come to claim my family's building," I told him.

Herr Münch looked nonplussed, perhaps even slightly amused. "This building is owned by the German railways—what are you talking about?" he replied in a somewhat belligerent-sounding tone.

With all the self-confidence I could muster, I delved into my coat pocket and took out the only evidence I had connecting me to this building.

"Take a look at this," I said, and handed him a copy of the page from a 1920 business directory with the listing, "H. Wolff, Berlin W8, Krausenstrasse 17/18."

"H. Wolff—Herbert Wolff," I told the man. "He was my grandfather."

In truth, I was bluffing, as investigative reporters learn to do. I could show that my grandfather had been in the fur business and once had an office in that building—but I had nothing to prove that my family had actually *owned* the building. I believed we had, and my grandmother Nellie had believed it, but, in a legal sense, I had nothing.

Still, my assertion of the name Wolff was enough to make Herr Münch turn pale. "You'd better come in," he said. He led me through the security turnstile and down the long corridor that led to the staff canteen, where he asked me to wait while he went to telephone his superiors at the head office in Bonn.

Alone in the canteen, sitting on a plastic chair surrounded by ugly, flowered wallpaper and row upon row of white metal tables, I felt I had stepped back in time. Although only a short cab ride from the bright lights and glittering shops on Berlin's main street, I was back in the drab Communist East Germany of the 1950s.

My emotions were all but overwhelming. I was in the Wolff family building—*our* building—which none of us had entered since the 1930s. I walked to a window and gazed out at the courtyard. Towering above me, I could see all six stories rising to the sky. The red-brick exterior was covered in grime and looked as if it had been untouched for decades.

This was not the magical place my mother remembered from her childhood when she visited her father, Herbert, and her grandfather, Victor, at their offices here. By then, Victor had built one of the most successful fur businesses in Germany. His agents circled the globe buying the finest animal pelts to be made into fur coats to adorn women of wealth in Europe and the United States.

One of Victor's successes had been to develop a process to dye cheap pelts, such as rabbit or even hamster, so they could pass for more expensive products, such as mink and sable. His faked furs became wildly popular. It wasn't that he fooled anyone. The coats and stoles just looked expensive and people thought they were a great bargain.

In those days, huge piles of furs awaited sale in the building's basement. My mother still recalled, as a girl of four or five, being driven with her father and grandfather in the chauffeured Mercedes to visit the company headquarters and jumping up and down on the soft exotic furs.

"You can jump on the rabbit furs but don't you go jumping on the ermine and mink," her father would warn.

After 20 minutes Herr Münch returned. He beckoned me over and we sat down at a small square table. Immediately, I detected a change.

He grasped my hand and said, "I have spoken to head office. I know now that you are telling the truth. We have been waiting for this to happen. This place has always been known as the 'Wolff Building' but no one really knew why. Head office has just informed me that they knew this building was once owned by Jews, but the person who I spoke to didn't know if anyone had survived. Tell me your story."

Thus began an extraordinary half hour. Brimming with emotion, I told him about my mother's father Herbert Wolff who, soon after Adolf Hitler took power in 1933, had taken his wife, Nellie, and their three children to live in safety in the British-controlled Holy Land, known then as Palestine. And I mentioned Herbert's brother, Fritz, an idealistic German who had refused to flee the Nazis.

Herr Münch listened intently. Every now and again, when I reached another tragic point in the story, he would interject "*Scheisse*" and then bid me to carry on. I knew enough German to translate, "Those shits!"

I told Herr Münch that it was for my mother, who at that time was retired and living in London, and for the memory of her Uncle Fritz that I was determined to win back our building.

When I finished, he said something I thought very brave for a long-time East German official, "Yes, you must get this building back for your mother."

Touched by his decency, I confessed I had found none of the official documents we would need to prove our ownership.

"Oh, the documents exist," he said. "You have to find them, but they exist." Like all German bureaucrats, he knew about the German obsession for record keeping.

I left the building walking on air. Surely, Herr Münch was right and the records were somewhere. I would find them and justice would be done.

Back in my hotel, I called my home in London and regaled my husband, Simon, also a journalist, with my day's success.

"I'm going to find the documents," I told him.

"I'll help you," he replied.

I never doubted he would.

It wasn't going to be easy, of course. We were claiming a building, which for more than 50 years successive governments—the Nazis, the Communists, and finally a united Germany—used to house entire agencies with hundreds, even thousands, of employees. I wanted the building as a matter of principle, not for any mercenary reason, but the fact remained that a six-story building in the heart of Berlin had to be worth a great deal. Governments, even the best of them, do not willingly surrender such real estate.

I had just fired the first shot in a battle that would continue for years.

2

H. WOLFF

The story begins with the birth of my great-great-grandfather, Heimann Wolff, on October 20, 1830. In 1850, at the tender age of 20, he established a fur company that for almost 80 years bore his name, H. Wolff. Unfortunately, few details of his life survive. The people who knew him are long dead, and the documents that might have memorialized him have been lost or destroyed. Still, his success makes clear that he was an ambitious, intelligent, and talented businessman. We know that he married Johanna, who was eight years younger, and their son Victor was born in 1858, when Johanna was only 20 years old.

We have a picture of Heimann as an old man; well dressed, solidly built, with a fine head of white hair and a thick moustache. In the picture, he looks satisfied; he had every right to be. By the time he died in 1913, at the ripe age of 83, he had seen his son Victor guide the company he founded to international success.

It was Victor who, in 1907, bought a large plot of land in central Berlin, a section that was home to many Jewish businesses and shops. Victor hired a top architect of the day, Friedrich Kristeller, to design the impressive building that would serve as the headquarters for the family's worldwide fur company. It took more than a year to complete and like other important structures in Berlin stretched back a whole block. With two large, interior courtyards, it extended from Krausen-strasse to the street that parallels it to the south, Schützenstrasse.

Many years later, a diligent Berlin researcher, Manolya Ezgimen, gathered facts for me about the early days of the company. Among her findings was a feature celebrating the new building in the April 1910 issue of the magazine, *Berliner Architekturwelt (Berlin Architecture World)*. Photographs make clear its scale and beauty. Inside the main entrance hall were marble flooring, carved wooden ceilings, and mirrored walls.

Victor Wolff's new building clearly elicited enormous interest in the world of architecture. It wasn't long before I found a November 1910 Berlin edition of *Blätter Für Architektur und Kunsthandwerk (Architecture and Craft Gazette)*. There was a superbly clear photo of the magnificent archway at the rear entrance on Schützenstrasse, with three little carvings and "*H. Wolff Confection Feiner Pelzwaren*" ("H. Wolff Fine Fur Products") on the wall. To my delight, there was also an accompanying article explaining that the owner had spent RM 1.2 million on the construction, which had lasted from October 1907 to March 1909. The entrance doors were bronze, and the intention was to use half the building for the H. Wolff fur business and the other half would be rented out to other firms.

As recently as October 2015, I visited the New York Public Library on Fifth Avenue where, to my amazement, I was able to read original, leather-bound, copies for the years 1908–1911 of *Fur Trade Review*, published over a century earlier in New York. I found full page advertisements for the H. Wolff fur business listing the location of the company's many representatives around the world—including in Paris, Moscow, Palermo (Italy), Copenhagen (Denmark), London, and even Melbourne (Australia)! The advertisements proclaimed the firm H. Wolff as "THE LEADING HOUSE IN GERMANY." I spotted, to my great amusement, that the telegraphic address on Victor's *Fur Trade Review* adverts was "Selfmademan Berlin".

The magazines contained multiple glamorous photos and drawings of models wearing H. Wolff–designed fur products—coats, hats, stoles, and muffs.

Volume 38, covering the years 1910–11, contains a chapter titled "Coming and Going," in which an announcement appeared that declared, "Mr Max Thorn returned from Europe on March 17 on the 'Lusitania.' A son of Mr. Victor Wolff of the firm of H. Wolff, Berlin, will arrive in New York in April to study the market under the tutelage of Mr. Max Thorn." The January 1911 edition even had a photograph of Mr. Thorn, and fellow fur trade delegates, on a visit to Washington.

Who was this illustrious Max Thorn with whom Herbert trained? Further research revealed that he was a leading light in the New York fur trade. According to the book *The Fur Trade of America and Some of the Men who Made and Maintain It* by Albert Lord Belden, Max Thorn became president of the Associated Fur Manufacturers in 1912. This body was established "To foster trade and commerce and promote the interests of those individuals, firms and corporations who are engaged in the manufacture of furs and skins and the sale of goods made therefrom."

The early 1900s was evidently the heyday of the H. Wolff fur empire. It was so successful, in fact, that in 1912 the City of Berlin conferred the honorary title of *Kommerzienrat* on Victor, denoting him as a distinguished businessman.

Meanwhile, Herbert, having returned to Berlin from New York, took responsibility for the company's offices in London, Manchester, and Glasgow.

The building at Krausenstrasse 17/18 was a monument to the success the firm H. Wolff achieved in the years leading up to World War I. That war, of course, would be a turning point for the company, for Germany, and for all of Europe.

Not only did the war seriously disrupt the fur business, it also called away Victor's eldest son, Herbert (who was already an army reservist, and had served in the Field Artillery Regiment of Prince Leopold von Bayern for a year before his trip to New York). Herbert joined some 100,000 other German Jews (of whom 12,000 were killed) who fought for the Kaiser during the First World War.

Herbert served in an artillery regiment on the Russian Front where he lost part of his hearing because, as he told it, he stood too close to the howitzers. Sergeant Wolff was awarded the Iron Cross Second Class, but he always laughed and said the army gave that honor to everyone. After catching typhus and subsequently being hospitalized for four months in 1916, Herbert was sent to an English language interpreters' school where he passed his exam "very well." He would later tell stories of life in the trenches, such as how the soldiers would use string to hang meat above the ground so the rats wouldn't steal their dinner. At the end of the war, Herbert returned to work for his father.

No record has turned up to show whether Herbert's younger brother, Fritz, served in the war. Almost certainly, as a pacifist and a Communist—and an engineer perhaps needed for vital war work in a factory rather than as cannon fodder—he would have avoided service.

Economic and political forces unleashed by the war hurt the Wolff business and countless others long after the shooting stopped. The 1919 Treaty of Versailles imposed both loss of territory and huge reparations on Germany. The Allies decreed the defeated nation pay compensation that, valued in today's money, amounted to more than $400 billion. American and British leaders counseled against these punitive demands but the French, who had suffered terribly in the war and shared a border with Germany, insisted.

These financial strictures outraged and embittered German citizens. Even though Germany did not pay the full amount demanded, the payments it did make were enough to wreck its economy, which led to soaring inflation and widespread unemployment. The economic disaster hastened the rise of Hitler. The French, by demanding such draconian revenge, helped create a monster which, two decades later, accomplished the military defeat of France—and the humiliating occupation of Paris—by a resurgent Germany.

The business environment was dire, as reflected in H. Wolff company reports that Victor wrote in 1919, 1920, and 1921 titled "Special Survey for the Trade in Furs." His words spoke with admirable candor about the challenges his company faced in the postwar world.

A few highlights:

1919: "The New Year brought fresh domestic political problems for the company. Although the National Assembly was elected without difficulty, pessimists who believed no peaceful future existed seemed to be correct. No prudent businessman could have faith in a resurgence of commercial fortunes. Under these conditions, prices fell but still no one was willing to buy."

Further on in his report, Victor recounted how representatives of H. Wolff visited the fur fair in Utrecht, Holland, between February 26 and March 8 ". . . but it was not well attended." Next was the Lyon trade fair but this was "a big fiasco" and then from March 15–27 was the Lucerne fair. "Everyone was hoping there would be businessmen from England and France but England refused to issue visas and so no one came and France sent only five businessmen. The Frenchmen were really dismissive towards the Germans."

1920: "Since the beginning of the World War, German commercial life in general and particularly the fur industry has never had such an unclear future as in January 1920."

A major worry was the falling value of the German mark, while at the same time having to deal with the ever-rising price of furs, silk, cloth, and wages.

The April 1920 entry refers to the failed *Kapp Putsch* that had taken place the previous month in an attempt by right-wingers to over-throw the Weimar government of Friedrich Ebert. Victor referred to this as "The insane military coup" that had "greatly disrupted the further growth of the entire German economy." ("*Der wahnsinnige militärische Putsch hat die ruhige Weiterentwickelung der gesamten deutschen Wirtschaftslage stark erschüttert.*")

All of this political disruption led to a situation in April 1920 where the currency's buying power had worsened.

In his May report, Victor wrote that not only his business, but also all German companies were suffering from "uncertain and speculative foundations."

The start of Victor's January 1921 report declares, "The current situation of the whole market in our industry can only be described in one single word 'uncertain.'" The new season had begun but he was unable to say whether prices would remain stable, either within Germany or abroad. He predicted he would have a better idea ". . . after the London auction later in January."

Yet, he allowed himself a hint of optimism when he wrote that he had purchased many furs from America and would soon be able to supply his salesmen with "an excellent collection" and many new products. He appealed to his friends in the business world to send their orders and promised to offer very attractive prices.

Toward the end of his report for 1921, Victor took the opportunity to make a political comment about the state of global unemployment. "The biggest political issue in Germany is unemployment though not only here but also across the entire world." He described how in Switzerland there were 134,000 people out of work, in the Soviet Republic 2,125,000 people were without work, and in the United States 4 to 5 million people were unemployed, and Victor noted, ". . . the President wants to convene a special conference to address the problem."

An English language version of a lavishly illustrated Wolff company brochure declared that F. G. Tanner of 72 Oxford Street, London W1—still a prime business address today—represented H. Wolff in Britain. In stilted language, it said, "The actual political and commercial situation still shows a depression of the whole world's trade." Noting the weakness and fluctuations of the German mark, it goes on to report: ". . . it has become more and more necessary to calculate and to sell in foreign currency, principally in [British pounds] sterling."

The currency fluctuations had its advantages, too. "But still the prices quoted in Germany are by comparison very advantageous as the cost of production and overhead charges have very much declined when reckoned with the actual currency rate."

Victor Wolff declared in the brochure, ". . . international commercial confidence is increasing, and this fact as well as the hope and keen desire for peace in all Europe are indeed conditions which cannot be overlooked and which are showing the way out of the chaos."

My mother was always skeptical that Herbert's brother Fritz ever took part in the business. But to my surprise, in my research I found a trade publication titled *Fur Age* published by Fur Vogue Publishing Company in 1921 in which, under a chapter headed "German Fur Trade Opposes Export Tax-Offers Substitute," there appears the following:

"At a recent national convention of the German fur trade, it was decided to render bills to foreigners in foreign money valuations . . . One of the speakers, Mr. Fritz Wolff of Berlin, recommended a 50:50 proposition. He has rendered half of the bill in foreign and the other half in German money valuation. This would balance the profit and the loss account with both parties to the transaction. Mr. Wolff claimed that this method had worked very successfully so far."

Although it's not definitive, it seems likely this was the very same Fritz Wolff who was my mother's uncle.

Manolya Ezgimen, my Berlin researcher, discovered an antiquarian bookseller in Germany, who had a listing on his Internet site for an H. Wolff catalog for 1910–1911. I purchased the brochure, which featured a magnificent array of photographs of models wearing glamorous luxury fur coats from the H. Wolff fur company at Krausenstrasse 17/18. The catalog listed company addresses in Paris and London.

H. Wolff also published Christmas calendar books to send to favored customers. Their woodcut engravings illustrated the company's far-flung, often exotic, activities. The cover of the 1920 edition shows two fashionable, fur-clad clients visiting the company's offices, while the back cover has an elegant gentleman in a top hat sitting on a trunk smoking a peace pipe with a Native American wearing a feathered headdress and an animal skin slung nonchalantly over one shoulder.

The page for July—again suggesting H. Wolff's worldwide reach—shows two buyers bartering for animal skins with other Native Americans in full tribal regalia, with teepees behind them in the distance. The initials "HW," honoring founder Heimann Wolff, were engraved on the suitcases of the company buyers in the calendar. Despite the world's and the firm's economic challenges, Victor Wolff put a brave, optimistic face on its operations.

3

MY MOTHER'S BIRTH

It was into this uncertain postwar world that my mother was born on January 22, 1922.

Her father, Herbert Wolff, the son of Victor and his wife, Lucie, was born in 1890. In March 1921, Herbert married Nellie, who was eight years younger and, much to her distress, she became pregnant on their honeymoon.

Nellie, the daughter of a prominent lawyer, was a beautiful, exuberant, often flirtatious woman. She loved parties, expensive clothing, fine antiques, and all of the other luxuries she'd known since birth. Nellie had a fine aesthetic eye, which she honed by taking a job, after graduating from high school, in an antique shop where she developed considerable expertise. Due to the severe recession at the time, many people had to sell their antiques to make ends meet financially.

When the war ended, Nellie attended finishing school in England. Being a devoted Anglophile she had a wonderful time, though finishing school was no preparation for any kind of career. When she returned to Berlin, Nellie lived at home with her parents, dabbled in antiques and, like virtually all women of her class in Germany in that era who were groomed for an early marriage to a prosperous man, she waited for a proposal.

Herbert Wolff—handsome, dashing, a war veteran, heir to a thriving company—was such a man, a fine match for Nellie. She was ready for marriage, but she was not at all pleased at the inconvenience of becoming a mother just two months shy of her 24th birthday. In that respect, she differed from her husband and his father, both of whom urgently wanted a son to carry the Wolff family business into a fourth generation. They viewed Nellie as an ideal mother for that heir. Her father, Norbert Danziger, came from a family that owned valuable grain mills in East Prussia. The family of Nellie's mother, Henrietta, owned a thriving Berlin department store.

Still, in terms of money, it was Herbert who brought great wealth to the match, while Nellie furnished the more impressive social status. The Wolff family, however, was not without its own social prestige. Victor had, after all, been awarded the honorary title of *Kommerzienrat* given only to distinguished German businessmen. His wife Lucie's brother, Alfons David, a tall, aristocratic-looking man, rose through the legal ranks to become a senior judge at the Imperial Court of Justice (*Reichsgericht*), the supreme civil and criminal court of Germany, which was located in Leipzig. His professional standing at the pinnacle of German society, however, did not shield him from anti-Semitism. My mother told me that on one occasion, when he was walking past several lawyers, one of them said to the others, "There goes a true Aryan." Alfons stopped, bowed, and announced, "Gentlemen, I am a Jew."

When Nellie gave birth on January 22, one of the midwives excitedly told her that she had a daughter, which was not the news she wanted to hear. Then, minutes later, another midwife added to her distress by exclaiming, "Wait, there's another one coming!"

No one had any inkling that Nellie was carrying twins. The midwives wrapped the newborn in cotton wool, placed her in a cigar box, and put her to the side. The second girl weighed less than five pounds. "This one won't survive," a nurse cruelly told Nellie.

This is how my mother entered the world, a tiny baby, soon expected to die. But in fact, my mother grew to be a woman of exceptional mental resolve, physical endurance, and forceful character.

The situation of the two little girls and their exhausted mother was made even worse by events outside the maternity home. The Weimar

Republic was descending into chaos. All across Berlin, Communists, emboldened by the Russian Revolution of 1917, were rioting in the streets. As a result, municipal services sometimes didn't function. The water supply was cut off in the neighborhood around the hospital, forcing Herbert and other new fathers to trudge to a communal pump and bring back water in buckets.

Despite the pessimism of some nurses, the younger of the two girls was holding her own, but needed to gain weight. The doctors urged that she be fed goats' milk, which was believed at the time to be more digestible by tiny babies. Victor Wolff bought goats and kept them on the grounds of his villa in the Berlin suburb of Wannsee. Given this steady supply of goats' milk, the newborn indeed began to thrive.

Soon, the twins and their mother went home to their parents' large, comfortable apartment just off the Kurfürstendamm, a prominent, prestigious avenue in western Berlin that is the equivalent to Fifth Avenue in New York or the Champs-Élysées in Paris.

The older girl was named Marianne, the younger (my mother), Annemarie. These were not traditional Jewish names, nor did their secular parents intend them to be. In fact, the names were suggested by a popular operetta Herbert and Nellie had seen that featured a lyric about "a delightful pair of twins" named Marianne and Annemarie. Sadly, the story of the Wolff twins ended in tragedy when Marianne, the older and seemingly healthier twin, died of a kidney condition at the age of six months.

When Marianne died, Nellie desperately wanted her to be buried in the Wolff family plot in Weissensee, the huge Jewish cemetery on the outskirts of Berlin. But, for some now unknown reason, her father-in-law, Victor, refused her request. My mother never knew where her twin lies buried.

Marianne's death was a cruel blow, but better news arrived almost three years later when Nellie gave birth to a son. His proud father named him Heinz, thus continuing the family tradition of a son answering to H. Wolff. His family and friends usually referred to Heinz as Heini. Three years later, another daughter, Marion, arrived. The family now seemed complete and, despite the nation's worsening economic and political conditions, the fur business continued to support them comfortably.

Annemarie and her younger siblings lived a pampered existence. There were nannies to care for the children, so Nellie could maintain her active social life and both parents could attend parties, plays, and concerts. Herbert and Nellie were Anglophiles who spoke excellent English and wanted their children to do the same, and so they hired only English nannies.

Nellie's mother and father, Henrietta and Norbert, often came to visit their grandchildren, and they and the nannies would take the children on walks to nearby parks. Not all of the nannies Nellie hired were a success. My mother had a vivid memory of one she disliked intensely, who only seemed to like little boys and was hostile to her. When this nanny took my mother and Heini out for their afternoon stroll to the Tiergarten, she insisted three-year-old Annemarie walk the entire way, while Heini rode in the huge baby carriage.

When my mother protested to her grandmother, Henrietta brought a stroller to the apartment and pushed the little girl to the Tiergarten, or to the family's little herb garden on a community plot near their home where children could grow their own plants and vegetables. The Tiergarten is a major park in central Berlin. Originally a royal hunting estate, its name can be translated as "Animal Garden" or, more loosely, "Garden of Beasts" which is the basis for the title of Erik Larson's best-selling book.[1]

My mother had many happy memories of those early childhood days. She told me about sometimes watching out their apartment window as a hurdy-gurdy man performed in the courtyard below and residents threw money to him from their windows.

A special treat for the children was to visit their paternal grandparents, Victor and Lucie, in their magnificent, red-brick mansion with huge wrought iron gates at Conradstrasse 1, in Wannsee, ten miles southwest of central Berlin. In the 1920s, the house was surrounded by what my mother described as a "park," one with sweeping lawns, plenty of horse-chestnut trees for the children to climb, and tenderly planted flowerbeds to admire. Old photos show the Grecian marble statues that

---

1. Larson, Erik. *In the Garden of Beasts: Love, Terror, and an American Family in Hitler's Berlin.* New York: Crown, 2011.

graced the parkland. One of these statues was of the Three Graces and another, a particular favorite, my mother recalled as, "A lady holding a jug, and when we were older we somehow got hold of a lipstick and painted her lips!"

The children had their own big playground with swings, a slide, and a sandpit. One year, for a Christmas present, my mother and her siblings were given a little hut in the style of the fairytale, *Hansel and Gretel*. It had a door, windows, and curtains, as well as gingerbread motifs stuck on it; the children would crawl inside and play. The gardens filled an entire block, with the small Wannsee Lake, known as the *Kleiner Wannsee*, at one end, and at the other end, the major König-strasse thoroughfare with the large Wannsee Lake (*Grosser Wannsee*) immediately to the north.

A small army of gardeners kept the grounds in pristine condition. They tended to the vegetable garden, the fruit trees, and the rolling lawns, and looked after the hothouses, where grapes, peaches, and melons were grown. The staff kept chickens and bantams; the latter laid small eggs that my mother and her siblings adored. The estate also included separate quarters for the Wolff family's large staff. The chauffeur and head gardener had apartments above garages that had once been stables. The maids' quarters were in the basement of the main house.

The children delighted in exploring the house. Upstairs was a dining room, a sitting room that housed a grand piano, sofa, and chairs with petit-point needlework, a library with a wooden ceiling and a whole wall covered in beautifully bound books, a conservatory with chandelier and stained-glass windows, and multiple bedrooms.

The home was full of valuable antique furniture and on the living room wall hung a Gobelin tapestry. Nellie played the grand piano and later arranged for Annemarie to have private piano lessons. My mother particularly remembered the graceful stairway with its long, curved, banisters that she enjoyed sliding down.

The family's life changed abruptly early in 1928, when Victor died at the age of seventy. His widow, Lucie, a vigorous sixty-year-old, decided she couldn't live alone in her vast mansion, so she asked Herbert to leave the apartment in Berlin and bring his family to join her in Wannsee.

Neither Herbert nor Nellie could reject such luxury. By then they lived mostly separate lives, because they were not, and had never been, as my mother used to describe it, "true companions." They had little by way of shared interests and were very different people. But this arrangement was not uncommon in their social circles where women were expected to marry well and have children who were largely raised by nannies. Nellie had married a good provider, while Herbert had what he wanted, a pretty and vivacious young wife. This did not stop him from enjoying affairs, which he probably saw as his entitlement. His wife turned a blind eye to his dalliances. She loved skiing holidays with her women friends, but Herbert disliked skiing and instead adored sailing. When they wished to entertain or to be together as a family, Lucie's estate was a perfect stage for them.

It was a pleasure for the family to share the house with Herbert's mother because Lucie was a lady in the truest sense of the word. She, together with her older siblings, sister Franziska and brother Alphons, were orphaned as young children. Both of their parents died by the time Lucie was two years old, and she and her sister had been sent to a boarding school where they were brought up.

My mother adored her elegant grandmother who, despite her wealth, was totally unostentatious. Lucie would tell her, "A lady doesn't wear jewelry during the day, at most just a string of pearls." Lucie's lifestyle reflected old money and she disdained the pretensions of the nouveaux riches. She was a generous, loving, and modest woman.

On a typical weekday morning at their new home, Herbert would enjoy breakfast and then sit in the back of the Mercedes while his chauffeur drove him on the half-hour trip downtown to the Wolff building. Before his father died, Herbert sometimes journeyed as far as Canada and Russia to buy pelts. His travels were basic to learning the business—and were also a fine way to see the world. After Victor's death, Herbert was the nominal head of the business, but he was content to let his managers run it.

My mother recalled her father—based on what she saw and what Nellie told her in later years—primarily as a playboy, a good-looking man who loved fast cars, elegant clothing, expensive boats, and beautiful women. He was charming, but totally unreliable. Nellie confided to my mother a long time later that she had known full well her husband had often been unfaithful to her.

She remembers her father not as a business tycoon, but as a man overly fond of luxurious living, and particularly sailing on Lake Wannsee with his friends. At home he would find time to read to her. Because she looked so much like him, she was his favorite child and he lavished praise and affection on her.

Herbert knew how to live the good life. Indeed, I found black-and-white film footage from the 1920s of him and his best friend Bernhard Bleichröder, owner of a prominent insurance company, on a sailing holiday in the Baltics. The footage shows Herbert looking suave—a pipe clenched between his teeth, wearing a beret, dressed all in white, smiling directly into the camera and nonchalantly turning the steering wheel while his friend gleefully dived naked into the chilly water.

My mother also told me that her parents often attended the theater and the opera, and that Nellie particularly loved concerts and the great museums of Berlin, Paris, and London. Later, when I was a schoolgirl living in the West London suburb of Ealing, Nellie would often take me to see exhibits at the British Museum in Bloomsbury, art exhibitions at the Tate and the National Gallery, ballet at Covent Garden, and concerts at the Royal Albert Hall in Kensington.

Herbert's chauffeur, who lived on the estate with his family, was Herr Siebecke. My mother sometimes visited the chauffeur's quarters to play with Ilse, Herr Siebecke's daughter, who was about the same age. Ilse was born with congenital glaucoma, and her eyesight was failing. Victor, who was a kind and generous man, paid for the finest ophthalmologist in Berlin to operate on her. She wore thick spectacles for the rest of her life, but her sight was saved.

After one visit, my mother reported to her parents that the Siebeckes put a yellow spread on their bread that was, in her opinion, much better than butter. Her mother, Nellie, explained that the spread was margarine and it was what the servants ate, but the Wolff family preferred butter, which was of higher quality. Annemarie didn't agree and continued to envy the Siebecke family's margarine.

One of the darkest moments in Herbert's seemingly charmed existence occurred in 1930 while he was driving to Leipzig to visit one of the H. Wolff subsidiary offices. For some reason, Nellie's parents, Norbert and Henrietta Danziger, accompanied him. The chauffeur was also with them, but Herbert insisted on driving the Mercedes himself, although he was a careless, often dangerous, driver. "He always wanted speed, speed, speed," my mother remembered.

On the highway, Herbert tried to overtake a truck but somehow collided with it instead. The resulting crash instantly killed Norbert Danziger and shattered Henrietta's pelvis, an injury that kept her hospitalized in Leipzig for months. Henrietta had been a champion tennis player—my mother was occasionally her ball girl—but she was never the same after that terrible collision. Herbert and the chauffeur walked away without injuries. Charges were brought against Herbert, but nothing came of them. Obviously this disaster was heartbreaking for Nellie, and it put an even greater strain on her marriage. As my mother later saw it, money was what kept her parents together.

Annemarie witnessed precious little of the Depression devastating Germany and much of the world. Her grandmother told her tales of how, during the rampant inflation in the early 1920s, she had had to keep piles of cash in washing baskets to pay for even basic household purchases. At that time, if a maid were sent to buy bread in the morning, the price of that same loaf might have soared by the afternoon. From Annemarie's perspective, in the cosseted world she lived in, no matter what the economy was doing the Wolff family seemed unaffected.

Everyone my mother knew lived, as the Wolff family did, in mansions with many servants and owned expensive cars to drive or be driven in. She took swimming lessons at a private club on the Wannsee Lake and was treated to shopping trips at the finest department stores, such as KaDeWe or Wertheim, to buy a new winter coat or a smart dress. These occasional excursions were among the few times my mother stepped outside the privileged world her family's wealth provided.

The Wolffs, like most of their Jewish friends, were almost entirely secular in religious terms. My mother was ignorant of her Jewish heritage and cultural background. "I never celebrated any Jewish festivals. Not only did I know nothing about Judaism, I didn't even know I was Jewish. We had no Passover, no Hanukkah. We were totally assimilated." She was never taken to a synagogue during her early life. She simply considered herself German.

My mother recollected, "Like most of their friends, my family was not in the least religious. My grandparents on both sides had paid for what they called a 'seat' in the synagogue but they were nominal members."

Neither pair of grandparents observed any Jewish rituals, but this was not unusual. In Germany, wealthy Jews were totally assimilated. Many married non-Jewish partners. There were tiny pockets of religious people, but on the whole the educated upper-middle class was secular. They all celebrated Christmas, though more as a winter festival than in any religious sense.

In Germany, everyone is obligated legally to declare their religious affiliation, if they have one, and a portion of their taxes is distributed to their community. The Wolff family paid their dues, but were not regular attendees of synagogue services. For the Wolffs, membership at a synagogue was clearly motivated more by social, rather than religious, reasons.

My mother told me, "Once a year my parents would dress up and go to the synagogue. The men wore top hats. I would say 'Where are you going?' And they'd say 'To the synagogue.' It must have been Rosh Hashanah (Jewish New Year) or Yom Kippur (the Day of Atonement). That was the annual visit to the synagogue."

For the Wolff family, Christmas was a highlight of the year. A huge tree was always put up in the dining room, reaching to the ceiling, but the children couldn't enter the room until the celebration officially started on Christmas Eve. There was always tremendous excitement because the tree was beautifully decorated and parcels were piled high beneath it. The maids usually received material to make a dress and the cooks and the chauffeur came in for their gifts as well. The family opened their presents last.

The Christmas Eve dinner was carp, as it was everywhere for prosperous Germans, and after it was finished the members of the staff who wanted to go to church or to see family were free to leave. On Christmas Day, the family enjoyed the luxury of goose for lunch. Christmas was not a religious event but simply a festive time to be shared with other Germans. Easter was the same. The daffodils were in bloom and the staff would hide eggs all over the spacious garden. When a child found one, he or she could eat it on the spot. The children loved that.

Sunday brunches at the Wannsee home were a tradition, with family and friends in attendance. The cooks always prepared lavish meals, sometimes consisting of venison, considered a great delicacy, and meringue cakes with strawberries on top. Annemarie, as the oldest of the children, was allowed to sit at the table and was expected to make polite conversation. Her manners, from a very young age, were impeccable. Not only had her strict English nannies tutored her on the correct use of different pieces of cutlery for each course, but they had put a ruler down the back of her dress in order to drill into her the importance of always sitting up straight during meal times. The two younger children were expected to circle the table and talk to all the guests while little Heinz, as was the custom in those days, had to kiss the outstretched hands of the ladies. Nellie enjoyed entertaining and being a fashionable young hostess, sharing the limelight with her charming and urbane husband.

Herbert's brother Fritz, younger by just a year, often attended these luncheons. Both he and Herbert were slender, attractive men. My mother described her uncle to me: "Fritz was a very tall, thin, nice-looking man, undoubtedly Jewish. My father was quite different, shorter, darker, extremely handsome and not at all Jewish looking, more like an Italian perhaps. He looked like a movie star."

The brothers had grown up together, blessed with the same comfortable lifestyle, but their lives had taken entirely different paths. Fritz had trained as an engineer, and worked in the fledgling aeronautical industry, but more importantly he was an idealist whose hatred of social injustice led him to Communism. Politically, he turned his back on the family, but his love for his mother, Lucie, brought him to the Sunday lunches. According to my mother, Fritz was a sweet-natured, unpretentious man who would always bend down low to talk to her. He lived modestly in Berlin and by then had no interest in the family business or his brother's flamboyant social life.

Fritz remained a bachelor until just before his 40th birthday. Lucie would sometimes introduce him to Nellie's English nannies—usually attractive, well-educated young women—in hopes of promoting a marriage. A photo of Fritz, standing in the garden with one of the

English nannies shows them to be a handsome couple. But Fritz looked elsewhere for romance.

In July 1931 he married a non-Jewish, working-class German woman named Charlotte Schwarz. To Nellie's horror, Charlotte's father was a lowly concierge, but Fritz and Charlotte seemed entirely happy.

Given my mother's fond memories of those idyllic years in Wannsee, it's deeply ironic that their gilded enclave was only a short walk from another mansion now remembered as the site of the infamous Wannsee Conference of January 20, 1942. There, a meeting of 15 senior Nazis, chaired by Reinhard Heydrich, chief of the Nazi security apparatus, planned the implementation of the "Final Solution"—the deportation and murder of millions of Jews. Four months after the Conference Heydrich was fatally injured in Prague, the Czechoslovak capital, during an ambush by a British-trained team of partisans. He is remembered historically as among the most despicable Nazis of Hitler's regime. Today, fittingly, the mansion is home to a Holocaust Memorial and museum.

4

WELL-HEELED NOMADS

Early in 1930, both Annemarie and Heini fell ill with scarlet fever. After they recovered, Herbert decided to take his family—including his mother, Lucie—on a grand tour of Europe. By then, the fur business was in sharp decline. At the height of the Depression, fewer women were buying expensive fur coats and furriers were not rushing to purchase pelts from H. Wolff. As a result, Herbert and his executives made a strategic decision, to transform the building entirely into a rental property. The tenants were almost all well-known, prosperous, Jewish-owned textile and clothing companies.

The impressive list of firms renting office space included established companies, such as Hermanns & Froitzheim, Dick & Goldschmidt, Ahders & Basch, Kraft & Lewin, Krahnen & Gobbers, and the insurance company Bleichröder & Co. owned by Herbert's best friend, Bernhard.

With more rental receipts coming in, Herbert left his managers to run the affairs of the building, while he spent more time at the Wannsee mansion, reading, playing Patience, solving jigsaw puzzles, and embarking on sailing trips with his various friends.

One day, Herbert announced that a trip around Europe would be a great adventure for the family and a worthwhile cultural experience for the two older children. In truth, the trip was mainly motivated by a far more pragmatic goal. By leaving Germany, Herbert and his mother would both greatly reduce their tax obligations. The family, therefore, spent almost two years visiting some of the most fashionable locations in Europe, from the ski slopes of Switzerland to the sunny beaches of the French Riviera.

For Herbert and Nellie, the tour added a new dimension to their glamorous lives and saved them money as well. So they plucked my mother, then just eight years old, and her younger siblings away from their comfortable home and their friends for what my mother would later recall as a travelling circus.

The circus included the chauffeur, Herr Siebecke, all five members of Herbert's family, plus his mother Lucie and, of course, a nanny. Herbert sat up front with Herr Siebecke, while his wife, mother, the nanny, and three children were comfortably accommodated in the rear, helped by backward-facing foldout seats for the little ones. Lucie's maid took a train to meet them in each new city.

The family traveled in a type 400 Mercedes limousine with a supercharged, four-liter engine, which experts say was the most luxurious model money could buy at that time. The huge touring car was not only filled with people, but also with luggage packed in its trunk and atop the roof. A glass panel separated the two men in the front seats from the women and children in the rear.

Their first stop was Zuoz, Switzerland, where they rented a villa and the children were treated to sleigh rides and skiing lessons. Zuoz suffered from frequent avalanches, and there was one that year. After the avalanche, all the men in the village, Herbert included, set out and thrust long poles deep into the snow to try to detect anyone buried underneath.

Then Marion, not yet two years old, came down with the scarlet fever the family thought it had left behind. She was admitted to a nearby isolation, or fever, hospital, but while there, the rental on the house the family had been living in ended. Rather than stay for a few more weeks until she was no longer contagious and could be returned to her parents, the entire family moved on to Geneva, leaving poor Marion all alone in the hospital. Nellie was not in the least maternal, and my mother observed that she never expressed any regrets at leaving her toddler behind with strangers. About six weeks later, the English nanny was dispatched to collect her. Thanks to her nannies, Marion spoke far more English than German, but while in the care of Swiss nurses she had forgotten her English and was doing the best she could with the local Swiss-German dialect, known as *Switzerdeutsch.*

The circus moved on to Zurich, then Villars, where the villa they rented was called *Joli Enclos*, which in French means, "Pretty Paddock." In German, *Klo* is slang for toilet so my mother and her little brother Heini translated this as "Pretty Lavatory" which they found highly amusing. Eighty years later, my mother would still laugh at the memory.

The summer season was spent at Juan-les-Pins on the French Riviera. Fritz and his fiancée, Charlotte, came to visit. My mother was thrilled by the local festival with colorful floats from which revelers threw cascades of flowers into the crowds that lined the streets. I have grainy, black-and-white footage of the parade and of my mother, together with her two younger siblings, sitting in a horse-drawn carriage decorated with flowers. She less happily remembered being enrolled in the local school despite not knowing a word of French. For her, that was the tour's great drawback. "Wherever we stopped I was pushed into somewhere new. That's how I lived for a couple of years." She would later say she attended 22 schools by the age of 11.

Finally, after nearly two years as well-heeled nomads, the family returned to Wannsee. It was 1932, and at the age of ten my mother looked forward to a normal existence in a local school. At first, she also studied with a private tutor to bring her up to speed in math and other subjects. Then she was enrolled in an exclusive, all-girls' establishment in the neighboring suburb of Zehlendorf. As it was near Potsdam, a traditional home of German culture and education, it attracted the daughters of the upper classes and of army officers who lived in the area. Annemarie continued to live at home and she commuted by train from the Wannsee station. My mother was the only Jewish girl in the school, but that didn't seem to matter, to her or anyone else.

But then, everything changed.

5

THE GATHERING STORM

On January 30, 1933, the president of Germany, Paul von Hindenburg, appointed Adolf Hitler to be the nation's chancellor after Hitler's Nazi party emerged as the largest single party in the previous year's legislative elections. Hindenburg thought by appointing Hitler he could placate the Nazis, while maintaining overall control himself. It was a tragic miscalculation. Hitler soon crushed the democratic government and replaced it with a ruthless dictatorship that unleashed an ever-expanding campaign against Jews, one that would relentlessly steal their rights, their property, and finally their lives.

These momentous events soon changed life for my mother at her new school. She was a bright, good-natured child who made friends easily, but once Hitler took office the other schoolgirls started to treat her differently. Suddenly she was identified as a Jew—the only one in the school, or so they thought—and her classmates began to harass her. She would open her desk and find a copy of *Der Stürmer*, a Nazi newspaper filled with vicious anti-Semitic cartoons, left there to taunt her. Girls would force her to stand on a chair, while they danced around her singing, *"Wenn das Judenblut vom Messer spritzt, dann geht's nochmal so gut."* ("When Jewish blood spurts from the knife, then things are twice as good.")

A lifetime later, my mother was remarkably forgiving of her tormentors. "They heard all the anti-Semitism that spewed forth on the radio," she said. "There was tremendous propaganda. They were only copying what was going on all around them. But it switched very suddenly from a normal life, where people mingled and had non-Jewish friends and Jewish friends, no big deal, and became vicious. I can't blame them now. They were 10 or 11 years old and they followed what the adults were doing."

She added, "There were teachers in my school who were perfectly pleasant, normal human beings but when Hitler came to power they took the swastika badge they'd worn under their lapels and put it on the front. Suddenly they were proud to announce that they were Nazis."

Although my mother was at first thought to be the only Jew in the school, soon all the students were required to bring in a copy of their *Stammbaum*, or family tree. The Wolff family has been Jewish forever—we have detailed family trees going back almost 300 years. Annemarie's status was clear. But a few of her tormentors faced a devastating surprise.

My mother told me, "Some of those girls, with very aristocratic names and lifestyles, discovered that they had a Jewish grandparent. Between the Franco-Prussian war and the First World War, a lot of aristocratic Prussian families, whose fortune was in land, did very badly, and they were happy to see their sons marry rich Jewish girls with a big dowry, and the girls were delighted to be accepted into the aristocracy. They got the new name with 'von' in front of it. Both sides felt they had a bargain. But now these little ten-year-old girls in an exclusive school discovered that they had a Jewish grandmother and began to lose their friends. There were floods of tears and hysterics at this terrible disgrace. The horror of having a Jewish grandparent!"

Hitler's vicious rhetoric had worked its spell. The taint of Jewish blood meant, among other things, that young people could not join the Hitler Youth. For some families, their unsuspected ancestry became a death sentence. Giorgio Bassani's novel, *The Garden of the Finzi-Continis*, and Vittorio De Sica's 1971 film adaptation of it, are powerful portraits of how the taint of Judaism destroyed one aristocratic family during Benito Mussolini's fascist regime in Italy.

As a result of the taunts she endured, my mother told her parents, "They say I'm a Jew, so I want to know more about being Jewish. I want to go to the synagogue."

Hence, one Saturday morning in the early months of 1933, Herbert and Nellie took my mother to the fashionable and liberal Fasanen-strasse synagogue, close to Kurfürstendamm, near the first apartment she had lived in with her parents. She clearly remembered seeing the engraved plaques there that identified the Wolff family seats. Its one-time rabbi had been the renowned Leo Baeck, considered the leader of Progressive Judaism in Germany. This was the spiritual home of many affluent Berlin Jews. One congregant was Dr. Heinrich Stahl, a long-serving board member of the synagogue who was elected president of the Berlin Jewish community, and served in that position during the agonizing period from 1933 to 1940. It later became significant to my mother's story that Dr. Stahl was also a director of the Victoria Insurance Company.

At the synagogue, my mother started to embrace what it meant to be a Jew, and continued as such, in a cultural sense, if not a religious one, for the rest of her life. The great Fasanenstrasse synagogue, however, was destroyed, along with hundreds of others, in the anti-Jewish riots of Kristallnacht in 1938. Since the end of the Second World War, it has been rebuilt as a Jewish community center.

Annemarie was living in a new Germany, with a new religion. Men in brown uniforms marched about menacingly on the streets and Nazi flags and swastikas were everywhere. Once she stood at the fence in their garden and watched a long line of huge cars drive past along Königstrasse. She recalled, "I saw Hitler standing up in an open car waving at people who lined the street outside our garden. But this meant nothing to me except the spectacle of it. What did I know? Even when they shouted, *'Die Juden, die Juden!'* ('The Jews, the Jews!'), I didn't identify with it. Did they mean me?"

Nellie and Herbert had never talked about money or politics in front of their children. But now my mother sometimes overheard her parents discussing the new political realities in Germany. They felt the rising anti-Semitism, but at first they couldn't believe it could affect "people like us, good Germans."

Herbert was a prominent businessman and a war veteran, and Nellie was every inch a German lady—a tall, blonde, blue-eyed beauty. In their minds, the Nazi demagoguery and the violence of its hoodlums was directed at "those poor Polish Jews" who kept arriving in Germany. Life had been so sweet for the Wolff family for so long, it was almost impossible to imagine it changing.

But the new realities could not be denied. Nellie found that many of her Christian friends would no longer visit her home or invite her to theirs, for fear of offending the Nazi elite and causing problems with the Nazis for their husbands or sons. Herbert, too, may have been a playboy but he was no fool; as he moved about Berlin, he grasped the new realities far more quickly than his wife and many other Jews.

For one thing, he could not ignore the dangers facing his brother Fritz.

On February 27, 1933, less than a month after Hitler's appointment as Chancellor (on January 30), a fire destroyed much of the Reichstag, the German parliament. Hitler blamed the fire on Communists and used it as an excuse to pass harsh laws against them and to arrest thousands. (It has long been believed by many that the Nazis started the fire to justify violent measures against their enemies, but the truth remains unknown.)

As the roundups intensified, Fritz and another Communist, his friend Boris Munk, the son of one of Nellie's friends, hid at the Wannsee home. Munk lived in a staff apartment above the garages, and pretended to be one of the gardeners. Nellie had a very wide social circle that included well-connected, long-standing, non-Jewish friends. Many of these women's husbands, sons, or brothers, were early members of the Nazi Party, and one of them took the honorable decision to give early warning that the police were planning on raiding the house in Wannsee in search of Fritz and Boris. The two men fled and were not to be found when the police arrived.

Another young man was also living on the estate, the son of Herr Siebecke, the chauffeur. It was said that he was first a Communist but later became a Nazi. A lot of people straddled the fence like that in the early 1930s, waiting to see which side won the bitter struggle for power. They were called "roast beef"—red on the inside and brown on the outside.

At that point, the Nazis were seeking Fritz for being a Communist. They soon caught up with him and sent him to what Herbert always referred to in later life as *"Festung,"* literally "fortress"—the Spandau prison, a grim citadel in Berlin where many Communists were held. Herbert and Fritz's wife, Charlotte, searched for Fritz for two weeks before they learned where he was incarcerated.

I have no idea how Fritz coped while imprisoned. But Egon Erwin Kisch, a Jewish Communist journalist who, along with a host of other Berlin Communists, was arrested immediately after the Reichstag fire and was taken to the same jail as Fritz, later wrote a vivid description of the conditions at Spandau. His report is chilling. The prisoners were held in single cells and were taken out for a half-hour walk in silence every day. During their exercise, they would look up at the prison wall and see the faces of friends not strong enough to make it to the courtyard after having suffered severe beatings at the hands of the *SA* (*Sturmabteilung*), also known as Stormtroopers, who were the paramilitary wing of the Nazi party. Political prisoners were denied any visitors. Alone for twenty-three-and-a-half hours every day, Kisch wrote that he started to feel like a madman and went on to describe hearing the cries of those held in the underground solitary cells, "Help! Help! People are being beaten to a pulp here!"[1]

Fritz was released sometime in May 1933, for reasons that are not clear. He and Charlotte moved to a working class neighborhood in the north of Berlin, where they tried to live inconspicuously. In addition to the political dangers he faced, Fritz suffered another distressing blow when Charlotte died of cancer in December of that same year.

Herbert was not at home when the police visited the Conradstrasse house in search of Fritz and Boris. However, the reality of that raid and of his brother's subsequent imprisonment led to his quick decision to take his family out of Germany. Even though the Nazis had not arrested Fritz for being a Jew, his plight gave Herbert a preview of what the regime was capable of and might soon do to Jews like him. Hitler had never concealed his virulent anti-Semitism and Herbert sensed it was time to take the Nazi leader at his word.

---

1. *Egon Erwin Kisch, The Raging Reporter. A Bio-Anthology* edited by Harold B. Segel, Purdue University Press, 1997.

In May 1933, before Fritz was released from Spandau, Herbert left Germany. He first went to Switzerland to collect funds from his bank account there, and then traveled on to Palestine. He told his family they would be reunited in a few months.

Hitler had moved more quickly against the Communists than against the Jews, probably because the former were the more organized, potentially violent, political force but he always had his eyes on the Jewish wealth that he intended to claim.

The memoirs of Douglas Miller, the commercial attaché at the U.S. Embassy in Berlin at the time, published in 1944 under the title, *Via Diplomatic Pouch*, captured the atmosphere. Reporting in August 1933, a mere six months after Hitler came to power, Miller quoted Gottfried Feder, Germany's Assistant Secretary of Commerce, as having briefed a private meeting that the Nazi party had four objectives. These were:

1. Breaking the Versailles Treaty;
2. Restoring Germany's military superiority;
3. Ridding the country of the "Jewish pest";
4. Ending the "International Jewish" capitalistic system.

Miller reported how Feder explained that while the first two objectives could not be reached right away, "the party may still go ahead 'at full speed'" to achieve the latter two.

The Nazis were in the process of passing laws that provided the death penalty for German citizens who kept funds overseas. At the same time, the Nazis were creating new taxes that applied to Germans who moved abroad—these, they explained, were to compensate the state for future taxes it would not collect. The Gestapo was also keeping a close eye on Swiss bank accounts and finding ways to identify people, particularly Jews, who deposited money there. Herbert may have broken Nazi laws by taking advantage of the traditional secrecy of Swiss banks but the alternative was to let the Nazis rob him blind, as they did to many Jews in the years ahead.

All of her life, my mother marveled at how her often-irresponsible father took such decisive action. But Herbert was shrewd and cynical enough, and sufficiently realistic to reject the widespread illusion that the Nazis wouldn't be so bad, or that "good" Jews like the Wolff family could survive their regime. His brother's arrest spurred him to action; he told his family, "I'm not staying here. I'm not bringing up my children here. We're going."

Herbert and his family joined an estimated 37,000 Jews who left Germany in 1933 and migrated abroad. Much turmoil and pain lay ahead for the family, but Herbert's decision saved their lives.[2]

---

2. http://www.ushmm.org/wlc/en/article.php?ModuleId=10005276.

6

PALESTINE

Herbert's family and friends regarded him primarily as a playboy, yet he had grasped the new realities of Germany faster than countless others who followed politics more closely. He had quickly made a major decision, one that surprised many who thought they knew him well: to seek a new life, not in the United States or Britain, as Nellie wanted, despite having the money and the right connections, but instead opting for British-ruled Palestine.

In 1918, as the Turkish Ottoman Empire collapsed, the British had taken control of the territory known as Palestine, under a mandate from the League of Nations. British Foreign Secretary Lord Balfour declared in 1917—in what is known to this day as the Balfour Declaration—that Palestine should be the Jewish National Home.

Herbert agreed with this view. My mother believes he did so despite considering himself a good German, one who had worn his country's uniform in wartime, and contributed to its financial strength. To see Hitler denounce and target Jews was, to Herbert, a betrayal. He began, for the first time, to identify as a Jew, in an ethnic sense if not a religious one, and the strength of that belief drew him to the new homeland that was more a barren desert than a land of milk and honey. He wanted to be with fellow Jews. As my mother later said, "In Palestine he found his Jewish heart."

Herbert arrived via Switzerland in May 1933. For 1,000 British pounds (the modern-day equivalent of $28,464 each) he obtained from the British authorities what was called a "capitalist visa." At that point, the Nazis were still encouraging Jews to leave Germany and allowed them to take at least some of their money with them, as long as they paid heavy exit taxes.

For her part, Nellie packed five huge wooden storage boxes (called "lifts"), full of family heirlooms, antiques, paintings, furniture, clothing, glass, and silverware. To Annemarie, 11 years old and glad to leave the school that treated her so harshly, the move seemed a welcome adventure. Still, one August afternoon shortly before Nellie and the children were to depart, Annemarie sat on her swing in the garden of the Wannsee home, and wondered, "Will I ever come back here?"

My mother was leaving a fairy-tale childhood for an unimaginable future. Yet she told herself that surely life, even in distant Palestine, would be better than in hate-filled Nazi Germany. "It was a great adventure," she told me years later, "but it was also the end of my gilded life."

As Herbert was settling in, Nellie, the children, and a nanny travelled to Lugano, Switzerland, to visit friends. The nanny was, unusually, not only German but also Jewish. My mother believes she was hired as a way of getting her out of the country. While they were in Lugano, Herbert called Nellie with some awful news.

Herbert confessed that, soon after he had arrived, he met two Polish Jewish immigrants who persuaded him to invest in their invention: refrigerated display cases that would allow shops to show perishable foodstuffs. Incredibly, Herbert sank virtually all his money in this scheme. The next thing he knew, the money was gone. Whether the men were swindlers or honest men with a flawed idea, was never clear. Not that it mattered; in either event, Herbert Wolff was all but penniless. Once again, this foolish man displayed a deplorable lack of the commercial acumen possessed by his father and grandfather.

Nellie was never sure exactly how much money her husband lost, but it was clearly enough for them to have settled comfortably in

Palestine. All gone, thrown away. Nellie could hardly believe—and it is still difficult to fathom today—that Herbert, the once prosperous businessman, the man who had so wisely taken his family out of Nazi Germany, could then have made such a monumentally stupid decision upon arriving in Tel Aviv.

In Lugarno, Nellie was in shock. It was all but impossible for her to imagine a life without the wealth that had shaped and cushioned her since birth. She agonized over her future. Money had kept her with Herbert even after his recklessness had killed her father and severely injured her mother—but would she stay with him now, with the money gone?

She spoke of taking the children back to Germany, where she still had family and friends, but the worsening Nazi menace frightened her. And Herbert, despite the loss of a fortune, insisted that he could do well. It was their new home, he said, and she should bring the children and meet this challenge with him. In the end, she decided to take her chances with Herbert, which surely says more about the desperation of a mother of three than about her affection for her infuriating husband. The Jewish nanny who had accompanied Nellie to Lugarno did not want to continue on and so returned to Germany. She was never heard from again.

Nellie and the children made the last leg of their trip from Germany by boarding a ship in Genoa. My mother, not understanding the financial disaster, savored their journey. One highlight she recounted to me was becoming friends with several nuns with whom she shared a cabin, who were delivering a statue of the Virgin Mary to a convent in Palestine. "The statue was put in a special room and the nuns all trooped in each day and crossed themselves, and prayed," she told me. "I had never seen anything like it and I was intrigued. So I did the same, followed them in, knelt down, and crossed myself too."

Upon arrival at the port city of Jaffa, just south of Tel Aviv, Nellie and the children climbed down ladders into a small boat that carried them to the dockside, where Herbert greeted them with hugs and kisses, apparently overjoyed to be reunited with his family. But this loving reunion was soon followed by the newcomers' first disheartening glimpse of their new home. Herbert had chosen Tel Aviv because it was mostly secular, as opposed to Jerusalem which was, and still is, considered a holy city. But Tel Aviv at the time was also dirty and crowded.

Annemarie recalled, "Tel Aviv in those days was a dusty, sandy village. We went to a fifth-rate boarding house, the Pension Dan, that was nothing like the luxurious Dan Hotel that it later became. It was nasty. We all slept in one room."

My mother looked on with astonishment as camels walked the streets, and Arabs sold fish and vegetables from sidewalk stands, mingling with religious Jews with their side curls and fur hats. For children who had grown up in Wannsee, it was like landing on another planet.

Without the nannies she had always employed, Nellie couldn't cope with three children. By selling some of the valuables they had brought from Germany, the family was able to put eight-year-old Heini and five-year-old Marion in a boarding school outside Tel Aviv. Tossed into classrooms where they knew no one, and speaking not a word of the Hebrew that everyone else spoke, they were desperately unhappy.

Marion has this recollection of their departure from the school:

Every group of newcomers got bullied by the "Oldies" and Heini was in a group of *Yekkes*, which meant Jews of German-speaking origin. There was a big fight between the *Yekkes* and the *Sabras*, who were the native born Jews. Heini got hit by a stone just above his eye, and had a scar to the end of his days.

Next morning, before dawn, he was standing next to my bed. "Get dressed, we're leaving!" I was six and a month or two, and Heini wasn't yet nine. We started off with quite a group, some eight or nine children, all about the same age, who wanted to escape. We walked from Ramat Gan to Tel Aviv and, of course, we went the route the bus drove, not a shorter way. By the time we reached our street it was dusk. We were limping along when a horse-drawn carriage came past and the lady inside thought, "Look at those poor children" before she realized they were her own children! It was Nellie. The rest of the way home we went in luxury in the carriage. Few people had a phone in those days and Nellie hadn't known we were missing until she saw us on the street. The next thing I remember we were out of that school and started in another one.

A few weeks after their arrival in Palestine, Herbert managed to move the family into a four-room flat on Mazeh Street. With no servants, Nellie tried to learn to cook on a small, kerosene burning, Primus stove. Meanwhile, Annemarie was enrolled in a Hebrew-speaking school, and it was there that she was astonished to find that her teacher disapproved of her name.

"Don't you have a Hebrew name?" the woman demanded.

Taken aback, my mother remembered once meeting a girl named Aviva. She thought it was a pretty name—it means "spring" (as in "renewal") in Hebrew—so she adopted it on the spot and kept it for the rest of her life. Annemarie had been fine for her secular life in Germany but, in staunchly Jewish Palestine, Aviva was the right name.

Herbert's professional skills were those of the fur trade, but few women were buying fur coats in the heat of Palestine, so he set out to learn Hebrew and the insurance business. In time, he was bringing home a little money from insurance sales. The transition to this new life was more difficult for Nellie. She was frequently depressed—clinically depressed, my mother later believed. Miserable, lonely, and poor Nellie would say to her young daughter, "Let's just take some pills and not wake up in the morning." Aviva was forced to grow up fast.

Next, the three children were sent to live at Ben Shemen, an agricultural boarding school in central Palestine. (Shimon Peres, the future president of Israel, was later a student there.) They were separated by age and put in different dormitories. All the teaching was in Hebrew so they learned the new language quickly.

If Aviva's original name had not been acceptable in her new homeland, Heini faced an even more painful problem. The other boys constantly tormented him because he was not circumcised. Back in Berlin it had been the other way round, many secular German Jews frowned on circumcision. Parents feared it might cause their sons embarrassment in later life. But at Ben Shemen, the other boys gave Heini absolute hell for being so alarmingly different. Whenever possible, he would have his older sister stand guard outside the communal showers to stop other boys from seeing him naked. By the age of ten he couldn't stand being bullied and teased any longer, so he found a doctor who performed the painful procedure upon which his social survival seemed to depend.

Aviva, by contrast, was entirely happy at their new school. "For nine months I never went to classes. I made friends with a young British policeman who was there as a guard and who had a horse for his patrols. I loved riding and he was happy to find someone who could speak to him in fluent English. We struck up a friendship and he let me ride instead of going to class. Several months later my parents came to school and asked the officials how I was doing and they could find no record of my having attended classes. I had been a naughty girl and they weren't going to tolerate that. So I was taken out of Ben Shemen."

Nellie heard of the religiously observant Evelina de Rothschild School in Jerusalem, which became Aviva's next stop. It was modeled on the very best English girls' schools, and teaching was conducted in both Hebrew and English. My mother was sent to live with a devoutly religious Jewish family that had come from Frankfurt. Every day, dressed in her summer school uniform of white stockings, white shoes, a long-sleeved white blouse, blue cotton tunic with box pleats, and a white straw hat with a black ribbon, my mother trotted off to her posh new school. In winter, she changed from white shoes to brown ones and wore a white pullover, a blue beret, and blazer. Living in such an ultra-religious environment, she encountered customs that struck her as utterly bizarre.

The family she lived with relied on an alarm clock to "ping" on a Friday evening to remind them to switch off all electric lights before the Sabbath began. Hot food was put in the hay box on Friday afternoon so that the family could have warm food on Saturday, as they were forbidden to light a stove to heat anything up. This was another world to my mother, but she had had no choice but to adapt to it. As she later reminisced, "It was all alien to me, I didn't know anything about the festivals or reading Hebrew or *Tanach* (the Bible). I could have been in China."

The headmistress, who originally came from England, was Miss Annie Landau. A renowned hostess, she enjoyed entertaining the elite social circles of Jerusalem with regular dinner guests, including the British High Commissioner and visiting UK dignitaries. Importantly, she was very keen to put on a good display at her parties. Lacking money, Nellie managed to persuade Miss Landau to accept payment for tuition in the form of pieces of the expensive silver and linen she had shipped over from Berlin. Slowly, the hundreds of beautiful items she'd brought in those five huge containers were sold to keep the family financially afloat. Some German Jewish families in Palestine, when their crates were empty, were reduced to living in them, according to my mother.

As she learned about Jewish rituals at her new school, Aviva was also learning about the political turmoil that raged outside its walls. Local rumor had it that the Mufti of Jerusalem, the Muslim leader, was offering a few cigarettes to local Arabs as a bribe to incite an anti-Jewish riot. Nellie would sometimes share a taxi for the 40-mile trip from Tel Aviv to Jerusalem and report the car had been shot at along the way. My mother recalled making that trip herself and seeing British soldiers stop traffic when bullets were flying.

Back on Mazeh Street, Herbert and Nellie's marriage was falling apart. They quarreled constantly. In Berlin, the family money had kept them together, but here in Tel Aviv, that adhesive was gone. Herbert may have had mixed feelings. He often asked Aviva's advice, what should they do? Plain spoken even then, and with the confidence of youth, my mother told her father that he and Nellie should divorce. She couldn't stand the constant rows.

Her advice was probably less decisive than Nellie's discovery that Herbert had secretly bought himself a car, which he parked several blocks from their apartment. His secrecy—and Nellie's growing awareness that he was using it to see other women—was the last straw. She threw him out and began divorce proceedings. From then on, my mother was estranged from her father. Although he continued to live in Tel Aviv, Herbert took virtually no interest in either her or his other children and very rarely saw them.

Nellie's was a brave decision, but it meant that, more than ever, she had to live by her wits. When the family had first arrived in Tel Aviv, she had taken a job as a saleslady in a shoe store, but that hadn't lasted long. After she and Herbert parted ways, she set out to exploit her knowledge of fashion. She became friendly with a woman who imported high-fashion clothing from Europe for sale to upper class Arab women, often the wives of high-ranking Egyptian officials, who visited Tel Aviv.

Her new friend was an elderly Jewish woman who owned and operated a boutique in a fashionable quarter of Tel Aviv. Nellie assisted in running the shop. She would model the latest fashions, and speak knowledgably about them in French with the well-educated Arab women customers.

Nellie also appealed to her mother, Henrietta, to leave Berlin and join her. Henrietta was in her 60s and had suffered greatly, starting with her husband's death in the car driven by her son-in-law, Herbert. Beyond that tragedy, and her own injuries in the crash, her family had lost most of its money in the 1927 German stock market collapse. And, by this time, she understood the increasing dangers she faced in Germany.

Given all this adversity, and being an enterprising woman, Henrietta agreed to join her daughter and three grandchildren in Palestine. Before embarking, she took a course on how to make chocolates by hand, a skill she hoped might help her and her loved ones survive in the distant land that would be her new home.

My mother remembered her grandmother, the one-time tennis champion, arriving in Tel Aviv, her body bent over as a result of her injuries in the car crash. But despite her infirmities, while Nellie was away, Henrietta kept house and helped with the children when they were home from school. She also started to help bring in some much needed income.

On Mazeh Street, Nellie and Henrietta began what they called a "lunch table" for some of the many single Jewish refugee men from Europe who often waited months for their families to join them. The two women cooked, offering inexpensive meals in congenial company. It was a touch of home for lonely men, and it provided much-needed income. No doubt Henrietta's handmade chocolates were a special treat for the guests.

Many of the men they served were well-educated German Jews, doctors, lawyers, and scholars who had found safety in Palestine, but not the kind of work for which they were trained. Often these men were reduced to laboring on construction sites where it was reported that, as they passed bricks to one another, they would say with exaggerated politeness, "*Bitte schön, Herr Doktor . . . danke schön, Herr Doktor*" (translates to "If you please, Doctor . . . thank you, Doctor.") They told a joke about two dogs, a Chihuahua who meets a St. Bernard and boasts of how important he was back in Germany, "At home I too was a St. Bernard!"

My mother told me that, somehow or other, Fritz managed to send money from Germany to help Nellie whenever he could. She had no idea how this was arranged, perhaps he found trustworthy refugees willing to take money to Palestine on his behalf but, however he organized this, Nellie was grateful for his assistance.

In time, Henrietta and Nellie managed to save enough money to make a move out of the four-room apartment on Mazeh Street in Tel Aviv to a new home in Haifa. There, they rented a large house from Shabtai Levi—a prominent lawyer who later became the first Jewish mayor of the northern port city. He moved to a residence in a more fashionable area, higher on Mount Carmel, the hill that dominates the area. The ever-enterprising Henrietta and Nellie turned the house into a rental business, offering individual rooms to officers of the British army and navy, several of whom became Nellie's lovers. Initially, Henrietta did the cooking, as full board was on offer, but as they became more established, a refugee from Vienna, who had previously been an art dealer, was hired as a cook.

The rooms were furnished with some of the beautiful antiques from Wannsee. Marion recalls how one naval commander, who she says drank a bottle of whisky almost every night, used his pocket knife to pass the time by picking out the pieces of wood delicately inlaid in a chest of drawers. The valuable antique was ruined.

Marion also tells how their new home, on what is now called Shabtai Levi Street, was just above the Arab suburb of Wadi Nisnas and that Nellie once sent her to buy sugar from a store there. She was wearing a summer dress, revealing bare shoulders. When the children in the village saw Marion dressed like this, they crowded round her and beat her on her back shouting, *"Yahoodi, Yahoodi."* ("Jew, Jew.") She quickly ran back home!

Although Nellie had little money, she did have wealthy friends, in both Germany and England, to whom she looked for help. She arranged for Marion to live with Dr. Emanuel Propper, a heart specialist, and his wife Johanna, who had come to Jerusalem from Switzerland. Unable to have children of their own, the Proppers wanted to adopt Marion. Nellie was willing for Marion to live with them because they were able to offer her a steady family life and home not far from one of the best schools in Palestine. Nellie was a highly attractive, stylish, woman who was anxious to remarry. She was conscious that having children living with her was not likely to endear her to any prospective husbands. But allowing Marion to be adopted by the Proppers was out of the question, and she refused all their requests to be legal parents to the little girl they grew to love so dearly.

My mother had not forgotten her friends left behind in Berlin. She exchanged letters with her best friend there, Ulla (short for Ursula) Donig. Ulla reported that she'd been forced to leave the school she'd been in and transfer to an all-Jewish one. Aviva, remembering her mistreatment in the exclusive school she had once attended, thought this sounded like a sensible move. Later, she better understood what the forced transfer meant to her friend as the pressures on Jews worsened. In fact, Ulla's family was eventually able to leave Germany and settled in California where Ulla, at 17, married a wealthy man. The two friends sometimes corresponded in later life and Ulla sent pictures of her children. But their lives were very different, and in time they lost touch.

Nellie had kept in touch with Edna Phillips, whom she had met when they were classmates at an English finishing school. Edna was married to Sir Samuel Joseph, a prominent businessman, and Lady Joseph, as she had become, was so touched by Nellie's plight she offered to pay for an education in London for one of her children.

Nellie knew immediately which child to send. It was 1936. She was a flirtatious divorcee of 38, and my mother had blossomed into a very shapely 14 year old adolescent. Nellie had been seeing a succession of British military officers, with the sincere hope that one would marry her and take her and her children to a good life in England. What the men did, of course, was enjoy her favors and then return home to their wives.

As Nellie saw it, her attractive teenage daughter might make her seem older and less desirable to potential husbands. Moreover, Aviva was outspoken in her disapproval of her mother's numerous gentlemen admirers. All of this made my mother the logical choice to benefit from Lady Joseph's generosity. She would receive an excellent education, and also be out of Nellie's way. Or, as my mother succinctly put it, "I was well developed and my mother didn't want a teenager around when she was having all sorts of relationships with British army officers. So she chose me as the one to send to boarding school in England."

Nellie, however, did not simply put her daughter on the next boat to London. She had more ambitious plans. She decided to accompany Aviva to England to personally thank her friend and benefactor, Lady Joseph. She also wanted to see old acquaintances in Germany. The decision was made that she and Aviva would detour through Berlin en route to England. However, in letters and calls to Berlin, she learnt that those who weren't Jewish were afraid to be seen with her, lest they run afoul of the Nazis. Nellie solved that problem by stopping for a few days in the northern Italian city of Bolzano, where several non-Jewish friends visited her in safety.

Despite these dangers, mother and daughter then proceeded to Berlin itself. Nellie was acutely conscious of the anti-Semitic environment, but she was headstrong. She wanted to see them all, and nothing was going to stop her.

The 1936 Summer Olympics were in progress, the games at which the African-American sprinter Jesse Owens enraged and humiliated Hitler by winning four gold medals in track and field events. Aviva came away from the trip with a treasured souvenir, a scarf with the five interlaced Olympic rings emblazoned on it.

Still, it was not a good time for two Jewish women to visit Berlin. Nellie's friends protested, "You must be mad! How could you bring such a Jewish-looking child to Germany?" It was true. Nellie was the very model of an Aryan lady, but my mother's appearance was quite the opposite. As she later told me, to Nazi eyes she looked the epitome of a Jewish girl. "For the first time in my life, I was really scared!"

The Nazis were not yet rounding up and deporting Jews. Nor had they started compelling German Jews to wear yellow badges as they would in 1941 almost three years after Kristallnacht, when Nazi mobs burned more than 1,000 synagogues and vandalized or completely destroyed more than 7,000 Jewish businesses, as well as hospitals and schools. But, already hostility was in the air. Uniformed Nazis were everywhere, and red flags with the swastika symbol adorned countless buildings. Nellie and my mother stayed with a succession of Jewish former neighbors in their Wannsee and Grunewald villas. My mother told me that by then people were not yet panic-stricken but they were certainly scared. Many had lost jobs, and their children had been forced to leave their schools. Nellie's friends spoke openly about the political situation and about trying to get out of Germany. Most wanted to immigrate to the United States, but they were discovering it very difficult to get visas.

But then, before they could leave Berlin, Aviva came down with jaundice. She was in no condition to travel, and Nellie, most irresponsibly, proceeded to England alone and left her daughter behind.

Nellie's dreams were soon shattered when she reached England. She had concocted the idea that Lady Joseph might not only pay for Aviva's education, but she would also set Nellie up as the owner of a fashionable women's clothing shop in London. In proposing such a scheme, she seriously overplayed her hand. Lady Joseph, offended by Nellie's presumption, not only refused the new request, but also withdrew her offer to pay for Aviva's education. She wanted nothing more to do with her one time finishing school classmate.

Meanwhile, my mother was still in Berlin imagining her wonderful new life in England. When she was well enough to travel, she boarded a train that took her from Berlin to Cologne, where she stayed a few days with her great-aunt, Franziska Steinert, Lucie Wolff's older sister. By then, Nellie had sailed back from England and met her daughter at Aachen, on the German border with Belgium. Together, mother and daughter made their way to the English Channel, and Aviva entered England on her mother's German passport.

Back in London, Nellie and Aviva stayed with their former nanny, Marion Teasdale, now Mrs. Parish. She was the attractive young woman with whom Fritz had once been photographed in the garden at Wannsee. Nellie was desperate. Even her daughter recognized her fragile condition. My mother never met Lady Joseph, and Nellie didn't tell her until she was an adult why her London friend's patronage had vanished.

Nellie searched for assistance. She took Aviva to visit some old Berlin friends, Paul and Lona Heller, and their daughters, Vera and Doris, who had come to London. My mother, fresh from Palestine and full of Zionist fervor, was horrified when she learned that the two girls were attending a convent school. This was not, in her opinion, what good Jewish girls should be doing, and she informed her mother she wanted nothing further to do with them!

Refusing to abandon hope of placing her daughter in a British school, Nellie contacted Dr. Martha Turk, a devoted supporter of a Jewish homeland in Palestine. Dr. Turk lived in Edinburgh with her sister Bertha, both having fled Germany when Hitler took power. Nellie had known them when the sisters had lived in Frankfurt. Martha and Bertha had a brother, Erich, who had moved from Germany to England in the 1890s and made a fortune on the stock market.

Erich often took in Jewish refugees and paid for their schooling. He had supported Peter Block, the son of a mutual acquaintance, who had died of cancer. Peter's father, Marcel, simply could not cope with a child after his wife died, and he was struggling to find work under the Nazi regime. Peter had often come on holidays to stay with the Wolff family at Wannsee, and later Erich had paid for Peter to go to Mill Hill, a top English boys' school. Seizing on these connections, Nellie talked to Martha Turk, who spoke with her brother who agreed to pay my mother's fees to attend Babington House, a private school in southeast London. It was a magnificent opportunity.

But there remained the question of where she would live. Marion and Raymond Parish owned a modest house at 39 Charldane Road, in the London suburb of Eltham, not far from Babington House. Mrs. Parish agreed, for a price, to let Aviva live there while she attended the school so, after about a month in England, Nellie was able to set sail and return to Palestine.

My mother had made a remarkable journey from wealth in Berlin to the hardships of Palestine and finally to London and the prospect of a decent education. War was coming, and many more challenges besides, but the future looked brighter than she had dared dream since she and her family left Wannsee three years earlier in search of a new life.

7

ENTJUDUNG

From the moment Hitler seized power, his goal was to force the Jews to leave Germany and expropriate their wealth. This campaign started quickly, sought to present a façade of legality, and became ever more violent, concluding with the genocide of the "Final Solution."

Starting in April 1933, the Nazis passed laws that barred Jews from the civil service, from the legal and medical professions, and from teaching in schools and universities. The Nazis sponsored boycotts of Jewish businesses, forcing many to close and later burned down those that remained. The Nuremberg Laws of September 1935 stripped Jews of their rights as citizens, and made it increasingly difficult for a Jew to own or operate a business.

U.S. diplomat Douglas Miller, in his book *Via Diplomatic Pouch*, quoted from one of his dispatches cabled to Washington in October 1935, ". . . a new wave of pessimism and despair has swept over Jewish businessmen in Germany. The newspapers are full of advertisements offering Jewish enterprises for sale. Buyers are few and are able to dictate prices which are only nominal ones: five or ten percent of the ordinary value of the property in question."

He added, ". . . the Jews are forced out through general political and economic pressure which is applied extra-legally at this time but which may be given more definite legal sanction in the specific provisions of the new anti-Jewish laws which have not yet been made public."

A British official, Eric Mills, wrote a 14-page report, dated November 12, 1935, after visiting Berlin in the previous two months: ". . . while before I went to Germany, I knew that the Jewish situation was bad, I had not realized as I now do that the fate of German Jews is a tragedy which for cold, intelligent planning by those in authority takes rank with that of those who were out of sympathy with the Bolshevist regime in Russia: or with the elimination of Armenians from the Turkish Empire."

Mr. Mills's report makes for dreadful reading. He understood the full implications of what he had learnt and observed on his visit.

> The [Nazi] Party ensures that Aryans and Jews may not enter relations as buyers and sellers. Hence a Jew cannot purchase the necessaries of life from an Aryan seller; similarly the Jewish seller cannot buy the replenishment of his stock from an Aryan. Land transactions are not approved on the ground that the sale is contrary to public interest. Hence a Jew is fortunate if he can sell his immovable or movable property for a "song." Such a sale amounts to informal confiscation . . . For the Jew it may be said that there is no rule of law . . . The Jew is to be eliminated, and the State has no regard for the manner of the elimination . . . I could not, on my return to England, remain silent and inactive after having been in intimate contact with people who are the direct objects for coldly intelligent evil.

These realities caught up with the Wolff family in 1936.

In 1929, the widowed Lucie Wolff, as the owner of the Wolff building at Krausenstrasse 17/18, had obtained a mortgage loan from the Victoria Insurance Company, a prominent German company that deliberately sought, and often obtained, the insurance coverage of major Jewish businesses. The amount of the loan was RM (Reichsmark) 1.2 million (about $285,000 in 1929 and perhaps $3.7 million today) to be repaid quarterly.

The loan was needed to ease the company's transition from the dwindling fur business to its new emphasis on renting office space. It was granted because Wolff executives could show that the company's rental income was sufficient for it to make the payments.

In August 1934, Herbert wrote from Palestine giving power of attorney to his brother Fritz over his affairs, which of course included responsibility for the Wolff family's building on Krausenstrasse. But Fritz, by then released from Spandau prison, left the day-to-day management of the building to Ludwig Salomon, the lawyer who was the appointed administrator of his mother's will.

Two other lawyers, Dr. Hans Fritz Abraham and Max Michaelis, assisted Salomon. For several years, these three men struggled against increasingly restrictive anti-Jewish laws to keep the business solvent. Fortunately, the building's elegance and central location enabled it to continue to rent space to prestigious textile and clothing firms. And, despite the many growing economic pressures on Jewish companies, the rents continued to be paid and the Wolff family's building at Krausenstrasse 17/18 managed to survive.

At several points, when rental income receipts were insufficient, portions of the family's Wannsee estate had been sold to help meet the payments to the Victoria. This suggests the determination of the family and its representatives to meet their obligations.

On May 4, 1935, Ludwig Salomon submitted his annual financial report to *Amtsgericht* Charlottenburg, the district court in the Berlin suburb of Charlottenburg. Included in his detailed list of all monies and rents received, he drew the attention of the court to his success in managing the building:

> . . . Keep in mind that I have succeeded in renting out all the available rooms, so at the moment nothing is empty, and on average I have managed to achieve rents which even the Victoria, in the present circumstances, consider good.

Then, in the summer of 1936, the Victoria abruptly demanded payment in full on the balance of the loan. The Wolff family lawyers protested that the quarterly mortgage repayments were being made and would continue. That did not satisfy the Victoria; its lawyers went to court in June and petitioned for a forced sale. The Victoria's lawyers made clear that they were not prepared to give the Wolff family any alternative. They certainly knew, as the Wolff lawyers did, that such payment terms were impossible and the family would be forced to surrender their property.

(This account of the takeover of the building is based upon court and legal documents that my mother's lawyers were able to obtain when she sought to win back the Wolff building in the 1990s.)

From a purely business point of view, demanding full and immediate payment of the mortgage made no sense, and suggested that some other motivation was behind the demand. At that time, however, whatever the Wolff family and lawyers might suspect, it wasn't possible to prove the true agenda. Nonetheless, the family's representatives put up a good fight to retain the building.

On September 4, 1936, Ludwig Salomon wrote back to *Amtsgericht* Charlottenburg to inform the court that all the land surrounding the entire estate at Conradstrasse 1 in Wannsee, which he had been administering on behalf of the heirs, had now been disposed of. He reported that he received RM 90,299 (about $36,400, nowadays $614,000).

But, on October 21, 1936, the Victoria wrote to *Amtsgericht* Charlottenburg about the mortgage on Krausenstrasse. It was requesting that various sums due to them be put in different categories, and they also asked about early payment of RM 320 (which, at about $130 at the time, seems an absurdly small amount to be making a fuss about).

Yet on October 31, 1936, the Victoria made an entry in the land registry document for Krausenstrasse 17/18 that a forced sale was pending.

On November 2, 1936, Ludwig Salomon again wrote to the court. As he reported, matters had taken a most ominous turn:

> Herewith I respectfully inform you that today, at the request of the Victoria, the sequestration of the property Krausenstrasse 17/18 has been ordered, and the official receiver has been placed in possession of the house.

With this move, Salomon pointed out that his role, as administrator of Lucie Wolff's estate on behalf of her heirs, had become redundant, "This is the only significant asset of the estate and the purpose of administration of estates becomes illusory."

Pathetically, he went on to say that he had no money to dispose of, not even to pay his own fees. "However, on the express wish of the Victoria, I am prepared to continue administering the estate for a short time so that matters can proceed without difficulties."

Salomon reported that he had already collected all the rents due on November 1, 1936, and all the monies had been disbursed as soon as they came in. And it seems that the Victoria valued his expertise in the handling of the estate. According to this letter, the Victoria was prepared to wait for further rental payments to come in and the company would even pay RM 1,450 ($580) still owed to Salomon in unpaid fees.

On November 27, 1936, Max Michaelis wrote to the court in protest about the insurance company's demand for payment, and argued that the threatened forced auction was unnecessary.

"The building was constructed in 1907–08," he wrote, "by Kommerzienrat Victor Wolff on four parcels of land. It is one of the best business buildings in the City of Berlin."

He went on to state that, according to the attached certification, its value that day was RM 2.7 million (nearly $1.1 million in 1936 U.S. dollars). The mortgage of RM 1.2 million was taken out in 1929 when the building was valued at RM 2.565 million. To rebuild such a building would cost more than RM 3 million.

An additional problem, predating the Nazis, then emerges from the correspondence. This was the so-called Brüning Laws, which came into effect December 8, 1931. In an attempt to alleviate the suffering in the aftermath of the 1929 Great Crash, these laws were enacted to enable tenants with commercial rental contracts to simply cancel them. This is what had now happened. Originally intended to improve the competitiveness of German industry, the impact of the laws was effectively to devalue the Reichsmark by lowering wages, salaries, interest rates, and rents. The net result was a catastrophic rental market, especially in the city of Berlin. Tenants exerted extreme pressure on landlords, who suffered heavily.

The impact on rents at Krausenstrasse 17/18 was recorded in detail by Max Michaelis. The total rental income for 1931 was RM 308,585 (around $73,000 in 1931 U.S. dollars) but this had diminished to RM 213,549 the following year, when these laws were only partly activated. One year later, rental income had fallen to a mere RM 104,100. Yet by January 1, 1937, the worst was over and total rental income showed a recovery, albeit small, to RM 118,500.

But even so, in early 1937 the big firms, which had rented space in the building at RM 40 or more per square meter (about RM 430 per square foot—around $170 in 1937 U.S. dollars) prior to the introduction of the Brüning Laws, were continuing to exploit this law to keep down their rents to RM 15 per square meter (about RM 160 per square foot) or even less. For example, the fashion house Ahders & Basch had, until December 31, 1934, paid RM 66,000 for the third floor of the building, yet by 1937, it was paying a mere RM 15,800.

By this time the courts and the laws were stacked against any Jewish claimant. It took courage for a Jewish owner or lawyer even to object to the Victoria's demand. Most Jewish lawyers had been banned from practicing law. The main exceptions were those with several decades of experience and veterans of the First World War. The Wolff lawyers apparently belonged to one or both of those categories.

Michaelis insisted the Victoria Insurance Company's sudden decision to foreclose was a reversal of their stance only a few months earlier, and had taken the owners by surprise. To support his case, that prospects for the Wolff building were excellent, Michaelis argued that German commercial life, particularly in Berlin, was entering a period of revival despite the worldwide Depression. Many new government buildings were being constructed, such as the enormous Air Ministry (which still stands today, now serving as the Ministry of Finance). Also there was a block between Leipziger Strasse, Wilhelmstrasse, and Zimmerstrasse, where buildings had been taken over by the Reich for a big central post office. Several premises were bought on Mauerstrasse next to the Ministry of Propaganda as well. The shortage of private business rental properties was further exacerbated, claimed Michaelis, by Hitler's Four-Year Plan, which saw the introduction of new laws forbidding privately held premises from being altered from domestic to business use.

Space used for the expansion of government meant that the number of buildings suitable for commercial rental was reduced. Already there was a dire shortage of available properties, Michaelis pointed out, so rents should start to increase, for the Wolff building and everyone else.

According to Michaelis, Krausenstrasse 17/18 was "in ship-shape order" ("*in tadelloser Ordnung*"), all taxes paid and not a single creditor asking for payment. He argued that this valuable family-owned property should be given a chance to survive the economic crisis that was ending. He made clear that the Victoria Insurance Company's demand for foreclosure would ruin the longtime owners. Given that the rental clients would certainly not wish to deprive themselves of the floor space, he asserted that the building could be increasingly financially successful.

The tenants, almost all of whom were very prestigious firms, had already occupied the building for many years and, explained Michaelis, they would surely rather agree to pay increased rent than have to embark on an expensive relocation. The principal tenants were Dick & Goldschmidt and Ahders & Basch, the former having rented there since it was built. Dick & Goldschmidt occupied the best rooms on the ground and first floor. It was because of the Brüning Laws that a crisis had arisen, but the Wolff heirs had sacrificed everything to try to keep up their payments. Parcels of land on the Wannsee estate were sold off and all of the monies had been passed to the Victoria Insurance Company. It appeared that the Victoria had been perfectly content—until now—with Ludwig Salomon's financial management on behalf of the heirs, but that an apparent change of heart suddenly occurred.

Michaelis ended his plea to the court by pointing out the Victoria was being unnecessarily harsh, particularly because there were minors involved—the three young Wolff children who were in difficult financial circumstances at that time.

"Immediately after the last parcel was sold from the Wannsee property, the last debt was paid to the Victoria [but] suddenly the applicant, in opposition to a statement made shortly before to Salomon, initiated a forced sale and forced administration. If the applicant continues with this decision, the heirs will lose the property which, since the building's construction has, without interruption, belonged to the family and which was administered in an orderly fashion."

Backing up Herr Michaelis, Ludwig Salomon wrote, on December 1, 1936, to the district court in Charlottenburg informing them the entire Wannsee estate had been sold, with the agreement of the heirs, to cover monies due to the Victoria Insurance Company. He provided an itemized list of all the rents being received from the many companies with offices in Krausenstrasse, including some very well-known names, such as Hermanns & Froitzheim, Heymann Welter & Co, Gertrud Isenburg, Dick & Goldschmidt, Ahders & Basch, Kraft & Lewin, Krahnen & Gobbers and, of course, Herbert's friend the insurer Bleichröder & Co.

And, Salomon added, despite having paid the Victoria the sum of RM 9,000 (about $3,630 in 1936 U.S. dollars) on October 1 that year, he was surprised to receive, at very short notice, a compulsory administration order. He believed he was turning the business income around, and he argued that he should be given more time to pay off the remaining mortgage to the Victoria Insurance Company. He added that all that remained of the Wannsee estate were a few household items, which were of very little value.

A series of letters followed from Ludwig Salomon to the district court in Charlottenburg. On February 8 and March 6, he sent updates on rentals received. On March 10, 1937, he wrote plaintively about how hard it was, on account of the Victoria's actions, to administer the estate and, due to the forced administration, he had no monies to pay out on accrued expenses. The only asset he retained was the company typewriter that had been valued at RM 90 (about $36 at that time). Because he needed the typewriter for his work, he was ready to buy it himself, and would deduct it from the wages he was owed dating back to November 1, 1936. The situation was clearly dire.

Perhaps not surprisingly, all of the Wolff family representatives' arguments fell on deaf ears. The court's ruling went against them, as everyone involved must have known that it would. The Wolff lawyers had no choice but to accept the foreclosure and to transfer ownership of the building not to the Victoria but directly to the Reichsbahn, or German Railways, for the use of the Nazi government. At that point, it became clear what was afoot, but there was nothing to be done: no appeal, no recourse.

Contemporary newspaper accounts of the atmosphere of that time amply illustrate what any Jew was up against. In the *Berliner Tage-*

blatt newspaper of May 16, 1937, the classified and sales section had an advertisement that read, "Glove factory with large machine park, established for 30 years, to be sold at very low price from non-Aryan proprietors." The economics section had a special column reporting on compulsory auctions, "The area belonging to the traders Chaim Brumberger and David Hecht, purchased by Mrs. Ottilie von Oertzen."

And it was in this disastrous business environment that, on May 25, 1937, Ludwig Salomon handed over a full list of tenants to the Reichsbahn, and assured its officials that those tenants had paid all due rents and many of them were still in the building.

On May 26, 1937, Ludwig Salomon and Dr. Hans Fritz Abraham appeared in the district court on behalf of the Wolff heirs; Dr. Harry Koppin and Albert Fatrot, Reichsbahnoberinspektor (railway inspector), appeared on behalf of the German Railways. The official record states: "This agreement has been read out to those present and has been signed by them."

The land and building was sold for RM 1.8 million ($725,800 at the time) to the Reichsbahn, and thus, became the property of the German Reich. From this figure, RM 1,405,603 ($566,775) was paid to the Victoria. This covered the RM 1,200,000 ($483,870) mortgage, and interest of RM 200,603 ($80,888) as well as RM 5,000 in fees ($2,016). Another RM 331,723 ($133,759) went to pay off two bank loans. A further RM 28,167 ($11,357) went for an interest payment and fees to lawyers. The residual RM 29,065 (about $11,700) was left over for Fritz, but he had to use what was left to pay other legal fees. There were a few additional small expenses as well, so at the end of it all he was left with RM 1,629 (just under $400 in those days).

The agreement stipulated that the German Railways were not to be held liable for any mortgage due to the Victoria Insurance Company, and all necessary payments to the heirs had been made to Ludwig Salomon, their lawyer. Salomon was to notify all tenants of the sale, and immediately start negotiations for their departure from the building. Both parties agreed that the property would be fully vacated by October 1, 1937.

Ludwig Salomon and Dr. Harry Koppin signed the formal sales agreement, dated May 31, 1937. It stated that, based on the May 26

contract, the German Railways in Berlin would henceforth be registered as the new owner.

The humiliation of the Wolff family continued on June 10, 1937,
when the Victoria wrote to Dr. Abraham to inform him they had
received an advance payment from the Reichsbahn of RM 1,405,603,
covering the mortgage and interest and payment to Ludwig Salomon.
The letter ends with the Nazi sign-off, "*Mit deutschem Gruss.*" (Translation: "With German Greetings.")

There were still a few loose ends to tidy up.

On July 16, the German government appointed an administrator to
run the building. His name was Bärenfänger (literally, bear catcher).
He reported to the government that he had made the required payment to the administrator representing the heirs of Lucie Wolff. Herr
Bärenfänger took the trouble to underline his contempt for the former
owners by adding a handwritten note on the letter, making reference to
Ludwig Salomon and adding an exclamation point after his name—a
little flourish to emphasize that he was dealing with a Jew.

On July 23, Herr Salomon wrote a final reckoning for the district
court accounting for all the monies taken in and paid out. Despite all
the evidence that the Wolff building had been a viable concern, the
family was left with virtually nothing from its glory days. The Wolff
family, like so many others, was a victim of what the Nazis called
"*Entjudung,*" the removal of Jews from the German economy.

The bottom line was the building had been taken from its owners by
the Nazis, like countless others, in a legal process that was a travesty
of justice.

During the course of my quest to find out what happened in the
prewar years, I discovered the fate of some of the tenants who had
operated their companies from Krausenstrasse 17/18. In September
1993, our lawyers informed my mother that they had found a book
by Uwe Westphal, published in 1992, *Berliner Konfektion und Mode:
Die Zerstörung einer Tradition, 1836–1939* (*The Berlin Garment and
Fashion Industry: The Destruction of a Tradition, 1836–1939*). Apart
from Bernhard Bleichröder's insurance business, all the other tenants
renting office space in Krausenstrasse 17/18 had been Jewish garment

manufacturers. The owners of Cohen & Kempe and Anders & Basch had immigrated to the United States sometime between 1933 and 1938, while the proprietors of Dick & Goldschmidt went to London in 1937. Some had clearly escaped but as for the rest, I can only surmise their ultimate fate.

8

"WHAT WOULD I DO WITHOUT THE LÜNEBURGER HEIDE?"

In the early 1990s, little was known about Fritz after his release, in May 1933, from three months' detention in Spandau prison. I would discover more over the years, as later pages will reveal, but most of what we knew came from a few legal documents and correspondence, as well as family lore. Some of the letters Fritz wrote to Herbert and Nellie in Palestine survive. They reveal a man who was generous, kind, and concerned for Nellie and her children's welfare, but above all he was profoundly unworldly.

A letter to Nellie in March 1934 began by wishing her a belated happy birthday. He was late, he says, because, "I could unfortunately not derive from my astronomical calendar" the correct date, until his Aunt Franziska, Lucie's sister, provided it. He goes on to joke that this correspondence, "has not got the character of a 'birthday letter' but you surely did not expect and could not have expected such a bourgeois tableau from me."

He makes clear that he wants to help Nellie all he can, and he offered a suggestion. His wife, Charlotte, had died just a few months earlier.

"Having dissolved my little household now I started to wonder whether you would wish to be sent the blue and white china as well as mother's seal fur coat, for which I am afraid I have no use now." He adds, "It would not be worth it to send over the *Schwechten* piano, would it?" This was the grand piano that Nellie had played and Aviva had taken lessons on in the Wannsee mansion.

Fritz's comments on Nellie and Herbert's decision to live in Palestine are humorous but disapproving.

> I would like to state my opinion on your emigration to you. You know Herbert left at a time when I was prevented from talking to him and offering him advice. [That is, Fritz was in Spandau prison.] He did mention the possibility of going to Palestine at some point, to which I replied that I could not see any future in that overpopulated stone desert. I advised you to follow him not only because it was Herbert's urgent wish but also because I was plagued by pressing and well-founded worries about your personal welfare if you had stayed behind.
>
> I do not know what Herbert takes to be "the idea behind it." [He apparently means Zionism, the drive to rebuild a Jewish homeland.] If he is referring to Jewry's pacifist world mission as sung about by biblical prophets, I do not believe that this can be achieved by returning to barren pastures that had been abandoned millennia ago and have not turned fecund in the meantime. In the history of the world, no people has ever done this out of "reverence," or, if it has, it has been punished with shambles and oblivion—but only from a position of power acquired by strength of body and mind.

Having expressed his doubts about the Jewish homeland, Fritz offers an alternative:

> For these reasons my mind returns to the possibility of you coming back here, even more so now that more and more emigrants are returning to Germany. Certainly it should not be a problem for Herbert as an Iron Cross–decorated veteran.

He reports that Aunt Franziska "is asking whether Herbert could not work in journalism, for which, in her opinion, he would be well capable."

He adds, "My address remains the same because I am renting a room in the same house," and closes with, "My most heartfelt regards to all of you."

At some point in 1934, Fritz moved again. This time, he lodged with Dr. and Mrs. Hierl, who had been friends with the Wolff family for many years. Fritz's decision to live with them is amazing for one reason: Dr. Hierl's brother, Konstantin Hierl, joined the Nazi party in 1928 and had become close to Hitler. In June 1935, Konstantin became the head of the Reich Labor Service, which was responsible for constructing military fortifications, supplying front line troops, guarding prisoners, and laying minefields. He remained in that role until the end of the war, achieving the rank of *Reichsleiter*, a status immediately below the Führer himself in the Nazi hierarchy. In February 1945, he was awarded the highest honor the Nazi party could give—the German Order. (After the war, he was tried for war crimes and sentenced to five years' hard labor.)

Why would Fritz, a Communist who feared arrest and imprisonment, run the risk of living in the home of this prominent Nazi's brother? Nellie told Aviva it was because Dr. Hierl was anti-Nazi and a man who scorned his brother's politics. Years later I found another possible reason Dr. Hierl and his wife took Fritz into their home—and perhaps why Fritz felt safe there. On June 23, 1937, Fritz withdrew a sizeable sum from his account at the Deutsche Bank in Berlin and gave RM 5,000 (more than $2,000) each to Dr. Hierl, his wife and another family member identified as H. W. Hierl.

Early in 1938, Fritz moved again, this time to Zepernick, an outer suburb of Berlin. At that time, a fresh wave of legal maneuvers was enacted by the state to further deprive Jews of their dignity, rights, and possessions. On April 26, the Decree for the Reporting of Jewish Owned Property meant that every Jew with assets valued at over RM 5,000 had to declare these to the state, including not only those within Germany, but anything owned abroad. Declarations had to be made to the official designated body by June 20, and failure to comply could lead to imprisonment as well as a fine. And, if someone were found to have willfully ignored the order, the punishment was up to ten years' hard labor. Without a doubt Fritz's assets exceeded RM 5,000. He certainly filled in the form, as I was to discover.

In August 1938, the Nazis ordered that, by January 1939, all Jews who had Germanic names that did not immediately identify them as Jewish would have to adopt the middle name "Israel" if male, and "Sara" if female. In October, all German passports owned by Jews had to have a letter "J" stamped in them. By November, Jews were excluded from all cinemas, concerts, theatres, libraries, swimming pools, parks, and gardens. Signs saying, "No Jews Allowed" were quite common on park benches, in restaurants, and in hotels. All Jewish children attending public schools were expelled, by order of the Minister of Education, and forced into Jewish-only educational establishments. By the close of 1938, Jews had to apply for, and carry at all times, an identity card.

Fritz may have managed to avoid contact with the Gestapo until now, but he could not evade their attentions after Kristallnacht, the "Night of Broken Glass" on November 9–10 when Jewish-owned shops, communal properties, homes, schools, and synagogues were wrecked and set on fire. The Nazis decreed that Jews could not make a claim on their insurance to repair the damage. In fact there was even a special tax levied on Jews to pay for the clean up.

The roundup of some 30,000 Jews following Kristallnacht affected Fritz as well. On November 22, 1938, he was detained for at least his second time, although Herbert later wrote that it was Fritz's fourth occasion. I have not found records for the two other arrests. This time, Fritz was sent to Sachsenhausen concentration camp, 22 miles north of Berlin, which had opened in 1936.

It was only in July 1995 that my mother received definitive, official proof that Fritz was sent to Sachsenhausen. The International Tracing Service in Germany, which at that time was managed by the International Committee of the Red Cross, wrote her stating that new documents had been provided to them:

After evaluating these documents, the following information about the imprisonment of your uncle could be determined:

WOLFF, Fritz, was born on 4.10.1891

On 22 November 1938 he was brought to the Sachsenhausen
concentration camp, Prisoner number 13677 and he was released
from there on the 6 December 1938 Category: Jew.

Conditions in Sachsenhausen in late November/early December 1938
have been described as "nightmarish." The number of prisoners surged
to 14,000 due to the 6,000 extra inmates brought in after Kristallnacht.
What must have been going through Fritz's mind as he entered this
frightful place, circled by a stone wall, dotted at intervals by guard tow-
ers, and with an inner electric barbed-wire fence to stop anyone escaping?

Surprisingly, Fritz was released after two weeks. Why? The Nazis
were prepared to let prisoners go free, under the condition they com-
mit themselves to emigration. And that was exactly what occurred in
his case. Herbert later explained that he had written to the German
authorities and informed them that he would obtain the paperwork
necessary for his brother to live in Syria, which at the time was controlled by France. Fritz was duly released on December 6 and must
have given assurances that he would soon leave the country.

But Fritz had residual business to conduct. Even though the building had now left the Wolff family's hands forever, the authorities were
hounding him to clear up the odds and ends of the former Wolff business empire. He continued working on this aspect of his family's former life late into 1938.

In a letter dated December 6, 1938, from Ludwig Salomon to the
district court at Charlottenburg, Salomon had to explain that Fritz had
been unable to deal with his affairs on account of having been arrested
and sent to Sachsenhausen: "Fritz W is prevented at the moment from
sorting out his business affairs."

On December 10, 1938, Fritz, now back in Zepernick, wrote a letter
to Ludwig Salomon clearing up the final loose ends from the forced
sale of the Krausenstrasse property. I have a letter where he writes
Salomon that he is gifting the typewriter to the heirs of Lucie Wolff.

On that same day, Fritz also wrote, explaining to the district court,
why he had failed to respond to a request for a document, ". . . on

account of the action which took place in the meantime, unfortunately it is no longer possible to provide the requested letter . . ."

The Nazi laws were progressively tightening their noose around the remaining Jews in Berlin. At the end of December, all unemployed Jews had to register to work. Despite all of this harassment, instead of leaving the country, Fritz moved to Dresdener Strasse 97, in central Berlin, where he was living on May 15, 1939, when the Nazis threatened him with an ultimatum. Fritz had four weeks to get out of Germany or he would be taken back, as he had been the previous year, into "protective detention" (*Schutzhaft*).

On May 31 he wrote again to Herbert in Palestine. He made one statement that suggested that his idealism was nearing a state of pure fantasy:

"I maintain that this whole quarrel is a love quarrel between nations . . . If there is ever any question about which nation I belong to, the only answer is Germany."

Fritz loved Germany, and refused to leave it, because he apparently didn't accept that his life was in real danger.

My mother recalled, "My father used to tell me that he was constantly writing to Fritz asking him to come out and join us. He had managed to get him a visa to Syria, but Fritz wouldn't hear of it. He wrote back saying, 'What would I do without the *Lüneburger Heide*?'"

That is an area of beautiful heath and woodland in Northern Germany where, in happier times, Fritz had gone every summer on walking holidays. Its peace and beauty must have become more real to him than the horrors he faced in the hell of Nazi-ruled Berlin.

9

MAKING HER OWN WAY

Marion Parish, the former nanny who had taken Aviva into her south London home, proved not to be the ideal landlady. My mother described her as "a really nasty anti-Semite who used to make horrible remarks about Jews all the time." For example, Jewish dance bands were popular in England at the time, but Mrs. Parish dismissed them all as "Jewboys." As a strong-minded teenager, just arrived from Palestine, Aviva fiercely objected to the woman's racist remarks. But the two managed to coexist, because my mother needed a place to live and Mrs. Parish needed the rent money. In her mid-teens, with little money and few friends in London, she could not make trouble with the woman who had put a roof over her head.

Moreover, Aviva found that she was happy at Babington House. Her three years there were the longest she had ever spent in one school. As a penniless Jewish refugee, who had previously attended numerous schools in Germany, Switzerland, France, and Palestine, she had little in common with the other girls in her class. Her recent experiences had made her far tougher and more mature than they could possibly be. She made few close friends and it didn't help that Mrs. Parish banned her from inviting any friends to the house. The result was that none of the girls ever invited her to their homes.

She spoke excellent English of course, thanks to her nannies. She developed a love for English novels and plays, and made the top grades in her literature classes. Her favorites included Thomas Hardy, Shakespeare, Jane Austen, and George Eliot. Not everything was smooth sailing however. Aviva vividly remembered one incident when the entire school was told to sing the hymn "Onward Christian Soldiers" during morning assembly. "I just stood there with my lips shut," she told me. When the headmistress spotted the one girl not singing, she made the assembled throng sing the hymn no less than three times, because she was so determined to make her join in. But my mother refused. So she was summoned to the headmistress' room and given a sound telling off!

Aviva had a bit of trouble with math, but a Scottish teacher gave her special tutoring that got her through. Her performance was such that before graduation she was made a prefect, which was a considerable honor at the school.

She received one pound every month (equivalent to $4 at the time) for spending money from an English friend of Nellie's, and she was sometimes invited for tea with her benefactor, Erich Turk, at his apartment on fashionable Cadogan Square. Babington House was a wonderful experience for this young refugee, but when she graduated in the summer of 1939 her future was uncertain. "I sometimes had dreams about going to university," she explained to me, "but they were totally unrealistic. Who would have paid for me?"

It was never going to be her father, Herbert, although he wrote her long, effusive letters telling her how much he loved her, and how important he considered a good education.

My mother received some helpful advice: "After she stopped being a nanny, my landlady, Mrs. Parish, had trained as a nurse and she told me that was what I should do because it would put a roof over my head and that was a major consideration."

Aviva thought that sounded like good advice and she soon learned that two women whose opinions she valued agreed with Mrs. Parish. She had been going up to Edinburgh to visit the Turk sisters each vacation. That summer of 1939, after her high school graduation, she went to Edinburgh again seeking advice. As my mother later recounted to me:

Dr. Martha Turk had been a pediatrician in Germany and she was keen on the idea that all the refugee children she was helping should get training they could carry with them. She urged me to become a nurse. She saw it as a way to gain professional training I could use anywhere in the world. She arranged for me to train at the Princess Margaret Rose Hospital in Edinburgh. I wasn't at all unhappy there, although it was very hard work. I lived in the hospital, had one day off each month and earned about £40 ($160) a year. Then the war broke out.

The Netherlands, Belgium, and France quickly fell to Hitler's armies. By the spring of 1940, England faced the threat of a German invasion, one that might be aided by an advance guard of spies and saboteurs. Winston Churchill, the new prime minister, issued orders to "collar the lot." Unfortunately, my mother, as a German—even a teenage Jewish girl who had fled Hitler—was numbered among "the lot" to be collared.

All Germans living near the British coast were ordered to relocate inland or face internment. The government's fear was that German spies might report on the movement of ships and submarines. Because Edinburgh, Scotland, is on the Firth of Forth, which at the time was the site of an important naval base, there was also legitimate fear of spies gathering information on military installations.

Aviva returned to London and made the rounds of hospitals, hoping that her few months of nurse training in Edinburgh would earn her a job. Everyone turned her down because of her status as an "enemy alien." She was only one of countless frustrated job seekers, including many German Jews who might have been doctors but now, as in Palestine, were waiters or construction workers. She found that British doctors, not wanting competition, often opposed the hiring of German doctors, however well qualified.

After experiencing many rejections because of her status, my mother suddenly enjoyed a burst of good luck. She was called before a tribunal that she feared would send her, like so many refugees—including her old friend from Berlin, Peter Block—to internment on the Isle of Man, off the coast of northwest England.

Instead, she learned that her parents, whom she hadn't seen since 1936, had become subjects of the British Mandate of Palestine. Because she had been a child at the time they achieved this status, she, too, was now a "Palestinian." Thanks to this she was no longer viewed as a security threat, and she was recruited as a nursing trainee at the Royal Cancer Hospital (now the Royal Marsden) on Fulham Road.

In the summer of 1940, Hitler's *Luftwaffe* tried to achieve air supremacy over the British Royal Air Force in advance of invading Britain, just over 20 miles across the English Channel from Nazi-occupied northern France. But thanks to the skill and bravery of the RAF pilots, in what became known as the Battle of Britain, the tactic was unsuccessful. Hitler decided to switch to night bombings of London and other English cities instead, in an attempt to break the spirit of the British people.

During the nights of mass bombing raids, known as The Blitz, through the winter of 1940 and spring of 1941, Aviva was busy at the Royal Cancer Hospital. She lived in the hospital and at night could hear the Germans trying to bomb the nearby Battersea power station beside the River Thames. Many of the patients she worked with were in advanced stages of cancer, and in great pain. She did what she could for them and, as the most junior trainee on the night duty roster, part of her job was to lay out the dead. It was a wretched task for a teenager. There was a total blackout during the bombings; not even flashlights were allowed, lest they help guide the enemy flying above. It was both a terrifying and an exhilarating time, as bombs fell, London burned, and no one knew what the future held.

The RCH allowed aspiring nurses to take only half their training in London and insisted they complete the course in Sheffield. Aviva rejected that plan. "I had discovered that training at the Royal Cancer Hospital didn't give the same status as training at one of the major teaching hospitals like University College Hospital. That meant a lot to me, so I traipsed round the hospitals again and UCH said they'd take me but they didn't recognize the training I'd had up until then. I'd have to start over from scratch."

She decided the UCH nursing qualification was worth it. Soon after she turned 20, my mother started her training over at UCH. She never regretted it. "I learned a lot and had a fine time too. I had boyfriends who were training to be doctors at the nearby Middlesex Hospital.

They would come and visit me when I was on night duty. They would climb up the fire escape and I'd give them coffee or cocoa in the ward kitchen. Of course all that was strictly forbidden. But you don't think of that when you're in your 20s. It was fun.

"I started nursing in the private wing at UCH and one day a patient said to me, 'You remind me so much of two girls at Henrietta Barnett, the school where I teach.' I asked their names. 'Vera and Doris Heller,'" she said.

Of course my mother remembered them! These were the girls she had visited with her own mother on first arriving in England in 1936. No longer at the convent school, they had moved to a respected all-girls prep school in North London.

It was one of those coincidences that emerged during the turmoil of a World War. Aviva called the Hellers and soon became close to the family. "Lona Heller regarded me almost as another daughter. This was the first time anyone had treated me as a proper parent should. She let me hold my 21st birthday party in her house. For the first time in my life I was having a real family life."

As the war raged on, parts of UCH were evacuated to the Ashridge House estate in Hertfordshire. Makeshift huts were erected on the grounds of this stately, old country house—the kind that recalls Brideshead or Downton Abbey—and turned into wards where severely injured soldiers were treated. Aviva and the other nurses would wheel recovering soldiers out into the gardens to enjoy the sun. This was Aviva's home for two years, and a time she remembers fondly.

She had a boyfriend there named Donald Phillips who had been a medical student at London's Middlesex Hospital, but was evacuated to a nearby village. With strict gas rationing, the only way to travel the several miles from the village to Ashridge was by bicycle, and Donald had one. Their romance lasted almost two years, but the problem was that Aviva couldn't stand Donald's snobbish mother, who visited sometimes and made it clear that no nurse was good enough for her darling boy. "He asked me to marry him but I turned him down because of his mother," my mother told me. To her delight, Donald eventually married another nurse.

In the fall of 1944, by then a registered nurse with an annual salary of £60 ($240), Aviva kept her promise to the Turk sisters to come live and work in Edinburgh. She enrolled in a one-year midwifery-training program at Simpson Memorial Maternity Hospital, part of the Royal Infirmary of Edinburgh. For the first six months, she delivered babies under supervision at the hospital.

After that she was sent out "on the district," to live with a midwife and accompany her as she delivered babies in women's homes. Unfortunately, she was assigned to help a mean-spirited woman who wouldn't even let Aviva give an aspirin to women in labor. She justified her cruelty by citing Genesis 3:16 which says, ". . . in pain you shall bring forth children."

Fortunately, the woman was lazy and often left deliveries entirely to her young helper. Aviva worked in Leith, now a fashionable section of Edinburgh, but back then it was a slum where people lived amid poverty and horrible insanitary conditions. She would walk those dirty streets at any time, day or night, tramping up and down the grimy stairs of dilapidated tenement blocks; often she would find women in labor lying on paper on the floor, with fleas leaping about and dirt everywhere. Sometimes she would tell the husband to go outside and sit on the stairs while she delivered the baby, but first, she would ask him to give her his shirt to wrap the newborn in.

Despite the dire conditions, my mother, dressed in her nurse's uniform and carrying her delivery bag, was always treated with the utmost respect. These people were nearly all destitute, and many were uneducated, but they felt great esteem for the nurses and midwives they so depended on.

The mothers were almost all married—illegitimacy was rare and frowned upon—but often they were so uneducated that they would ask, "Nurse, where is the baby going to come out?" She was tempted to tell them, "It's coming out the same place you made it!" Some believed the baby would emerge from their belly button.

A week or so after a birth, Aviva would go back and examine the mother and child, and offer what advice and assistance she could. After that, the mothers were on their own. How those women would be able to raise their children troubled her greatly. She often reflected on how different those babies' lives would be from her own childhood back in Berlin.

10

AFTER THE WAR: LOVE AND MARRIAGE

The July 1945 elections in Britain resulted in a surprise defeat for Winston Churchill and his Conservative Party. Clement Attlee's Labour Party was elected with a large majority. Among the many post-war reforms introduced by the new Labour administration was one that was to propel Aviva's life in a new direction. The new government decreed that everyone who had done war work could apply for a grant to attend university. Fortunately for my mother, nursing qualified as war work and so she applied for, and was given, a grant to study social sciences at Edinburgh University.

In September 1946, I began one of the best times of my life. I lived in a little basement flat and had a wonderful time. I joined all the clubs I could and became president of the Cosmopolitan Club, which was for foreign students. In my second year I moved in with a woman called Margaret Henderson. She had two young children and a husband who was a doctor at sea with the Royal

Navy. She was lonely so she rented me a small windowless room with a skylight. It worked out well for both of us.

In the summer of 1947, my mother became a naturalized British subject. Her transformation from German citizen to Palestinian national to British passport holder was complete.

Aviva wanted to qualify as a psychiatric social worker and to do so she had to take a one-year mental health course. Only two universities offered the course, Edinburgh and the London School of Economics (LSE). She was accepted at both.

During her spring break from Edinburgh University in 1948 she traveled to London to visit the LSE and was invited to stay with her old friend from Berlin, Peter Block, who was a student there. When Peter had been interned on the Isle of Man, he learned that one way out was to volunteer for dangerous military duties. Peter joined the paratroopers and after training was dropped into France to work with the Resistance. (His father, Marcel, had escaped to France during the war, been captured by the Nazis there, and was deported and murdered in Auschwitz.)

Now, with the war over, Peter was sharing a house on Burrard Road, West Hampstead, with several other ex-servicemen. One day, he asked his friend Dan Gold if he could share his room when Aviva came to visit. Dan asked Peter if she was "a looker."

Peter assured him that she was.

"I've got a much better idea," Dan announced. "You stay in your room and send her to stay in mine!"

Peter laughed and replied, "You don't stand a chance, mate." He explained that where Aviva and boys were concerned, the boys were "like bees round a honeypot."

Dan Gold was a slim, athletic, handsome young man with dark, wavy hair. Peter rejected the sleeping arrangement he proposed but, nonetheless, when Dan and Aviva met, they felt an instant attraction. They exchanged letters after she returned for her final semester in Edinburgh. Every day he would write, helping with her work in math and statistics, which weren't her strengths but were his. "Marry me," he promised, "and you'll never have to do math again."

He came to Edinburgh for my mother's graduation ball, where he wore a borrowed dinner jacket. They hitchhiked back to London together and she subsequently moved into his room in the house on Burrard Road.

Dan's grandfather had come to England from Eastern Europe, and started a small business that sold tailors' supplies in the East End of London. In time, Dan's father, took over and wanted nothing more than for his own son to follow in his footsteps. But my father, born in 1921, never saw that as his destiny. He was very different from his parents. He was an outstanding student and extremely musical, although denied music lessons, which were deemed as having no practical value.

Aviva recognized a major cultural clash looming between her family and Dan's. She viewed the Wolff family, although no longer wealthy, as educated, cultured people who knew something of the world, but to her the Golds were small-minded, utterly conventional Eastern Europeans. The Golds, for their part, were appalled that this young woman, who looked likely to become their daughter-in-law, wore long pants instead of dresses or skirts, and was indifferent to Jewish religious ritual and observances. Worse still, she had a mind of her own and no money.

When war had been declared between Britain and Germany on September 3, 1939, Dan had immediately volunteered for the RAF. He was given an aptitude test that showed he was strong in science, and that led him into training courses that he found fascinating. "A whole new world opened up," he said later. "Why hadn't they told us about this at school? This was science in action and I reveled in it." His wartime service was spent with a unit that moved from one airbase to another to maintain Lorenz Beam landing systems.

Unlike many of his contemporaries, who spent their leisure hours in bars or chasing girls, my father spent his free time taking courses that qualified him for university when the war ended. He entered LSE on the same grant program as my mother, and he studied economics and statistics.

In the immediate postwar years he, like many other Jewish ex-servicemen, was outraged to find that despite the defeat of Hitler, some British people still had fascist sympathies. The former leader of the British Union of Fascists, Oswald Mosley, and several of his followers, had been interned during the war. Within months of the war's end, pro-fascist rallies were held across London and southern England. Jewish men returning home after six years of fighting a bloody war were not prepared to put up with this activity. Many remembered that, as boys, they could be insulted or attacked by fascist thugs if they just happened to walk down the wrong street.

After all of this sacrifice, and particularly the horrific news coming out of Europe about the deaths of six million Jews, it was unacceptable to my father and his fellow Jewish ex-servicemen to have fascists once again strutting about, holding rallies, waving Nazi-style flags, and spewing their messages of anti-Semitic hate.

Dan became one of the founders of the 43 Group, named for the number of men who attended its first meeting. Soon their ranks numbered several hundred, including the then 17-year old Vidal Sassoon, later a celebrity hairdresser, who my father described as "a tough little fighter from the East End of London." They believed that the British government would do precious little to stop the fascist rallies. The argument was that freedom of speech was a fundamental right. The 43 Group didn't see it that way.

Well-organized bands of 43 Group members would tear down the platforms of the speakers. If the fascists were smart, they ran for their lives. If they tried to stand their ground, war-hardened men prepared to use their fists, and who often carried clubs or bricks to use as weapons, confronted them.

There's an excellent, 20-minute film entitled "The 43 Group" available on YouTube, which interviews many of the group's members and shows footage of rallies and street brawls. One of the old warriors comments that the fascists had always thought of Jews in terms of the "little tailor" who could be pushed around. The 43 Group disabused them of that notion.

At one point in the film a man, wearing a Mackintosh raincoat, who looks exactly like my father, can be glimpsed being pushed backwards by a policeman as police, fascists, and 43 Group members struggle in a street. The group had numerous members who didn't look at all Jewish and could infiltrate fascist meetings to learn their plans. My father looked too Jewish to do that, but became the head of the group's intel-ligence arm, as well as a street fighter at extremist rallies.

The fascists could not understand how the 43 Group always knew so much about their organization, their membership, their plans, and meeting places. My father told me that he had managed to insert not one, but two, Jewish agents into fascist planning meetings. The groups never realized they had been infiltrated, and Dan's moles were able to continue their invaluable work undetected. It became increasingly dif-ficult for the fascists to organize their rallies without disruption, and by the end of the decade, the fascist dream of a political revival was as dead as Hitler.

Living with Dan on Burrard Road, and busy at LSE studying for a certificate in mental health psychiatric social work, Aviva found definite drawbacks to being the only woman in an otherwise all-male house-hold. The men had previously rotated the chores, but now they liked to think their house cleaning days were over. One of the roommates, Val Sherman, was a dedicated Communist who, at age 17, fought with the Republican army in Spain. When asked to perform his share of the boring duties he always insisted he had to dash off to a party meeting. Later in life, his politics moved sharply to the right and he became an economics adviser to Prime Minister Margaret Thatcher, was knighted, and thenceforth became known as Sir Alfred Sherman.

Dan's parents didn't approve of their son living with Aviva, much less the prospect of their marrying. David Gold told his son that liv-ing together was wrong. "You don't do that sort of thing with the girl you're going to marry," he insisted.

To which Dan replied, "Well, who else do you want me to do it with?"

"It's not nice," his father persisted.

"No, you're wrong, it's *very* nice!" Dan fired back.

On one occasion, Dan's mother took Aviva to lunch. She spoke at length about all the wonderful girls who wanted to marry her son, and how this one's father would have bought them a house, and that another's would have taken him into his business. Finally, my mother could stand it no longer and burst out laughing, saying, "But he doesn't *want* to marry any of those girls!"

It wasn't that the couple was opposed to the institution of marriage, but each had a grant from the university as long as they were single— but not if they married. Money was too tight to sacrifice those grants for the sake of the respectability of marriage.

But Dan's parents persisted, and finally the lovers capitulated. Aviva went to Hampstead Town Hall and obtained a license to marry the following Saturday. When she reported back to Dan, he was shocked. "Saturday? That's Shabbat. You can't get married on Shabbat!"

Aviva was indifferent to the fact that Saturday was the traditional Jewish day of rest. The wedding was booked and she wasn't going to change it. Dan yielded and the marriage went ahead on July 17, 1948. My grandparents, David and Dora Gold, refused to attend. Those present included my mother's brother, Heini, by then an officer with the Israeli merchant marine, my father's sister Sheila, Peter Block, and Stanley Clements. Stanley was a blond, blue-eyed, rugby-playing veteran of the RAF. He was also a member of the 43 Group and one of two Jews who had gone undercover and sat on the fascist committees.

Dan's housemates were happy to welcome back the newlyweds, but Aviva became increasingly unhappy with the situation. "Living in the shared house as a married couple was a nightmare. All the other boys in the house still saw me as a friend and would come into our room and share all their problems with me. Dan got pretty fed up with that."

Dreaming of privacy, my mother spotted an advertisement for a caretaker for an apartment building on Upper Montague Street in Central London. The job came with a basement apartment—two rooms and a bathroom—free gas and electricity and rent the equivalent of just $2 a week. All that was required was that the caretakers clean the staircases and common areas. To Aviva, this sounded like heaven. She and Dan applied. They got the job—and with it their own home.

The Golds, however, were horrified. Their son, a caretaker! Living in a basement with a poor refugee girl, who came into the family without a dowry. For my mother, a lifetime of being patronized by her in-laws had begun.

After they were married a year, Aviva was working as a newly qualified psychiatric social worker, and Dan was midway through a two-year program that would lead to a master's degree in statistics. It bothered him that his wife was supporting them, so he quit graduate school and took a job with the National Coal Board in Newcastle, in the far north of England. His first task would be to set up a statistics department. One major attraction of the job was that it was a long way away from Dan's family.

True to their Socialist ideology, my parents bought a miner's cottage close to a coal mine in the village of Forest Hall in Northumberland.

Aviva found work in a number of Northumberland mental hospitals. As a student at LSE, she had trained at the Maudsley Mental Hospital, and she found that the hospitals in Northumberland, while well intentioned, were not as modern as those she'd known in London.

In one, severely troubled men were made to stand outside with nothing to do except a bit of gardening that didn't interest many of them. My mother suggested they be given a football to kick around, which proved popular with the patients. She also suggested they be given simple carpentry work—like sandpapering chair legs—to do outdoors. This led to the introduction of other forms of occupational therapy. Aviva and Dan stayed in Northumberland for seven years before they eventually returned to London in 1958.

With the war finally over, Aviva began to learn what had become of family members and friends with whom she had lost touch.

Her parents, Herbert and Nellie, had divorced in 1936. Herbert remarried and in 1940 his new wife, Eva, gave birth to a son, Michael, a much younger half-brother for my mother. During the war, Herbert had falsified his birth date to make him seem younger so he could gain a job as an account clerk for the RAF at an airbase in Cairo.

In his later life in Israel, Herbert attended classical music concerts— he never managed to learn enough Hebrew to attend the theater—bred cocker spaniels, read extensively, and researched the Wolff family history. His house in Ramat HaSharon, a suburb of Tel Aviv, was like a relic from another era, full of mementos of his life in Germany. He would often reminisce about past glories.

My mother had last seen her father in Palestine in 1936, at the age of 14, when she said goodbye to him before leaving for school in England. In 1952, he suddenly turned up in London at her friend Vera Heller's wedding; at that time, Aviva was 30 years old. Her father was still very handsome, and laid on the charm. After he returned to Israel, he wrote asking her to give him power of attorney to negotiate restitution of the family properties in Germany. She signed the papers without questioning him.

Like many other Jews, Herbert received a pension from the postwar German government. But what he really wanted was to obtain compensation for the Wannsee villa and estate. The mansion had been converted into apartments and several family homes had been built on the grounds.

A year went by without any news on the state of her father's claims before my mother wrote to her father's lawyer and asked him what was happening. In reply, she received a furious letter from Herbert asking, "How dare you get in touch with my lawyer?"

She replied that she simply wanted to know what was going on. She never did receive a reply from the lawyer and assumed that her father was trying to cheat her in some way.

And she was right, although it took many years to find out exactly how he was trying to do it. Half a century later, I unearthed a letter, dated August 21, 1947, from a Berlin realtor and property developer representing Herbert Wolff. The letter stated that Lucie Wolff had two sons, Herbert and Fritz, who were her joint heirs. One, Fritz, had been killed during the war, and the other, Herbert, had asked this man to make enquiries on his behalf about a certain address: Krausenstrasse 17/18. Clearly, Herbert was preparing to make a claim on that building.

"The scales fell from my eyes," my mother told me. From then on, she regarded him with suspicion and had virtually no relationship with him.

11

THOSE WHO SURVIVED AND THOSE WHO DID NOT

Fritz was arrested for the last time in February of 1943. My mother knew nothing of what happened after that, but had to assume he had been murdered in a concentration camp.

Boris Munk, Fritz's fellow Communist, who in 1933 had hidden from the Nazis at the Wannsee estate, left Germany for Palestine where he was a frequent visitor at Nellie's Tel Aviv apartment in Mazeh Street. But his heart was not into starting a new life in the Middle East, and he never settled. With the outbreak of the Spanish Civil War in 1936, Boris returned to Europe to fight with the Republicans battling General Franco's pro-German, Nationalist movement. He eventually ended up in Cuba, where he became a professor of economics after Fidel Castro took power.

Lucie Wolff's brother, Alfons David, was forced from office when the Nazis took power. The eminent lawyer, who had once proclaimed to his fellow judges, "I am a Jew!" had little choice but to flee from Germany. In March 1933, shortly before his removal from office as a Supreme Court Justice, he was quoted as saying: "I am deeply mortified that I am to leave office before I reach the mandatory retirement age, under such humiliating circumstances, after I have felt and acted my whole life like a 'real' German. Loyalty can be found in every religion and every race. I think statesmen should preserve loyalty like a holy flame, regardless of where they may find it."[1]

He eventually settled in California with his daughter, Luise Amalie David, and her husband, Rudolf Minkowski, a brilliant physicist who was fired in 1935 from his professorship at Hamburg University. In California, Rudolf forged an outstanding new career as an astronomer.

Lucie's sister, Franziska, had married Ferdinand Steinert and lived in Cologne, but was already widowed when Aviva visited her in 1936 during her detour through Germany on the way to England. Franziska was deported from Cologne on June 15, 1942, to the Terezín concentration camp in Czechoslovakia, where she perished the following February. Her son, Ernst, was deported in July 1942 to the Minsk ghetto and died there. Her son, Karl, escaped to Paris but was captured and sent to Auschwitz where he was killed.

Dr. Heinrich Stahl, the Wolff family's friend at the Fasanenstrasse synagogue who had been president of the Berlin Jewish community from 1933 to 1940, was deported with his wife, Jenny, to Terezín in June 1942. Just before they left Germany Dr. Stahl wrote a letter, dated June 10, to his children and grandchildren living in Brussels saying,

. . . we had to renounce all our possessions and transfer our money to the Reich and leave like beggars into an unknown future . . . I am writing this letter to you today, my dearest, on the eve of our execution, in order that you and others will know one day why your father and grandfather together with your good mother and grandmother had to suffer and were driven to their deaths.

Wir haben hier auf jeden Besitz verzichten müssen, alle Gelder dem Reich übereignen müssen & gehen als Bettler in die ungewisse

---

1. http://www.ruleoflawus.info/Nazi/Law%20and%20the%20Holocaust.pdf.

Zukunft . . . Das schreibe ich heute am Vorabend unserer Exekution
für Euch, meine Lieben nieder, damit Ihr & Andere einmal erfahret
weshalb Euer Vater & Grossvater in Gemeinschaft mit Eurer guten
Mutter & Oma leiden musste & und in Tod getrieben wird.[2]

Heinrich Stahl died in Terezín in November 1942. (Stahl's papers
are part of a collection at the Center for Jewish History of New York's
Leo Baeck Institute.)

Herbert's close friend Bernhard Bleichröder, the insurance executive, escaped from Germany in 1938 with his wife and one daughter. Their son and other daughter were already at boarding schools
in England. The family settled in London where Bernhard launched
a new insurance business. In England, Bernhard's son Adolf took
the name "Tim Bleach," and in 1940, as a German "enemy alien," he
was deported to Australia. Tim was later able to return to England by
enlisting as a paratrooper with the British armed forces. He fought in
North Africa and Italy, before being killed in September 1944 during
the Allied attack on strategic bridges over the Rhine River at the Dutch
town of Arnhem. His body was never found. He was 22 years old.

Of the three lawyers who battled so hard on behalf of the Wolff
family in the 1930s, Ludwig Salomon, the executor of Lucie Wolff's
will, disappeared and was not heard from again. The same is true
of Max Michaelis, the appeals court lawyer who fought the Victoria's claim on the Wolff building. The Memorial Book in the German Bundesarchiv (National Archives) lists five male Berlin residents
named Max Michaelis. Four were deported to their deaths, and one
committed suicide on January 31, 1939. Three men with the name of
Ludwig Salomon are listed. Two were deported from Berlin to Auschwitz and one to the Minsk ghetto. None of them survived. But the
third lawyer, Dr. Hans Fritz Abraham, a distant relative of the Wolff
family whose older son, Peter, was a former playmate of my mother's
in the gardens of the Wannsee estate, managed to leave Germany
with his wife and two sons and settle in Tasmania, Australia.

---

2. Letter, June 10, 1942; Heinrich Stahl Collection; AR 7171; box 1; folder 11; Courtesy of the
Leo Baeck Institute.

After Nellie refused to let Dr. Emanuel Propper and his wife adopt Marion, they adopted Barbara, a girl from Germany who took their name, but they continued to care for Marion until she was age 14. The two girls lived together like sisters for three years. Barbara, born in 1930, was three years younger.

At the age of 16, Barbara entered Neuchâtel University in Switzerland and later returned to attend the Hebrew University in Jerusalem. In 1950, she joined the Israel Defense Forces and in 1952, as part of her military service, Barbara went to the Negev desert where she was a founding member of Kibbutz Sde-Boker (this later became the retirement home of David Ben-Gurion, the first prime minister of Israel). In July of that year she was discharged from the military and joined the kibbutz full time as a civilian. She and another woman took turns shepherding the sheep and goats of the kibbutz.

Barbara was known for her intellectual interests, and she often read while she watched the herd. On the morning of September 23, 1952, she took the animals out to graze at Wadi Halikum. At 10:20 A.M. a shot rang out. Kibbutz members seized their rifles and ran to the scene, where they found Barbara lying unconscious. She died on the way to a hospital. She had been reading *Through the Looking-Glass* by Lewis Carroll.

Two Bedouin Arabs were captured while trying to flee. At their trial they said that Druze soldiers had impounded some of their herd. (The Druze are a religious minority in Israel whose members serve in the Israeli military.) The accused said they thought the Druze had given their sheep to the kibbutz and went to steal them back. Barbara was wearing her work clothes of khaki trousers and a cap and the Bedouin said they mistook her for a man. They claimed that, in keeping with their religion, if they'd known she was a woman they would not have shot her. One of the men died in prison and the other escaped. Barbara is buried at *Har HaMenuchot* ("Mount of Those who are Resting"), which is known also as Givat Shaul cemetery, on the outskirts of Jerusalem. A poem was written about her called "She Fell in the Fields." The Wadi is now called "The Shepherdess Wadi" in her honor.

My mother's sister, Marion, completed the last two years of her education at the missionary-run English high school in Haifa. Until then, she had lodged with the Proppers and attended the same Jerusalem school, Evelina de Rothschild, where my mother had been a student. Marion remembers that, during the 1936–1939 Arab Revolt against Jewish immigration, Nellie would often make the dangerous journey from Haifa via Tel Aviv to Jerusalem to bring her home for a vacation. She recalls how four buses would travel together, with protection provided by armed British police in cars at the front and rear of the convoy. If Arab fighters opened fire, the British would announce, "No more travelling." Marion can remember everyone having to stay overnight in the safety of Kiryat Anavim, a Jewish village midway between Jerusalem and the coastal plain.

My aunt was very happy living in Jerusalem but when the German army, commanded by the legendary General Rommel, advanced into Egypt, threatening the Suez Canal, Dr. Propper sent 14-year-old Marion back to live with Nellie because he did not want to be responsible for her safety if Nazi forces reached Palestine. Dr. Propper was also a grand duke in Freemasonry, and Marion has told me how he burnt all his Masonic-related papers in fear of a German invasion.

Despite her best efforts, Nellie never remarried. Running a boarding house for British officers in Haifa did not endear her to the local Jewish community, who had come to regard the British occupying forces as the enemy. Between 1942 and 1945 Nellie also worked in Haifa for the Red Cross, which was run by the wives of the British Mandate of Palestine administrators. With her fluent German and excellent command of English and French, she did secretarial work and translation, including writing 25-word messages, the only form of contact allowed between Jews who had left Germany and their relatives left behind.

At the end of the war, when the full horrendous truth emerged about what had happened to Jews in Europe, 17-year-old Marion was receiving private lessons with a tutor in preparation for her high school final exams. She vividly remembers how devastated this man was and how he would arrive to teach her but then say, "I am sorry, I can't teach you today," because he was just too traumatized.

In 1945 a British Royal Navy commander with whom Nellie was in the midst of an affair, offered to find her daughter a job at his base. Three years later, at age 20, Marion got married and in 1952, shortly after Barbara Propper's murder, she left with her husband for Brazil. There they established a successful business dealing in semiprecious stones. Marion's husband urged her to cut all ties with her family and, much to her mother's distress, all contact was lost for many years. Nellie tried, but she was unable to get in touch.

After the war, Nellie briefly returned to Berlin and, with the help of a lawyer, claimed a small pension, as did Henrietta. She wasn't happy living in Germany, and after her pension arrangements had been sorted out, she left the country for good. In 1949, Nellie returned to England and saw Aviva for the first time in 13 years. Mother and daughter hardly knew one another, and were entirely different in temperament. The 14-year-old girl she had left in London to fend for herself was now an educated, married, highly independent woman. Nellie lived on memories of the past. Aviva lived for the here and now. She didn't want her mother settling in England because she feared Nellie would disrupt the life and stable marriage she had created for herself.

Nellie had long hankered to establish herself in England, but now she discovered that her long cherished dreams of the life she might lead there could never match the reality she found herself in. In her vivid imaginings, she had conjured up an existence for herself similar to the one she had enjoyed as a young woman at finishing school in London immediately after the First World War. Now she was middle aged and hard up. The social whirl she had once enjoyed eluded her in the austere years following the Second World War. My mother's psychiatric training meant she began to detect Nellie's mood swings and diagnose that she veered between alternating bouts of depression and mania. It was hardly surprising, after all she had been through, that her mental state was frequently unstable but, from time to time, when her depression became too severe she had to be admitted to a psychiatric hospital for treatment.

With the help of her German pension, Nellie was able to buy three small apartments, two in Putney, a suburb of London, and one in Haifa, Israel. She would live in one and rent out the others. Henrietta came to live with her for a time in Putney.

Once, when Nellie was in Putney, Aviva's mother-in-law came for a visit. Dora Gold, still scornful of her daughter-in-law's family, was barely in the door when she expressed horror at all the "horrid second-hand furniture." In fact, the items in question were fine antiques that had been carried from Berlin to Tel Aviv to Haifa and finally to London.

Eventually Nellie spent summers in London and winters in Haifa, near her son Heini and his wife and two children. When she reached her mid-70s she settled in Haifa permanently. Before she stopped visiting England, I often stayed with her in her Putney apartment. During my high school vacations, the two of us would frequently enjoy London's movies, ballets, musicals, and art galleries. And of course our regular trips to the elegant patisserie on the Brompton Road opposite Harrods. There Nellie could all too fleetingly forget her radically changed circumstances and instead indulge herself with cream cakes and coffee, imagining herself on Berlin's Kurfürstendamm back in the old days. And while we sat gazing at the customers dressed in haute couture, which Nellie could no longer afford, she would entertain me with stories of prewar Berlin and the property she hankered after. If I mentioned to my mother Nellie's talk of winning back the building, she would say that was just a fantasy. She never believed a word of it, and urged me to ignore Nellie and all her tall stories.

PART TWO

12

A QUESTION OF OWNERSHIP

At the end of the war, Krausenstrasse 17/18 was in the Soviet zone of occupation of Germany, which in 1949 became the state of East Germany. In January 1949, the *Deutsche Reichsbahn* (East German Railways) commissioned a survey of the building. Architect Ferdinand Kalweit reported that 50 percent of the roof was destroyed during the war. This was perhaps a consequence of a direct hit suffered on the building immediately next door, Krausenstrasse 15/16, which had been reduced to a pile of rubble. Krausenstrasse 16 had also been owned by the Reichsbahn, and had been used to house cobblers, who made shoes and work boots for the personnel of the Railways Directorate.

This information came to light because on November 30, 1948, the ownership of Krausenstrasse 17/18 had been taken over by the *Treuhandstelle* (Trust Office/Administrators of the State) of what was then the Soviet occupying power. (The German Democratic Republic, also known as East Germany, was not founded until the following year.)

Worryingly, I found a letter from the *Deutsche Reichsbahn* Berlin to the *Treuhandstelle* dated January 12, 1949, which took issue with their instruction that nothing could be done by the *Reichsbahn*, because the legal ownership of the building at that time remained unclear.

This is an extraordinary historical irony: when the Soviet army entered Berlin in 1945, its soldiers raped and looted. But now the Soviet occupation authorities in Berlin were behaving in a scrupulously honest way about a legalistic detail.

The *Reichsbahn* argued that there was a sales contract and Ludwig Salomon had given permission (on behalf of the heirs) for the sale. The letter from the *Reichsbahn* stated that the sales contract for RM 1.8 million paid off the mortgage of RM 1.2 million to the Victoria Insurance Company and the family solicitor, Abraham. The remainder of the money went to Ludwig Salomon, who gave it to Fritz Wolff. Therefore, in the view of the *Deutsche Reichsbahn*, the 1937 sale was perfectly legal.

In November 1949, the available building area for occupancy was said to be 2,347 square meters, or just over 25,000 square feet. Although the owner was still listed as being the *Deutsche Reichsbahn*, the building now fell under the jurisdiction of *Die Deutsche Treuhandstelle zur Verwaltung des polnischen und jüdischen Vermögens im Sowjetischen Besatzungssektor*. (Translation: The German Trustees for the Administration of Polish and Jewish Property in the Soviet Occupied Sector.)

The *Treuhandstelle* then administered the building, because the *Reichsbahn* had acquired it through a compulsory auction during the Nazi era. With typical German attention to detail, the file notes that the building was meant to house several different departments of the postwar *Reichsbahn*:

- the railways' bank and building society staff (16 people);
- the railways' building office (9 staff);
- the land surveying office (2 staff);
- the railways' social welfare office (61 staff); and
- 14 rooms converted for use as office space for the production of punch cards (60–65 staff).

And, reflecting the secret police character of the new East German state, the building also housed an office of *"Die Eisenbahn-Volkspolizei (Personenzahl kann nicht angegeben werden)"*— translation: "The Railway People's Police (number of personnel cannot be specified)."

In August 1961, the Berlin Wall was constructed running along the street just one block south of the building's back entrance. Two hundred yards to one side was Checkpoint Charlie, controlled by the U.S. Army. The crossing point almost became a household name because, when American and Soviet tanks stared each other down during times of crisis, this is the flashpoint where the third world war could have started.

For the next 29 years, Krausenstrasse 17/18 was just another office block in East Berlin, a drab backwater compared to the bright lights and bustle of West Berlin, a mere few hundred yards away beyond the Wall. Instead of Mercedes cars, the few vehicles in the roads around it were mainly *Trabants*, the East German people's car. Across the street, four huge, and very ugly, apartment blocks were built for the workers of the socialist dream state.

But whatever the faults of the East German state and its Soviet masters, they had done me a favor by noting that the ownership of the building was disputed and awaited resolution.

So, when I came to Berlin in 1990 and took the cab to Krausenstrasse 17/18, those working there, who referred to it among themselves as the "Wolff Building," realized immediately the significance of my bold statement, "Herbert Wolff was my grandfather and I have come to claim this building." No wonder they quickly contacted the top bureaucrats at the Transport Ministry's headquarters in Bonn.

13

MY LIFE IN BRITAIN

By the time the Berlin Wall came down, much had changed. In the 1950s, my parents spent nearly a decade quite happily in the north of England. Then the National Coal Board offered my father a job at its head office in London, whereupon the family, which by then included my brother Adam and me, moved south and settled in Ealing, West London.

My father did statistical work at the National Coal Board and in his spare time he pursued the study of music. He had always loved the French horn, and as he neared the age of 40 my mother urged him to learn to play the instrument. He took lessons, practiced for an hour each night, and became good enough to play in the London Medical Orchestra, an amateur group that included many of his and my mother's friends.

He had also become fascinated with Buddhism. He joined the London Buddhist Society and became a prison visitor on their behalf. He wrote a correspondence course on the religion for prisoners to take. He remained, however, Jewish culturally and we belonged to a very liberal London synagogue.

My mother continued her work as a psychiatric social worker at various London hospitals, often helping seriously disturbed, psychotic patients and once participated in a research project for schizophrenia. She retired at age 60, not because she wanted to but because the Medical Research Council required it. She was soon busy as a potter and amateur painter, took Italian lessons, and attended lectures on art and literature.

I had a fairly conventional English education enlivened by the two years we spent in Geneva when my father was assigned to the United Nations. For a few years, I attended a rather posh girls' school, where I was far too outspoken to fit in. Then, at age 16, I entered Drayton Manor, a local (state) public high school, where I thrived, and at 18 years old, I headed off to university. In six years of study, I gained three degrees, the last from Oxford University, where I attended Corpus Christi College on a scholarship. The college had just gone co-ed, and I was the first woman to be awarded a degree since its founding in 1517.

During one of my university summer vacations, I went to Haifa to visit Nellie, who by then was living in a home for seniors on Mount Carmel. She had one room and shared a bathroom and kitchen with a grouchy, uneducated old woman. Nellie was not happy. She never adapted to the informality of Israeli life, and she spoke only very basic Hebrew. With her coffee and cakes at the local patisserie and her elegant and stylish attire and formal manners, Nellie was markedly different from the other old people. She still dreamed of one day recovering the lost building in Berlin, which she believed would restore to her life the grandeur that she had once known. She received a huge surprise in the late spring of 1974 when Marion made contact again. The first person Marion tried to reach was her older sister, my mother. My brother Adam, then a schoolboy, had answered the phone. "Hello," said the voice on the other end, "My name is Marion. You don't know who I am but I would like to speak to your mother."

"I know exactly who you are," Adam replied, "You're my mother's sister." When my mother came home from work that day, Marion called back and told her she and her husband had left Brazil, were separated, and she was now living in Germany. My mother immediately invited her to London and they met a few weeks later. It was the first time the sisters had seen one another since 1936. Thirty-eight long years had passed. In September, Marion visited Israel and was reunited with her parents. In November 1974, two months after seeing his daughter again for the first time in 22 years, Herbert died. Three years later, in the spring of 1977, Nellie was diagnosed with leukemia and by August she was dead. In her will, Nellie left me her one-bedroom apartment in Putney. It was basic at best, but I was grateful to have a home of my own, and that was where I lived when I began my first job.

All through university, I had longed to be an investigative journalist. My ideal was to work on a weekly BBC radio program called "Checkpoint" that took pride in aggressive, foot-in-the-door journalism. I loved listening to the tales of the corruption, fraud, and scandal its fearless reporters exposed. I noted they had no woman on their team and I thought they needed one—me!

Soon after leaving university, I landed my first job as a financial reporter for a magazine called the *Investors Chronicle*. It was a good start, but it wasn't where I really wanted to be.

In October 1979 I met Simon Henderson, a foreign correspondent for the *Financial Times*. He had recently returned to the UK from Tehran where he had spent five months covering the Iranian Revolution, the overthrow of the Shah, and the triumphant return of Ayatollah Khomeini. On November 4, just over a fortnight after our first meeting, the Iran hostage crisis began when Iranian students and militants seized the U.S. embassy in Tehran. Simon was dispatched straight back to Iran, this time for an uninterrupted six-month stint.

Obviously, this was not conducive to the perfect romance, but I was willing to wait. He and I kept in touch intermittently, courtesy of crackly phone lines that were most likely bugged. Simon returned to London in May 1980, and a year later we were married. By this time, I had sold the apartment in Putney that Nellie had left me in her will, and bought a small row house in Hammersmith, West London. Simon sold his apartment in Islington, North London, and moved into my house, which was near my parents. A year later we moved to a bigger house nearby.

Meanwhile, my dream job since college finally came through. I had applied to join the BBC's "Checkpoint" team, and I was hired. Now the team was five men and me! It was exciting work and we believed we were doing good—righting wrongs and tackling injustice. People across the United Kingdom would contact the program with their stories, and some would leak vital information to us.

Sometimes, though, it could be dangerous—on one occasion, Doberman Pinschers ran at me on a remote Welsh hillside when I was covering a story about loans sold fraudulently to farmers. I helped send crooks to prison, and I managed to free an innocent man, who was the victim of a trumped up charge of arson. I also helped victims of medical negligence and fraud win huge amounts of financial compensation. I learned the skills of investigative journalism—developing sources, interviewing techniques, confronting suspects, and meticulous research.

In 1984, I was offered a job doing the same sort of investigative journalism on the BBC's prime time television program, "Watchdog." After our son, Daniel, was born in 1986 I went back to work, leaving him in the care of a nanny. In October 1989, I was pregnant again when political convulsions began spreading across Eastern Europe as Soviet control weakened. Night after night, we sat watching the news, seeing the massive crowds demonstrating across East Germany chanting, *"Wir wollen raus!"* ("We want out!")

On October 18, Erich Honecker resigned as leader of East Germany and was replaced by Egon Krenz. Three days later, I went into the hospital and gave birth to our daughter, Rachel. The amazing events continued as East German travel restrictions were lifted on November 9. By midnight, crowds were streaming past the checkpoints into West Berlin. We watched as people poured into its brightly lit shopping areas and danced in the streets to celebrate freedom after decades under Communist rule.

Truly, these were events we had never expected to see in our lifetimes.

14

WHAT HAD MY GRANDMOTHER
ONCE TOLD ME?

In the midst of these historic developments, I found myself thinking intensely personal thoughts. I remembered what Nellie had so often said about a building on the other side of Checkpoint Charlie, and her passionate belief that it belonged to our family, although the Nazis stole it in the 1930s. I searched my memory for details of what she'd said, any scraps of information that might tell me if her story could have been true. I soon realized I had to find out. I was an investigative reporter, after all, and this might just be the biggest story I would ever sink my teeth into. Good luck intervened in January 1990 when Simon embarked on a two-month fellowship at Tel Aviv University to do research on Iraq, which, following the invasion of Kuwait in August 1990, resulted in his book, *Instant Empire: Saddam Hussein's Ambition for Iraq*. Rather than sit in wintry London with a newborn daughter and our three-year-old son, I decided to accompany him.

I was aware I had cousins in Israel but I hardly knew them. I had heard only one lived in Tel Aviv, Leor Wolff. (Leor is the son of Micky, Herbert's son with his second wife, Eva. Micky, therefore, is my mother's half-brother and Leor is my cousin.) Micky had gone to live on Kibbutz Shamir in the Upper Galilee. He married while in his teens, and fathered Leor not long thereafter. But the marriage soon ended in divorce, and Leor went with his mother to Kibbutz Yagur, near Haifa. He had no contact with his father.

Sitting in our rented apartment near the Mediterranean Sea in Tel Aviv, I looked through the telephone directory, found a Leor Wolff listed, and called his number. When he answered, I hesitantly began to explain who I was. He interrupted me, and in almost faultless English assured me, "I know exactly who you are. You're my Aunt Aviva's daughter from London."

Later that day, we met in a cafe near the beach. At first, as the waves of the Mediterranean crashed onto the nearby shore, each of us wondered how we would relate to each other. We soon realized, despite our totally different upbringing (him in a kibbutz; me in the London suburbs), it was as if we had known each other all our lives. It helped that we were both journalists—he worked at the time for *Yediot Ahronot*, the major Israeli newspaper.

We talked about the whereabouts of various relatives, but we quickly discovered that we shared a common passion. We were both immensely curious about the lives our grandparents had left behind in Germany before the Second World War. Inevitably this led us to exchange memories of the stories we had each been told during our contrasting childhoods. Then I told Leor I wanted to follow up on Nellie's claim that our family had once owned a huge office building in what had been East Berlin until recently, and that I was determined to find out if that were true. Leor shared my enthusiasm.

"I have an old suitcase at home," he said. "It's full of photos and scraps of papers from the old days. Do you want to see it?"

Of course I did! Maybe it held clues to the whereabouts of the building Nellie had so often spoken of. At that point, I knew almost nothing.

Leor told me that after his grandmother Eva, Herbert's second wife, died in August 1981, Herbert's son, Heini, and his wife, Ruth, cleaned out her house in a suburb of Tel Aviv. They found old Wolff family papers but, rather than saving all of them, they piled a large quantity up in the backyard and started a bonfire. Leor arrived later that day to find the fire still smoldering, but he managed to salvage papers that were blowing around the yard.

When we opened the old leather suitcase he had stored them in, the papers proved to be a treasure trove. Leor had rescued fascinating snippets of our family's life in Germany in the 1920s and 1930s. There were old family photographs including pictures of the house in Wannsee and assorted papers in German that we struggled to understand.

Leor and I hunted for any scrap of information that might lead us to an address for the building. Finally we found a singed, ripped, yellowed letterhead.

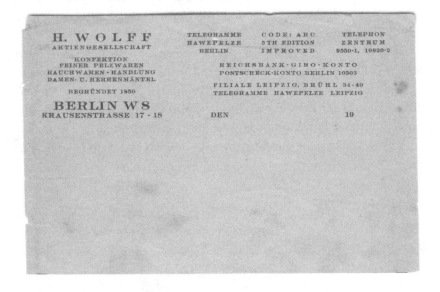

H. Wolff. Was this our grandfather Herbert? Or was it his grandfather, Heimann? Was Krausenstrasse 17/18 the building Nellie had referred to? It was a start.

Then we turned up another surprise. We came across a business card, faded and torn, but it contained more useful detail. The business card belonged to Herbert Reinhard Julius Wolff, our grandfather. I recognized the address on Conradstrasse in Wannsee. It was where my mother had lived as a child.

But where was Krausenstrasse? Was this the address of the building beyond the Wall that Nellie talked about? I found a map of Berlin. Yes, Krausenstrasse was in East Berlin, just beyond where the Wall had stood, a short distance from Checkpoint Charlie.

Among the charred papers, we found a long, legal document in German that neither of us could translate. It later proved to have been written by a lawyer in 1953, as part of Herbert's effort to win back family property in Berlin, and contained information about Fritz's arrest in 1933.

The document went on to say, "Since 1 April 1933, the situation worsened rather than improved and with Fritz's continued incarceration Herbert left for Palestine, where he arrived in May." Later in the same paragraph the lawyer added that Nellie and the children joined him in September.

Even these scorched scraps confirmed several things I had been told by Nellie and my mother. Some of the information I learned later, from documents I would uncover in Berlin, but to find that much evidence there in Tel Aviv, in such dramatic circumstances, filled me with excitement and determination. I began thinking about a trip to see, with my own eyes, the building that was now accessible to us in Berlin.

15

OUR INVESTIGATION BEGINS

Back in London with my maternity leave now finished, I returned to work at the BBC. I was assigned to a small team of journalists who worked on news coverage of special events, BBC-speak for national and local elections in the UK. Because of the collapse of Communism and the emergence of democratic governments in Central and Eastern Europe, the team was now covering elections there as well.

Events were moving with lightning speed. In May 1990, East and West Germany signed a treaty of monetary, economic, and social union that went into effect on July 1. A reunification treaty was agreed on August 31, and approved by the parliaments of both countries on September 20. The Law on the Regulation of Unresolved Property Issues (*Gesetz zur Regelung offener Vermögensfragen*) was passed on September 23, 1990, enabling owners, or their heirs, to file claims on former East German properties. Formal reunification was completed on October 3. The first national elections were set for December 2, barely a year after the Wall had come down.

In the summer of 1990, while preparing for the BBC's coverage of the German elections, I travelled to Bonn, which was then still the capital of Germany. While there, I hired a German researcher to help our BBC team. I also asked if he could help me on a private quest. Could he find out anything about the company my grand-father had once owned? The only leads I could give him were the information on the letterhead and business card that I had found with Leor's help in Tel Aviv, plus the fact my mother said the company traded in furs.

Within days, the researcher found old copies of a business directory from the 1920s—the *Deutsches Reichs-Adressbuch*. In English, it translates to the "All-German Address Book," the equivalent of the Yellow Pages. Looking at the volume for 1920, under the section *"Pelz"* (German for fur) we found the following entry:

Bingo! This was almost certainly the building Nellie had dreamed of recapturing. Nellie was dead now, but I felt myself making my way back into her world.

My mother needed to act fast. It was imperative she register a claim with the German authorities which, I was told, had set a deadline for such claims. In a newsletter she received from a charity she supported, the Association of Jewish Refugees, she spotted an advertisement from a firm of London lawyers (known in Britain as "solicitors"), Pritchard Englefield & Tobin, that specialized in restitution claims.

She wrote them and received a prompt reply from a partner in the firm:

16th July 1990

Dear Mrs. Gold,

Thank you for your letter of 11th July.

We shall be pleased to assist you but really need some more information. Is there reason to believe that this house actually belonged to your father's firm and they were not just renting it? Have you made any application to the West German authorities? In that event, would you have some papers which we could see?

We would like to point out that we are not doing this work on a success and percentage basis which is not permitted under [lawyers'] rules, but that we would charge you on a time basis for work done.

We do feel that enquiries should now be made.

Yours sincerely,
H. H. Marcus

Scrawled across the bottom Mr. Marcus had added: "I enclose a power of attorney in case you wish to proceed."

My mother was not enthusiastic. The prospect of having to pay hefty legal fees to pursue a claim that might fail did not appeal to her, so she didn't reply.

Two months later, Mr. Marcus wrote again.

Dear Mrs. Gold,

I wrote to you on the 16th of July. A time limit has now been set for the 13th of October. If you wish to proceed the matter is urgent and we enclose a power of attorney for your signature.

A deadline for claims on East German immovable property had indeed been set for October 13, 1990 (though this was later extended to end December 1992). After that date, the German authorities would assume that if there were potential claimants, they were either dead or not interested in claiming. Any entitlement to compensation or restitution instead would have to be made to the Conference on Jewish Material Claims Against Germany. Established in 1951, this body represents Jews worldwide in negotiations for compensation and restitution, recovers unclaimed Jewish property and allocates monies to organizations supporting Jewish survivors of the Holocaust. It was important that she meet the October 13 deadline.

With some trepidation, my mother wrote back:

17 September 1990

Dear Mr. Marcus,

Thank you for your letters of July 16 and September 11.

I enclose my Power of Attorney.

In your letter of July 16 you ask whether I am certain that the business housed at Krausenstrasse 17/18 actually belonged to my father. All I can tell you is that the firm was founded by my great-grandfather, then owned by my grandfather Kommerzienrat Victor Wolff and subsequently by my father, Herbert Reinhard Julius Wolff, and, to the best of my knowledge, was certainly owned by the Wolff family.

I should be grateful if you could let me have your accounts at regular intervals so I can keep track of how the costs of pursuing this claim are developing.

Yours sincerely,
A. Gold

Mr. Marcus lodged a formal application with the *Amt zur Regelung offener Vermögensfragen* (known as the *AROV*), the Federal Office for the Settlement of Property Issues, sometimes referred to as the *Vermögensamt* or German Assets Compensation Agency. By early November 1990, my mother received her claim number—25823.

The role of the AROV was to examine property claims in the former East Germany, and decide whether or not the claimants were entitled to compensation or restitution. It was an independent agency of the Federal Ministry of Finance, which controlled the budget from which compensation could be paid.

In our case, we learned the German Ministry of Transport was occupying the Krausenstrasse building and wanted to stay there. As a result, the Ministry of Finance was also involved, because it would have to find the money to pay my mother and the other Wolff claimants the full market value if the AROV found in their favor.

We had filed our claim, and I felt that we were making progress, but not everyone in our family was as supportive of my crusade as Simon.

"Grow up," my father said. "You can't take on a government and win. Who do you think you are?"

We had just finished lunch and I had begun to clear the table and make coffee.

"I'm not going to let them get away with it," I told him. "I won't give up that easily. I owe it to Fritz."

"You have a full-time job, a fourteen-month-old baby and a four-year-old, you just don't have the time for this," was my father's argument. "Just how much of your own money are you going to spend in pursuing this adventure?"

Simon was the only one who gave me full, unequivocal support. He understood the moral imperative of the issue, and he agreed I should give it my best shot.

With his support, I vowed to continue my investigation.

It helped, too, that Leor promised to assist me in any way he could in the search for supporting documents.

In December 1990, after being in Bonn with the BBC to cover the first unified German elections since Hitler came to power in 1933, I took a few days' leave and flew to Berlin. It was there I made my one-woman assault on our building and met Herr Münch, whose words had so encouraged me.

16

LAWYERS AND WILLS

Two months later, in February 1991, I arranged for my mother and I to meet face-to-face with her lawyer, Hans Marcus. I put together my slim file of evidence and information: the copy of the 1920 edition of the *Deutsches Reichs-Adressbuch* with its listing for H. Wolff, and the photographs and notes I had taken at the building in December.

Mr. Marcus had a great deal of experience with Jewish claims against Germany. With my photographs of our building, I was able to show him our case would be one of the biggest property claims ever made against the German government.

We discussed finances. His first letter said if his firm took the case, it would bill us for work done; they would not pursue the claim for a percentage of the financial settlement if we were successful. To our delight, despite what he had written earlier, he now said his firm would pursue the case for 15 percent of whatever funds, if any, were ultimately obtained. I took this to reflect the fact that 15 percent of the value of a six-story office building in central Berlin would far exceed what his firm would earn on an hourly basis.

He concluded by saying that if I could gather the papers necessary to mount a credible legal challenge, and if my mother would sign a contract giving him 15 percent of whatever sum she might be awarded, then he and his firm would act as our lawyers and legal advisers. He made clear that he wanted our active cooperation, and urged us to seek out any documents we could to support our claim.

At the end of the meeting, as Mr. Marcus showed us to the door, he declared, "Mrs. Gold, I think you're going to be a very rich woman."

His prediction was one that neither my mother, nor I, ever expected to hear. But as would often happen as our case progressed, our elation was short lived.

Other than a few family photographs, an old business card belonging to my grandfather Herbert Wolff, and a 1920s German business directory, I had nothing. I simply had no documents whatsoever to support my mother's claim for restitution.

Mr. Marcus urged me to find out as much as possible about the history of the building at Krausenstrasse 17/18 after Hitler came to power. Had the property been stolen by the Nazis? That was the crux of the matter. If Nellie had been wrong and the property had been legally sold, we had no case.

One factor potentially in our favor, was the presumption of duress applied to all transactions involving German Jews after September 1935, the date when the anti-Jewish Nuremberg Laws were passed. If the Wolff family truly had owned the building, my mother surely had a case. But we needed proof.

We faced an unexpected obstacle in May 1991, when Simon went to Israel to speak at a conference. While there, he also wanted to talk to my uncle, Heini, and his wife, Ruth, about our efforts to find information about the building in Berlin. Heini was either unable or unwilling to talk with Simon, but Ruth did. She said she thought the family had no claim, but in the event we did, Aviva would not stand to inherit anything—only Heini and Micky, Herbert's other son, would be heirs.

Herbert and Eva had had identical wills. Herbert died first but Eva's will clearly reflected his wishes. He left everything to Eva, who in turn left everything to his two sons, Heini and Micky. His daughters, Aviva and Marion, were left exactly one Israeli pound each. The point was, if a son or daughter were left nothing, he or she might challenge the will on the grounds that the deceased had inadvertently forgotten to include them. But if they were left a token sum, it would be much harder for them to argue that the will should be overturned.

Herbert almost certainly left Aviva the insulting one Israeli pound (about ten cents) because of his intense anger, years earlier, when he had asked her for her power of attorney, and she had later written to the lawyer asking what was going on. His treatment of Marion was probably due to her having cut herself off from the family for so long.

Given the fact of Herbert's will, leaving everything to the boys, it is understandable how Heini and Ruth assumed that, if the building in Berlin could be won back, it would go solely to the two sons.

Actually, we would all have surprises in regard to Wolff family wills and the allocation of any new windfalls. For my part, I didn't worry about what Ruth had said. Money wasn't uppermost in my mind. I wanted to know how true Nellie's stories had been about the great wealth and grand lifestyle the Wolff family had enjoyed in pre–World War II Berlin. Her stories fascinated and challenged me. I had heard them all my life, and I wanted to know the truth.

Our pursuit began as a matter of principle, a belief that a Nazi theft should not be allowed to stand, but it is undeniable that we all began to realize a great deal of money might be involved. My mother's brother and half-brother in Israel were certainly aware of that and, therefore, they insisted we had no claim and were wasting our time. It seemed clear they intended to pursue the issue without including my mother.

I felt that we were trying to redress a crime committed against the Wolff family, but I also knew that my mother, from the time she had left Berlin at the age of 11, worked very hard and never had much money. I thought it would be wonderful if she might finally be compensated for what had been taken from her and her siblings.

Naturally, our lawyers were concerned about the strength of Heini and Micky's possible claim. If our effort to win back the building succeeded, and my mother was one of the heirs, they stood to earn a large fee. If she wasn't an heir, they were wasting their time. They kept on with the case, but urged us to do everything we could to find the documents that would establish my mother's place in the line of inheritance.

In June 1991, my mother received a discouraging letter from Mr. Marcus. He pointed out the laws regarding restitution and compensation were extremely complicated. In his letter, Mr. Marcus wrote that in many cases,

> according to the legal provisions now in existence it is impossible to obtain restitution of the property. Generally speaking, restitution cannot be obtained if the property has undergone substantial changes, e.g. new buildings have been erected on bombed sites, or when the original buildings are used for social purposes, e.g. when an old villa is used by the local authority as a Kindergarten or Old People's Home . . .
>
> Our main problem at the moment is to obtain further information; this is a slow moving process because the authorities in Germany are flooded with requests for extracts from the German Land Register and other information.
>
> In practically all cases one has to prove entitlement by producing a Certificate of Inheritance . . . In all cases, birth, death and marriage certificates of the claimants and of the relatives under which they claim must be produced . . . We have to prepare the above for submission to the German Embassy and the claimants will have to make a declaration which is sent to a German court which issues this Certificate.
>
> Claimants should also think about possible witnesses or any other sources, material, old correspondence and the like which sheds further light on the property claimed.

His letter made it painfully clear that a difficult road lay ahead. We believed our claim to be valid, but many fraudulent claims were surely being filed, and the German government was justified in demanding solid proof.

17

THE SMOKING GUN

Apart from researching the history of the building, I needed to gather many documents to prove my mother was a legal inheritor. To obtain an *Erbschein* (certificate of inheritance), my mother would have to provide copies of her birth certificate, her parents' marriage and death certificates, relevant wills, and other official documents. Other than her birth certificate, she had none of these.

As journalists, Simon and I knew it was always important to go where the story was. So, in August 1991, we flew to Berlin to research the history.

Our first stop was the building itself. We contacted Herr Münch, the sympathetic official I met the previous December, and he agreed to show us around. It was not an easy tour. I was four months pregnant with my third child, and the elevator was one of those continuously moving ones with no doors, which required each rider to step in on one floor and step out—actually, jump out—at another.

The building still matched the description portrayed in a stilted English language brochure written by my great grandfather, Victor, in the 1920s, ". . . the bright distinguished halls of our showrooms on the ground floor of our house at 17-18 Krausenstrasse . . . The second floor of this building is occupied by the Department for SMALL FURS and the Skin Stores. In these rooms are working men who have had a world wide training in the art of selecting, grading and matching skins of every description."

It was not difficult to imagine the vibrancy of the business in its heyday, when Victor Wolff was at the helm. He wrote about fur wraps of sable, marten, mink or skunk, and smaller collars of mole, skunk, sable, or mole-dyed hamster. According to the brochure, the firm's "well-known speciality" was "the wonderful silverfox dye, scarfs of various width and length in unique and most effective elaboration."

Upwards the lift is leading to the Stores of Woollen and Silk Materials and the Department for LADIES' COATS and Cos-tumes. . . . Farther on our way is leading to the Department for GENTLEMEN'S COATS where heavy Winter overcoats, warm Travelling Ulsters, Waterproof Coat, Leather Coat and Jackets for motoring and Fur Lined Coat for day, evening and sports wear are to be seen.

Furs and skins used included raccoon, opossum, flying squirrel, white fox, grey fox, monkey, Persian lamb, ponies, and marmots.

"Fur Hats, Caps and Leather Hats are manufactured in rooms grouped round courtyards," the very same courtyards we found our-selves looking down on from high up in the building, as we wandered along corridors and past empty offices that probably hadn't changed much since the 1920s. And there, below, were archways through which horse-drawn carriages, and later motorcars, had once entered and exited at the rear of the building on Schützenstrasse.

One of the striking things about the building was that from its upper floors, there was a clear view into what had been West Berlin, a far freer and more prosperous world, cut off from the East by that ugly Wall. I wondered how many East German office workers had sat in our building dreaming of somehow crossing that Wall to freedom, and having no idea that salvation would suddenly arrive in 1989.

Later, in the lobby of a nearby hotel, Simon and I met one of the property speculators—who prefer to be called "property developers"—who were swarming around Berlin looking for a fast buck. This one said he might be interested in buying our claim, but would only pay a fraction of the building's value because the case might take years to resolve. Indeed, he said he would only pay a small portion of this sum on signature. The balance would come to my mother and her relatives when the claim was resolved. We politely rejected his offer. If our claim were valid, we didn't need someone like him.

The speculator was offended by our rejection and scornfully told us that, if we were going ahead on our own, we had to have the record of transfer of ownership. The only way to get that was to get a copy of the *Grundbuch*, or land registry document, the official record of who had held title to the property over the years. We assumed it would be lodged at the local land registry but the speculator said that, as private individuals, we could not get access to the registry. Only a lawyer could. On that smug note, he wished us luck.

Fortunately, luck was on our side. We learned a New York property mogul had hired an East German lawyer to track down the land registry documents of Krausenstrasse 17/18, as well as several other properties. The speculator apparently wanted to put in an offer to buy and renovate the building. If there were any truth to it, we needed to act fast.

Armed only with the telephone number of the lawyer, we called and said we wanted to meet him to talk about Krausenstrasse 17/18. He reluctantly gave us his address. We jumped in a taxi and drove deeper and deeper into the increasingly dingy, forbidding suburbs of East Berlin. When the driver finally stopped outside a big, ugly tenement block, we got out of the taxi with considerable trepidation. There was no elevator, so we climbed up several flights of stairs, passing rubbish strewn everywhere, wondering what on earth we had got ourselves into.

Breathless from our steep climb, we reached the man's apartment, knocked on the door, and waited nervously. A hostile-looking young man opened the door and demanded to know what this was all about. An awkward discussion ensued because our German was poor and his English was borderline non-existent. Somehow we managed to convey our request to be shown whatever documents he had relating to our building.

The man showed us a notarized copy of the *Grundbuch* for Krausenstrasse 17/18, bound with an official-looking clip and bearing an equally formal embossed purple stamp. It was clear that he saw value in these documents, and wanted to make some money from them.

Simon abruptly said, "How much?" The man, startled to be asked straight out what amount would close the deal, responded by holding up three fingers and saying, "dreihundert Deutsche Mark." That was 300 Deutsche Marks, or about $200 at the time. He apparently saw this as a considerable sum, but Simon surprised him by whipping out his wallet, extracting three 100 Deutsche Mark notes and handing them over. The deal was done.

Before our new acquaintance had time for second thoughts, we grabbed the *Grundbuch*, and exited the shabby apartment as fast as we could. Soon, we were safe inside a cab heading back to our hotel, where we finally had a chance to examine our purchase. What we found was startling.

Even with our rudimentary knowledge of German, it was clear from the document that for years the Wolff family had obtained an apparently standard mortgage from the Victoria Insurance Company. But, according to the *Grundbuch*, in June 1937, the building had changed hands. The Victoria never took ownership. The building passed directly from the Wolff family to the *Reichsbahn*, the German Railways.

This was the first hint we uncovered that supported the theory that the Victoria Insurance Company worked in concert with the Nazi government to seize the building. All of the people who had first-hand knowledge of the 1937 legal proceedings that handed our building to the Nazis—Herbert, Fritz, the lawyers—were either dead or presumed dead, their whereabouts unknown.

Was this a case of collusion between a huge insurance company and the Nazis? Much remained to be learned, but we were nearing the heart of the matter. Soon, we would find documents that would tell us more about the 1937 court proceedings and the Victoria Insurance Company.

A short, one-page letter dated November 30, 1948, attached to the *Grundbuch*, also encouraged us. After the war, the building was in the Soviet zone of occupation. Its ownership had, according to the document, been reregistered as the *Deutsche Treuhandstelle*, or (East) German Trust Authority.

Much can be said about the evils of the Soviet Union but, in this case, its occupation forces had arrived at a judgment that was extremely helpful to us, and potentially to others pursuing claims. In the case of Krausenstrasse 17/18, although the attached letter was in German, we knew it carried a significance that would ultimately assist our claim:

> . . . da der jüdische Vorbesitzer gezwungen war das Grundstück unter dem Druck der damaligen politischen Verhältnisse zu veräussern . . . Wir bitten Sie, sich jeder Verfügung über das Grundstück zu enthalten.

And while neither Simon nor I could read or understand much German, we could certainly translate the word "*jüdische*"—Jewish. We couldn't understand the rest of the sentence but we suspected it meant the Soviets knew the building had been stolen from Jews.

Back in London, we obtained a translation:

> The Jewish private owner was forced to sell because of the political circumstances of the time . . . we request that you do not make any disposition of this property.

We were elated. The Soviets had taken the view that in the 1930s Krausenstrasse 17/18 had been a Jewish-owned building that had been forcibly sold to the Nazis. Although the property came to be used for the administration of the East German railways, this note was intended to prevent any further sale until the true ownership was established.

If Soviet officials had recognized that fact, we hoped new Federal Republic of Germany officials would as well.

We reported our discoveries to my mother and her lawyer, Mr. Marcus. But once again, our euphoria was brief. After a business trip to Germany, Mr. Marcus wrote to my mother on November 5, 1991, and brought us back down to earth:

> Had a very interesting, rather depressing time in Berlin. We have to prepare ourselves for a long wait . . . All that matters is to get *Rückerstattung* (restitution) rather than *Entschuldigung* (apology)

and your prospect is not good as the railways are treated as *"ein gemeinnütziger Zweck* (a charitable purpose)." The compensation law is not yet published but all indications are that it will be only 1.3 times the 1935 tax value. We are trying to find out what this was but you can reckon generally that it is about 10 percent of the value today—still in your case a worthwhile sum but don't expect too much.

Depressing news indeed. Even if we could prove that the Wolff family had surrendered Krausenstrasse 17/18 under duress more than 50 years earlier, there was a distinct possibility that because the building was now being used as a government office, the German authorities would only be required to pay token compensation. Despite a valid claim, would we be cheated a second time? Germans of one political stripe or another had used this property, rent free, since 1937.

My spirits sank further when Mr. Marcus reported that some 150,000 claims had been registered with the AROV, and only 800 were currently being examined. We thought we had a relatively low claim number, because we'd registered early, but this was still not encouraging. The pursuit of my mother's claim was proving to be an emotional roller coaster. Every step forward seemed to be followed by a quick step backward.

At the onset of 1992, good news finally arrived in the form of an unexpected letter from Herr Bernt-Joachim Giese of the Berlin branch of the German Ministry of Finance, the agency that would have to pay if my mother's claim were successful.

Dear Mrs. Gold,

You have registered a claim for the above-mentioned property according to the law re property.

Whether you will come into possession of your property I cannot judge, as, regarding this, the Court dealing with the regulations regarding property has to decide.

The Federal Republic of Germany is, however, amongst other properties, interested in obtaining the property which you have registered. I request, therefore, that you contact me without obligation and propose to me an idea of a price.

In addition to this I request you, should you be interested in a sale, to let me know in what relationship you stand to the possible former owners and, insofar as you know, when and in what way they acquired possession.

This seemed to say that if we could prove our claim to the building, the Finance Ministry would be interested in buying it back from us. That was good news because, as a practical matter, it was unlikely that my mother or anyone in the family would want to own and manage a huge office block in Berlin. We were fighting this battle as a matter of principle, not because we dreamed of owning a spectacular piece of real estate.

Mr. Marcus was more optimistic when he wrote a few weeks later, "We have a certain nuisance value to the authorities and what we want to achieve is to sell . . . The property is worth a lot of money but one does not know what they are prepared to pay."

However, a new development soon arrived to complicate matters. My mother registered her claim to the building without reference to her brother Heini, her sister Marion, or her half-brother Micky. But she had repeatedly told Mr. Marcus that they were part of the equation. Now we learned that her siblings, without informing her, had together hired German lawyers to act on their behalf.

Mr. Marcus told us that all Wolff family claimants needed to present a united front, ". . . only a joint action and an inheritance certificate covering all parties will enable us to proceed."

I was not close to this side of the family. I hardly knew them, except for Leor, who had been so helpful in Tel Aviv. Leor was not in contact with other members of the Wolff family in Israel either. Nor was my mother. Since leaving Palestine for Britain at age 14, she grew up without a family, forced to fend for herself. The Nazis, the Holocaust, and the war had blown the family apart, but now it needed to come together in a common cause.

I managed to find a telephone number for Micky, my mother's half-brother, who was living on Kibbutz Lahav, near the city of Beersheva in the Negev desert. Micky gave me the name of the lawyers in East Berlin who were representing the Israeli side of the family, and the lawyers began to share information.

But it was becoming clear that, while we might join together for the legal action, we had different ideas about who should inherit what if we won. Heini and Micky still thought they were the true heirs, and they resented my mother's efforts.

Soon, we had another stroke of luck. A friend from my Oxford days was writing feature articles for the *London Evening Standard*, the capital's main afternoon newspaper, which in those days published a high quality, glossy magazine each month. He had been assigned to write an article for the magazine about claims being made on properties in the former Communist bloc. Hunting for leads, he contacted the law firm that was representing my mother, which had a reputation of being among the best UK lawyers pursuing such claims. They suggested several cases and he immediately recognized my mother's name. Happy to have found a claimant he knew, he called me and asked if we would cooperate.

I, too, was pleased, because I'm a great believer in the power of the press and I trusted this friend to write a solid story that would serve to our benefit. Thus, in early March 1992, my mother flew to Berlin with him, at the *Evening Standard*'s expense, for a visit that included Krausenstrasse 17/18, and taking photographs of her outside the building where she had played as a child.

While in Berlin, this reporter also visited the *Vermögensamt* (the Federal Office for the Settlement of Property Issues, or AROV), and spoke to Stephan Giessen, the deputy head of the department. Herr Giessen promised he would investigate my mother's file; all he said he needed to help him do this was the case number. We were jubilant. It looked as if the German authorities would take our claim seriously. Mr. Marcus called Herr Giessen in Berlin, outlined the legal issues, and encouraged him to indeed focus his attention on my mother's case.

The *Evening Standard* magazine article appeared in April 1992 under the headline, "Getting Their Own Back." I was mildly irritated to find my mother's story lumped in with those of an exiled Hungarian count trying to reclaim his family's mansion and of a Polish prince seeking to recover his splendid moated castle, which once had its own private army and orchestra. Fortunately, my mother was presented in more sympathetic terms: "Why is an Ealing housewife laying claim to an East Berlin office block worth millions of pounds?"

It was a good story and the photographer had taken wonderful pictures of my mother outside the main entrance, including one alongside the official plaque on the front of the building, which featured a black German eagle with outspread wings, a red beak, and red talons.

The reporter also captured my mother's no-nonsense attitude when he wrote that, upon first glimpsing the family building she showed "no obvious emotion." Then he quoted her as saying, "I am not some helpless little old lady. If you were expecting tears, then you have got the wrong person. I am fairly tough, you know, because I have had to be."

The article concluded: "'We are going to keep stirring this until justice is done,' says Dina Gold. The German government has found formidable adversaries in Mrs. Gold and her family."

It was exactly the message we wanted delivered to the German officials.

Mr. Marcus was delighted. He wrote to my mother, "I was very pleased to see the article in the *Evening Standard*. Have any steps been taken to bring it to the notice of the Ministry of Finance in Berlin?"

We learned that German officials had indeed seen the article and were annoyed because it made them feel under pressure. That was fine with us.

18

PROVING THE LINE OF INHERITANCE

We continued to search for the documents needed for my mother to be granted an inheritance certificate.

Our land registry search had revealed that Krausenstrasse 17/18 had been registered in the name of Victor Wolff, until his death in 1928. It then passed to Lucie Wolff and, after her death in 1932, the building was administered on behalf of the heirs until it passed directly to the ownership of the *Reichsbahn*.

Establishing the line of inheritance was crucial. My mother feared that documents we needed had not survived the Allied bombing of Berlin during the war. It turned out she was wrong.

In April 1992, she phoned the district court in the Berlin suburb of Charlottenburg and, in her impeccable German, asked the woman who answered if it would be possible to obtain the will of her grandmother Lucie Wolff, who died on February 25, 1932. To her astonishment, the woman calmly replied, "Would you like to stay on the line or would you like to phone back in ten minutes?" My mother said she'd call back.

Ten minutes later, she rang again. "Yes, I have the will of Lucie Wolff," the woman said nonchalantly. My mother was staggered. "Would it be possible to have a photocopy?" she asked. "Certainly," the woman replied, "I'll mail it to you." It would be an understatement to say, when she put down the telephone, that my mother was triumphant. She had managed to obtain this vital document. Despite intensive bombing by the Allied forces, these German records had miraculously survived.

That fact moved my father, proud of his RAF service during the war, to comment, "Obviously, we didn't bomb them enough!"

My mother always assumed that Lucie had divided her estate between her two sons, Herbert and Fritz. Instead, when the will arrived, it contained a stunning revelation.

Attached to Lucie's will was a declaration by Herbert that he renounced his half share of his mother's estate (the other half was left to Fritz) in favor of Nellie and their three children. Nellie's claims to be an inheritor of the building were entirely accurate.

We never found an explanation of why Herbert did this, but my mother always believed that Lucie, who was fond of Nellie and fully aware of her elder son's reckless ways, had been determined to guarantee the financial security of her daughter-in-law and three grandchildren and, therefore, had wanted Herbert's share to go to his dependents.

As soon as my mother received the copy of Lucie's will and her father's renunciation document, she forwarded it to Mr. Marcus. This changed all of the assumptions she had made about her status as a beneficiary. It was also going to affect her brothers' firmly held beliefs about their prospects as well. I saw trouble ahead. After all Heini's wife, Ruth, had told Simon that even if there were any validity to the claim, my mother and Marion were entitled to nothing, because Herbert had, for all intents and purposes, left his daughters out of his will. That wasn't how it looked any longer.

Hans Marcus agreed, and our lawyers were soon at work calculating the line of inheritance, and how any settlement funds might be divided. Simon telephoned Marion in Haifa and told her of our recent discovery, and how it would affect her likely share of the claim. She might, quite unexpectedly, be in line to inherit a great deal of money. She was naturally surprised and grateful. I treasure a letter she wrote to Simon and me in 1992 saying, "Congratulations on the wonderful work you have done."

Predictably, my uncles in Israel were angered by the implications of Lucie's will. They would soon declare themselves prepared to go to court to fight my mother's claim and, if they did so, the issue might not be resolved for years.

The documents we had found did, however, raise questions about Fritz's legal status. If he inherited half of the building from Lucie's will, and had died in 1943, as we had to assume, with no wife or children, who were his heirs? And for that matter, could his death be documented?

In hope of finding answers, Simon and I visited the Wiener Library in London, which houses Jewish and Nazi-era documents collected by Alfred Wiener, a Jew who had fled Germany in 1933. Initially he had settled in Amsterdam, where he established a library documenting anti-Semitism. In 1939, Wiener had fled again, this time to London, taking his collection with him. One of the librarians showed us four volumes the West German government had prepared and first published in 1986. Together the volumes are known as the *Gedenkbuch* (*Memorial Book*), although their official title is *Gedenkbuch-Opfer der Verfolgung der Juden unter der nationalsozialistischen Gewaltherrschaft in Deutschland 1933–1945* (*Memorial Book—Victims of the Persecution of Jews under the Nazi Dictatorship in Germany 1933–1945*). This invaluable resource is now available online.

It took only seconds to find the entry for Fritz Heinrich Wolff, date of birth (October 4, 1891), where he had been living (Berlin), date of his deportation (March 1, 1943), his destination (Auschwitz), and a statement of what had happened to him—*verschollen*—which means "missing" and is a bureaucratic way of saying, "murdered by the Nazis."

We needed a death certificate.

On March 23, 1992, my mother received a letter from the Bundesarchiv in Koblenz, in response to the letter she wrote two weeks earlier. The letter told her what we already knew, that Fritz had been sent to Auschwitz on March 1, 1943. But, attached were two documents we read with great sorrow.

German record keeping is nothing if not precise. Gestapo Transport List number 31 to the East included a code denoting which train Fritz had been on: BA, ZSg. 138/337. Included on the list of all the Jews on the train was Fritz Israel Wolff. After 1939, all Jews in Germany were required to add the name "Israel" (for men) and "Sara" (for women), if their own names did not appear on an official list of those defined as "typically Jewish."

Also enclosed was a copy of a letter from the Gestapo, the Nazi secret police, dated March 5, 1943, to the local tax office, which authorized the seizure of the assets of the transported Jews for the benefit of the state. A rough translation would be:

> In the attachment I send a transport list about those Jews whose property has been confiscated during the deportation from the German Reich.
> The property is not forfeited, but passed to the German Reich. It is about 31 Osttransport.
> At the same time I enclose the appropriate asset declaration.

In other words, Fritz, like all the Jews taken to their deaths on the railways, had paid for his own ticket to Auschwitz.

On April 6, 1992, a letter arrived from the International Tracing Service, the organization set up after World War II to track what might have happened to missing civilians. My mother had written to this agency as part of her quest for a death certificate for her uncle. This letter reported:

> Evacuated March 1, 1943, by the Gestapo in Berlin, 31 Osttransport, (Transport to the East) from Berlin to Auschwitz concentration camp.

> Category: Jew

> Of his fate after March 1, 1943, we unfortunately know nothing. Accordingly, we are therefore not in a position to issue a death certificate.

No death certificate because his fate was unknown? The fate of countless Jews sent to Auschwitz was all too well known.

Another insult followed on May 8, 1992, when my mother received a letter from *Amtsgericht* Tempelhof-Kreuzberg, a Berlin suburb. The official writing proposed Fritz's date of death should be officially recognized as December 31, 1945. My mother was stunned, as was I.

We couldn't accept this outrageous suggestion. We already knew Fritz had been sent to Auschwitz on March 1, 1943, at the age of 52. Were the German authorities seriously suggesting that he did not die until nine months after the end of the war? This was not even a remote possibility. It was likely Fritz had been sent to the gas chambers soon after his arrival in Auschwitz. If a death certificate were issued dated December 1945, it was as if the Nazis were absolved of his murder. Had he miraculously made his way back to Berlin after the end of the war and died in his own bed?

We rejected the December date. Hans Marcus's assistant, Inge Bahlmann, registered an official petition that Fritz should be declared dead before May 8, 1945—the end of the war in Europe. She explained to my mother that:

The law says that the court is only obliged to make their own enquiries about the probable date of death if there is an official petition. If not, they can choose December 31, 1945.

In other words, far from it being the whim of some bureaucrat to issue death certificates dated the end of 1945, it was official German policy! This struck me as despicable.

Millions of Jews across Europe had been slaughtered, with no record of what had happened to them. Any surviving family members either had no clue as to their fate or could, at best, surmise what happened to their loved ones. We were in a rather different position. Our research efforts had enabled us to discover the exact date, location, and train number Fritz had been on and where it had been sent.

Hans Marcus followed up Inge Bahlmann's petition with a letter of his own to a Herr Walter at the district court.

Please find enclosed a copy of the Transport List in which Fritz Heinrich Wolff is listed. After this date there exists no further sign of life from him . . . It is necessary to ensure that the designated time of death should be the most likely one. Because of the

Transport List, the most likely one is a time during the war. Fritz H. Wolff was deported to the concentration camp during the war and died there. This cannot possibly be after May 8, 1945.

It would appear that the German government had come to recognize the injustice of the law as it stood. Rather than automatically present family members with death certificates dated December 31, 1945, the law needed to reflect the culpability of the Germans for these people's deaths during, not after, the war. Automatically dating their death certificates for the last day of the war in Europe was the right and proper way to proceed.

Inge Bahlmann wrote on June 30 to tell us that a "new law will make it easier to apply for death certificates . . . It will be assumed that Jewish people who were sent to concentration camps officially died on the 8th of May 1945."

This seemed to us as an honorable move. But it did not affect our application for a death certificate. Unlike so many others, we had tangible proof that Fritz had been forcibly removed from Berlin on March 1, 1943.

On August 27, the court wrote to say that Fritz Wolff had been officially declared to have died on March 1, 1943.

We were proud of the progress we made in uncovering the facts about Fritz's death. However, we still had questions about his fate, and in time we would find more answers.

19

THE *REICHSBAHN'S* MOTIVE

One underlying question we faced was why the *Reichsbahn* had been so anxious to acquire our building. When we did find out, I was sickened.

In 1992, Simon went to Berlin to meet with Alfred Gottwaldt, chief archivist at the Transport Museum and a specialist in German railways. Dr. Gottwaldt was able to explain a great deal.

In January 1937, Hitler's architect, Albert Speer, was appointed General Building Inspector and charged with transforming Berlin into the grand capital of the Reich. As part of this redesign, the city's main stations and railway lines were to be reorganized and expanded. A new state railway directorate was established on May 12. The new *Reichsbahn* architectural planning department needed office space to enact Speer's plans. Krausenstrasse 17/18 was perfect for its needs.

Also, on that same day he appointed the 32-year-old Speer as the General Inspector of all things architectural, Hitler declared in a speech to the Reichstag:

I now state here that, in accordance with the restoration of equality of rights, I shall divest the German Railways and the *Reichs-*

bank of the forms under which they have hitherto functioned and shall place them absolutely under the sovereign control of the Government of the German Reich.[1]

In other words, the young Speer was already well known to be one of Hitler's favorites and whatever Speer said he needed, he got.

The adjoining building, Krausenstrasse 19/20, had already been bought by the *Reichsbahn* (from its non-Jewish owners) months earlier. With the Wolff building right next door, the railway officials saw ideal office space for its planning department that could be acquired without difficulty.

Dr. Gottwaldt made clear the specific motivation of the Nazi seizure of our building. This new *Reichsbahn* directorate existed solely to lend support to Speer's—and Hitler's—grandiose architectural plans for Berlin: To develop its north-south axis, to free up the railway areas for the magnificent buildings Speer planned, and to lay down new, modern railway facilities.

The combined buildings would house the numerous designers and architects working on the many plans underway for a grand new city to be called "World Capital Germania."

Given the central role of the railway system in the economy of any modern nation at that time, the *Reichsbahn* was one of the key components of the Nazi regime. Hitler had always viewed the railways as enormously important. In December 1935, he gave a speech in Nuremberg to mark the 100th anniversary of the *Reichsbahn*: "This enterprise, guided and organized according to high ethical and moral concepts, is at the same time the most modern transportation enterprise in existence today."[2]

Holocaust historian Raul Hilberg's seminal work, *The Destruction of the European Jews* (1985), points out that in 1942 the *Reichsbahn*,

---

1. "On National Socialism and World Relations" speech delivered in the German Reichstag on January 30, 1937, by Adolf Hitler, Führer and Chancellor, on the fourth anniversary of the Nazi takeover of power. German translation published by H. Müller & Sohn in Berlin.
2. *Hitler: Speeches and Proclamations, 1932-1945—The Chronicle of a Dictatorship* (Vol. 2, 1935-1938) Adolf Hitler and Max Domarus.

under the authority of the Ministry of Transport, employed half a million office personnel and 900,000 others operating the trains and tracks.

In May 1942, Albert Ganzenmüller, a close associate of Speer, became head of the *Reichsbahn.*

Though the *Reichsbahn* was central to the mass deportation of Jews to the death camps, to the best of my knowledge, none of the planning or operational control for this was conducted from Krausenstrasse 17/18. Still, to know that the family's building had even a tangential connection to Hitler's genocide was an appalling finding.

At the end of the war, although hundreds of Nazis from the military, the SS, and the Gestapo were put on trial for implementing the "Final Solution" and other war crimes, not one member of the *Reichsbahn* faced a similar reckoning.

Ganzenmüller was arrested in 1945, held briefly by the United States Third Army, but was soon released. It appears that many of the employees who arranged the "special trains" (those taking Jews to the death camps) were actually promoted in the post-war German Railways system.

Years later, the lack of punishment for the crimes of the *Reichsbahn* and its employees was finally publicized. An article in the *Berliner Zeitung* newspaper on December 19, 2007, was headlined, *"Tief in den Holocaust verstrickt: Bundesverkehrsministerium arbeitet erstmals die NS-Vergangenheit seiner Vorgängerbehörde auf."* ("Deeply mired in the Holocaust: Federal Transport Ministry to come to terms with its predecessor's past for the first time.")

Part of the article mentioned the building in Krausenstrasse:

One of the Federal Ministry for Transport's three offices is the building Krausenstrasse 17–20 in Berlin *Mitte.* During the Nazi era, it had already been taken away from its Jewish owner in 1937. 'Are the people who work there aware of this?' Transport Minister Wolfgang Tiefensee (Social Democrats) wonders. The predecessor of today's authority, the Reich's Transport Ministry, had never been some apolitical administration department. From the top down the employees participated in the preparation of the mass murder of the Jews.[3]

These facts were helpful to our case, by showing the motivation of the Nazis to seize our building—and it was also important knowledge to have for the historical record. One small example of the attitude of the German Railway toward Jews was seen as early as May of 1935, when it issued an order stating: "Advertisements of Jewish firms are no longer admissible within the precincts of the German Railway."

In time, of course, the railways would be used to carry millions of Jews—and other enemies of the Reich—to their deaths.

3. http://www.berliner-zeitung.de/archiv/bundesverkehrsministerium-arbeitet-erstmals -die-ns-vergangenheit-seiner-vorgaengerbehoerde-auf-tief-in-den-holocaust-verstrickt, 10810590,10526390.html.

20

CLAIMS AND COUNTERCLAIMS

The remaining months of 1992 were taken up with letters to various authorities attempting to find birth, death, and marriage certificates to prove my mother and her siblings were direct descendants of Lucie Wolff and, thus, beneficiaries of her will. Not long after we had started the hunt, Hans Marcus received a letter from *Amtsgericht* Schöneberg (yet another Berlin district court), which amazed me. It was the will of my mother's grandfather, Victor Wolff, dated April 14, 1926, written in his own hand and signed by him.

My cousin, Leor, in Israel, helped by obtaining Herbert's and Eva's wills. Meanwhile in London, Simon, and I were finding it a slow and frustrating experience. My mother feared that the German authorities, mindful of the potential cost of Jewish claims, were deliberately stretching out the process for as long as possible. If all of these old people died, perhaps their claims would die with them and Germany could save a great deal of money. Or were the delays simply the product of typical bureaucratic inertia?

My mother added a codicil to her will. If she died before this case was settled, I was to continue with the claim on her behalf.

My emotional roller coaster soon plunged downward again.

Due to his advancing age, Hans Marcus had delegated much work on the claim to one of his German colleagues, Dr. Karsten Kühne. Dr. Kühne made frequent trips to Berlin. On one visit in August 1992, having decided to open up a working relationship with the lawyers acting for my mother's Israeli siblings, he met with their two attorneys, Frau Suzanne Kossack and Frau Barbara Erdmann. These women worked in the legal firm of Dr. Friedrich Wolff (despite the name not, apparently, any relation), a renowned criminal lawyer, with a long and distinguished career as former chairman of the Berlin Bar Association in East Germany and a television personality. He also had the dubious distinction of having been one of three lawyers chosen in 1992 by East German General Secretary Erich Honecker to defend him against charges of having been responsible for the manslaughter and attempted manslaughter of people shot while trying to flee to the West.

Dr. Kühne returned to London with interesting information. In the early 1950s, as we always suspected, Herbert had initiated a legal action to reclaim the family's villa and estate in Wannsee. Shockingly, he had also made a claim on the building in Krausenstrasse, despite knowing full well that he had renounced any entitlement to a share in 1932. But because the building was in the Soviet zone and beyond legal reach, he and his lawyers had concentrated on reclaiming the house and grounds at Conradstrasse 1. Herbert's case was that the land had been sold off in parcels, under duress, and that because of Nazi anti-Semitic laws the family had been forced to accept less than the true market value. The arguments his lawyers submitted, with supporting documents, had languished with the Berlin Supreme Restitution Court until a judgment was finally issued in 1961.

That judgment did not make encouraging reading in terms of our claim. The court had found wholly against Herbert, declaring that the prices achieved had been lawful and correct. The court ruled that the family had begun selling parts of the grounds in 1932 to service its mortgage on Krausenstrasse, and these sales had continued for several years to cover the shortfall in rent received. The fact that anti-Semitic laws had devastated the businesses of the Jewish tenants renting office space in the building did not figure in the court's decision. The court seemed to assume that business continued as usual after the Nazis took power.

The court even quoted parts of a letter written by Fritz Wolff to Ludwig Salomon, dated June 4, 1936, congratulating the lawyer on the price he had received on the sale of one parcel of the estate. To imagine that Fritz, a Jew in Germany in 1936, could have received a fair price for his land, defies belief. The court failed to recognize that Fritz's letter to his lawyer was simply recognition of the severe difficulties he had overcome to achieve any sale at all. There might also have been a touch of irony in his congratulations.

Dr. Kühne had this to say about his meetings with the two lawyers, Suzanne Kossack and Barbara Erdmann, representing the Israeli branch of the family: "Their conclusion unfortunately was that there are only very little chances of being successful with restitution because of a serious financial crisis of the family after 1932."

Dr. Kühne also met Herr Bernt-Joachim Giese at the Ministry of Finance, who was representing the German government as a prospective purchaser of our property. He reported to us, "He is a somewhat untypical German civil servant: dynamic, efficient and helpful, about 30 years of age."

Herr Giese explained that he was the sole link to the German Ministry of Finance which would pay for any purchase. Nevertheless all details would have to be negotiated with the Ministry of Transport, which currently occupied the building and was supposed to administer it, should the German government decide to buy it in the event that the claim had merit.

We did not go into detail about the value of the property but he indicated that only the land in size of 5,700 square meters (over 61,000 square feet) in this location must be worth a fortune and my impression was that the figure of roughly DM 20 million [$13 million at the time] . . . was not unrealistic in respect of the whole property. Herr Giese then raised the question of how strong our claim was.

The dynamic, efficient, and helpful Herr Giese became a major player as our drama unfolded, although one whose views changed with alarming regularity.

Dr. Kühne reported that Herr Giese had concluded that my mother's case was fragile: "Like Frau Kossack, he had perused the documents and his impression was similar to the one of Frau Kossack although he was not as gloomy as she was."

Despite his apparent pessimism regarding our case, Herr Giese told Dr. Kühne that, because the original building was still standing, if we could prove our claim, "it would be a claim for restitution and not for nominal compensation."

Dr. Kühne tried to persuade him that the family's financial difficulties in the mid-1930s had been due to anti-Semitic Nazi policies.

My obvious answer to show the strength of our claim was that the family had suffered from anti-Semitic boycotts and that we would prove to him that our claim for restitution was justified.

Dr. Kühne reported to my mother that he was not encouraged by Herr Giese's response.

He (Herr Giese) did not accept that because he had found out from the files that the property had been let fully at the time and that the family could not have done better with the property . . . He mentioned that in 1935 the tax value had been reduced to about RM 800,000 ($5.6 million in 2014 US dollar values) and that in respect of this the sales price of RM 1,800,000 ($12.6 million in 2014 US dollar values) did not indicate that it was a forced sale at a low value.

Nevertheless, it appears that Herr Giese "was convinced it was likely that we had a claim" and he shared with Dr. Kühne a useful piece of information:

. . . to propose a deal to the Ministry of Finance he would not have to be convinced that our claim was safe but that there should be a likelihood of more than 50 percent that we had a valid claim. This indication is very important for us because then in all negotiations and letters we have to concentrate on establishing a chance of more than 50 percent and we do not necessarily have to aim for 100 percent.

If, in fact, the government was lowering the bar with regard to the amount of evidence required to win our claim, it was good news. But the government maintained the right to set the bar, and their standard seemed to us to be subjective and largely unclear.

Given his position as our only link to the Ministry of Finance, Herr Giese was surprisingly open with Dr. Kühne. He informed our lawyer, "His department was seriously under budgeted, but that a new budget was forthcoming in January and he was confident that payment of the purchase price could follow soon."

Herr Giese even told Dr. Kühne he could examine his file relating to our claim and have photocopies made of whatever documents he wanted. Dr. Kühne proceeded to make photocopies relating to the legal action in 1936–1937 that resulted in the Wolff building passing from the hands of the Wolff family to the German Railways. These were copies of the entire legal proceeding, with statements from the lawyers on both sides—the documents I used to reconstruct the legal proceedings earlier in this book.

These documents gave us a new and detailed account of how the Nazis forced our family to surrender the building. To have this account of the entirely unfair proceeding—this theft that was technically considered legal under the Nazi's Nuremberg Laws—was vital to our efforts to win back the building 60 years later. We probably would have unearthed these documents eventually, but to have them handed to us at that point in our investigation was invaluable. Why did Herr Giese do us this great favor? It seems most likely that he was simply a fair-minded man who wanted to do the right thing.

Dr. Kühne was encouraged by Herr Giese's suggestion that we might be awarded the building as early as January 1993, when his agency would have new funding. If we could prove our claim, we might be less than six months away from victory.

Contrary to what Herr Giese had said, Dr. Kühne reported to my mother:

... the rents had not decreased because of the collapse of the rental market only but because of the anti-recession legislation in Germany which gave the tenants a right to give notice with immediate effect without special reason. Obviously all the tenants had made use of this right and had threatened to move out of the building. Due to financial pressure on the family and the poor market, the rents had to be decreased to such an extent that the profits made on the building were almost wiped out. The personal representative in Germany (*Nachlassverwalter*) tried extremely hard to avoid the bankruptcy of the estate which was very difficult. According to a letter he wrote in September 1936 he had managed however to turn the corner and it looked as if by that time there was no further danger of bankruptcy. The main creditor, however, the Victoria *Versicherung* in Berlin surprisingly in November 1936 enforced their legal charge on the property and forced the family to sell the property to the *Reichsbahn* for RM 1.8 million. At that time the Victoria *Versicherung* were owed approximately RM 1,500,000 which they took from the proceeds of sale. It would be very important to prove that Victoria *Versicherung* acted at 'arms length' of the *Reichsbahn* and that they helped them to expropriate Jewish property. It remains to be shown however that the purchase price of RM 1,800,000 was not the appropriate market value at the time of the sale. It should be discussed with the client whether we instruct a historian in Germany to try to prove that Victoria *Versicherung* helped the Nazi Government. In my opinion this is most likely because all of the large German companies cooperated with the Nazis and it looks strange indeed that nobody else than the *Reichsbahn* acquired the property.

Dr. Kühne also visited the Asset Compensation Agency to meet Frau Mirus, and two of her colleagues, Herr Schnurbusch and Herr

Moisich. Their office would ultimately decide whether or not my mother's case was sound, and they would issue a legally binding finding.

> Frau Mirus concentrated only on the date of sale and as this was after September 1935 [the date of the Nuremberg Laws] she was convinced she had not to go into any details . . . Frau Mirus and Herr Moisich then put forward some arguments which might be dangerous in respect of restitution in kind because of considerable investment of the *Reichsbahn* in the buildings and because of the close connection of our building with the neighbor buildings.

Insofar as we could read her, Frau Mirus appeared to have an ambiguous view of our claim. She seemed to think the Nuremberg Laws gave us the presumption of duress on the sale. Yet she raised objections about improvements to the building, which we thought made little sense. Dr. Kühne also reported that she asked him if she and her colleagues should send their approval of the claim to Herr Giese directly or to him. What were we to make of all this?

Dr. Kühne continued:

> I suggested that they should send it to me. At the end of our discussion they referred to the article in the magazine of the *Evening Standard* which they did not like. I apologized for this article and agreed with them that the article makes life unnecessarily more difficult for everyone involved. (I shall suggest to the clients to stop the use of media at that stage where our position is still very fragile.)

Dr. Kühne asked us to hold back from further publicity for a while and indeed my mother turned down a request for an interview by a German documentary maker. Still, we did not regret the *Evening Standard* article.

Dr. Kühne seemed to have made a positive impression on the German authorities. He even managed to persuade Herr Giese to put aside his file for six weeks and wait for a legal opinion from the AROV, which he had been told would be in our favor.

In September 1992, my mother heard again from Dr. Kühne:

. . . Herr Giese of the Ministry of Finance who started very friendly talks with me was asked by his minister to give a written opinion. Herr Giese gave this opinion and the result had to be negative because Herr Giese has all the documents on his file which give details of the financial problems of the family. His report obviously has been distributed and Frau Mirus at the Assets Compensation Agency has a copy, too. When I tried to arrange a meeting with her on my next trip to Berlin on September 30 she told me that she had changed her mind and that it is very likely that there is no claim at all. . . .

We now have to take emergency steps and I am putting together a list of our arguments in favor of our claim . . .

Herr Giese mentioned on the telephone that he could still imagine to come to an agreement, even including a purchase price, all subject to proof of your claim of course.

Dr. Kühne was trying to keep lines of communication with Frau Mirus and Herr Giese open, and avoid a negative recommendation being made to the Minister of Transport, but the situation looked bleak.

On October 13, 1992, Dr. Kühne wrote what was essentially a holding letter to Frau Mirus stating the main points of my mother's claim.

He argued that the price paid, in May 1937, to the Jewish Wolff family, (of RM 766,93 per square meter) was not equivalent to the market value of the time. Non-Jewish sellers achieved 45 percent higher sales prices. This was the case with Krausenstrasse 19/20, the building immediately next door, which had been foreclosed on and sold for RM 1,100 per square meter. The owners had not been Jews. A similar building had been sold in 1938 for over RM 1,100 per square meter. He concluded that there was no doubt that the Wolff building had been the subject of a forced sale and that comparable sale values had been 45 percent higher than the price paid to the Wolff family. The only significant difference between the Wolff sale and the other two had been the religion of the sellers.

Our lawyer considered it highly significant that the Victoria Insurance Company never registered itself as the new owner. Indeed, it had never put the building up for auction to the highest bidder. Instead, the building passed directly into the hands of the *Reichsbahn*. Surely this was an example of German business interests colluding with the Nazis?

Dr. Kühne also believed that, if there had been an auction, the burden of proof would have been on my mother to prove discrimination. But because there was no auction, the burden of proof was reversed. It was for the German authorities to prove that there had *not* been discrimination. We could only hope the government would agree.

21

WHO'S WHO IN NAZI GERMANY

At the start of our quest to prove how the Wolff building had wound up in the hands of the Nazis, Simon said to me, "I've always wanted to hunt Nazis."

As a child, he had followed newspaper accounts of the trial of Adolf Eichmann, one of the architects of the "Final Solution" and, during his college years, he had read *The Odessa File*, Frederick Forsyth's thriller about a German journalist tracking down a Nazi war criminal, a book that had inspired him to become a journalist.

Now he really was hunting Nazis!

Early in 1992, Simon went to what was then the British Public Records Office (now known as the National Archives) located in Kew, a suburb of London close to Heathrow Airport. We knew the office housed a huge amount of material on the Second World War and the Nazis, and Simon hoped to find clues as to why the Victoria Insurance Company had wanted to withdraw the mortgage on a building that was paying off its loan. Clearly, it was not normal business procedure.

On his first day at the archive, he found something so astonishing that he rushed to a pay phone to call me at my office at the BBC. While working through a catalogue of the documents available in the vaults, he had spotted one entitled, *Who's Who in Nazi Germany*. He asked for it to be retrieved and the original duly arrived at his research desk. *Who's Who in Nazi Germany* was a slim booklet from the British War Office, dated May 1944 and marked "Confidential."

The book contained the names and brief biographies of about 1,200 prominent Germans in Hitler's Third Reich. Simon came across a section on Banking, Finance, Insurance. Thirty-two names were listed including one he instantly recognized: Hamann. Turning to page 70, he found the biographical entry: Dr. Hamann, Kurt. Chairman of the Board of the Victoria Insurance Company (born in 1898).

Nazi propaganda chief, Dr. Paul Josef Goebbels, and Hitler's designated successor, Hermann Göring, were on page 67 of the booklet. The head of the SS, Heinrich Himmler, and Adolf Hitler himself were on page 75. Sandwiched between them, Hamann was in bad company. Though, from the point of view of our case, it was fine company indeed.

The intelligence arm of the British war effort had classified the head of the Victoria Insurance Company as a leading player in Nazi Germany. Now, our lawyers could argue that the Victoria had unquestionably worked hand in glove with the Nazis. In other words, to use the German legal expression, the sale was "Nazi driven." What hope did the Wolff family have for retaining their building, when such forces in 1937 Germany targeted it?

We were to discover much more about Dr. Hamann and the Victoria Insurance Company, but we already had powerful ammunition for our lawyers to use to counter any present-day German official who believed that the Wolff family voluntarily sold its building for the greater glory of the Third Reich.

Later, as he was walking along Charing Cross Road in central London, Simon's instincts told him to go into a bookshop that specialized in Nazi Germany. There he found a reproduction map entitled "Berlin—Allied Intelligence Map of Key Buildings." It was a 1944 British War Office map of Berlin, marking the principal buildings and indicating whether they had been destroyed by Allied bombing or not. And Krausenstrasse 17/20 was marked, numbered as "139." On the other side of the map, the note for number 139 explained that the building came under the section "Reich Government," for which the first entry was Hitler's headquarters, the Reich Chancellery. Listed further below, under the subsection for the Ministry of Transport, was *Reichsbahn-baudirektion* Berlin (Berlin Division of the State Railways: Construction), and the address given as Krausenstrasse 17/20.

Back in the British Archives, Simon came across another interesting letter. This was a memo, dated December 14, 1936, addressed to I. A. Kirkpatrick at the Foreign Office, reporting on a visit the official had received from a Mr. E. F. Irgens of Messrs C. E. Heath and Company Limited, Bankside House, 107/112 Leadenhall Street. This company of insurance brokers and members of Lloyds was doing business with a firm of insurance brokers in Germany.

Mr. Irgens called in to report that their German counterpart was owned by Jews, and stated other German firms had been warned to sever their connections with it, and that "This will hit very hard the Jewish firm with whom Messrs Heath are connected." Clearly, Mr. Irgens was acutely worried that if the German company should be forced out of business, then C. E. Heath "might also be hit quite hard. In these circumstances Messrs Heath are sending a representative, Mr. C. C. Hardy, to have a look round and see if anything can be done ... The Department of Overseas Trade tell me that Messrs Heath are thoroughly respectable people deserving of every assistance ... Messrs Heath's German correspondent is Bleichröder and Company, Burchardstrasse 24, Haus Hubertus, Hamburg."

What had leapt off the page was the name "Bleichröder." Bernhard Bleichröder was my grandfather Herbert's best friend who had had offices in Krausenstrasse.

It all added up.

22

DR. HAMANN AND THE VICTORIA INSURANCE COMPANY

We began to receive, as a result of our many enquiries, an array of documents from other sources and archives that started to paint an interesting picture. First, there was the annual financial report for 1932 of the Victoria Insurance Company dated June 9, 1933, which contained a full list of the board of directors. Next, a legal document lodged on February 26, 1936, with a Berlin commercial court, listed seven board members and seven company lawyers who had power of attorney. At the top of the list was *Landgerichtsrat* (Magistrate) Dr. Kurt Hamann, a board member since October 1932, and another name of interest, Ernst Teckenberg, who joined the board on February 15, 1936. (Teckenberg had the title of *"Kaufmann,"* meaning "business-man.") Both these luminaries had been major contributors to the centenary celebrations. But more importantly, they had been on the board before the mortgage held by the Wolff family on Krausenstrasse 17/18 had been withdrawn.

Who exactly was Dr. Kurt Hamann, the illustrious chairman of the Victoria Insurance Company and its leader throughout the war, as noted by the British Government in *Who's Who in Nazi Germany*? It is incredible what can be gleaned by scouring the archives and libraries. Before too long, I was able to fill in the missing pieces of this man's inexorable rise to the very pinnacle of German commercial life.

In January 1993, my husband wrote to Dr. David Marwell, the then director of the Berlin Document Center (BDC) based at the United States Embassy Office in Berlin. The BDC was established in 1945 as a repository of Nazi Party records captured by the wartime western Allies—the United States, Britain, and France—and were held under the authority of the U.S. Army for use in war crimes and denazification trials. After 1953, it came under the jurisdiction of the Department of State, with all the expenses of its operation paid by the Federal Republic of Germany.

This collection of documents contains Nazi Party membership records. What could Dr. Marwell tell us about any on the list of 1930s wartime directors of the Victoria Insurance Company? We sent him 14 names; all in senior management positions at the Victoria Insurance Company at the time of the foreclosure on Krausenstrasse. Specifically, we asked him to tell us if, and when, any of them had been members of the Nazi party.

In early May 1993 Dr. Marwell replied with a bundle of documents that contained exactly what we were seeking. He drew a blank on eight of the 14 names. The rest all had connections to the Nazi Party.

The first piece of evidence was the official Nazi party membership document, complete with a black eagle holding a Nazi emblem on the front page: "Ernst Teckenberg, date of birth November 22, 1891, address Satzbrenner Strasse 25, Berlin Grunewald, joined the Nazi party on May 1, 1937, party number 5586511."

On the list were two other directors of the Victoria: "Wilhelm Seemann, date of birth April 9, 1888; address Zeltinger Strasse 15, Berlin Frohnau, party number 8013921."

And "Dr. Carl Hüschelrath, date of birth December 10, 1899; address Patschkauer Weg 56, Berlin Dahlem, party number 2085455."

Three other names from among a list of the company lawyers that we submitted to the BDC had files on them in its archives.

(Also in the batch of papers—a Kurt Hamann, date of birth February 20, 1898, who joined the Nazi party on April 1, 1933, membership number 1774003. Although it is the right year, this is not the same birthdate of the Kurt Hamann who had led the Victoria Insurance Company.)

So, Teckenberg had been in the company before, during, and after the war and had, along with five of his colleagues, been a member of the Nazi party.

But what about Victoria Insurance Company chairman, Dr. Kurt Hamann?

It was not difficult to find out about his glittering post-war career. A 1955 edition of *Wer Ist Wer? Das Deutsche Who's Who?*—which provides information on more than 15,000 personalities in politics, industry, and culture living in Germany—(". . . *gibt Auskunft über mehr als 15,000 Persönlichkeiten des politischen, wirtschaftlichen und kulturellen Lebens in Deutschland*") revealed that Dr. Kurt Hamann was awarded the Federal Cross of Merit (*Bundesverdienstkreuz*) in 1953—the highest civilian honor. A mere eight years after World War II, Dr. Hamann was again at the peak of German society. Not bad for someone who, as I continued to discover, had a less than wholly glorious past.

I was not finished with the German archives just yet. The Victoria Insurance Company board might want to forget about their history in the period leading up to and during the war, but it is highly pertinent to what happened to my family's property. Having successfully positioned itself as a leading insurer to the Jewish commercial sector, the Victoria was in a prime position to foreclose on these same business people who helped make it the successful insurance company it had become.

The pity of it all is that it was all done perfectly legally—at least within the terms of Nazi-era laws. It was certainly unethical, but in complete accordance with the law of the time. The German leadership was at pains to ensure the law was obeyed. No matter that the prevailing circumstances were such that Jews were barely able to conduct any normal business transactions.

Alongside the research of Dr. Marwell, we decided to commission a firm of property specialists in Berlin, Nagel & Partner, to compile a report on any information that could be discovered about the history of the Victoria Insurance Company. Specifically, what had the company been up to between 1933 and 1945? What emerged made disturbing reading.

The pile of documents and searches gave us considerable background into the business affairs of the Victoria during the crucial war years, as well as the immediate post-war period. The dossier contained copies of Berlin court records that proved the Victoria had foreclosed on many Jewish-owned properties, aided by Nazi race laws that stripped their owners of the right to do business under normal, legal conditions. Also, there were several pages listing businesses taken from their owners whose names were given, and often included "Israel," the name that the Nazis forced Jewish men to adopt so there would be no doubt about their religious and ethnic origins.

The letter from Nagel & Partner accompanying the submission of the documents, along with the invoice for the research, contained a most encouraging, and indeed somewhat triumphant, message:

> We are pretty certain that because of this documentation your dispute position is considerably improved and in view of this we wish you much success.

> *Wir sind zuversichtlich, das Sie anhand dieser Dokumentation Ihre Verhandlungsposition erheblich verbessern können und dürfen Ihnen in Hinblick darauf viel Erfolg wünschen.*

Indeed it did. They had uncovered some fascinating new material.

After the war, it had been business as usual for the insurance company. Many of the previously Jewish-owned properties on which the Victoria had foreclosed now fell within the Soviet zone. But that did not stop the Victoria petitioning to have their ownership registered in the land registry.

As some kind of perverse justice perhaps, the East German authorities took over these properties in the name of the *Volk* (People), but it did not take long for the Victoria to head back to court protesting that they wished to see their previous ownership of these properties duly recognized in the land registry.

The Magistrate in the Soviet zone of occupation was having none of it. Properties in what was now the Eastern sector that had formerly been "owned" by the Victoria were from now on to be registered as *"Eintragung als Eigentum des Volkes"* or the "Property of the People." In some instances, the Victoria even tried to argue to the court that they owned the land on which the property sat, but this was all to no avail.

Among our new stash of documents was yet another further fascinating discovery. In May 1949, the Magistrate of Greater Berlin in the Soviet zone had published a list of over 200 banks and insurance companies classified as war criminals and Nazi activists (*Kriegsverbrecher und Naziaktivisten*). As a result of this legal status, these companies were forbidden to conduct any business activity whatsoever in the Soviet sector and neither were they entitled to receive restitution or compensation. Recorded alongside a host of well-known names such as Deutsche Bank, Dresdner Bank and Allianz Insurance was the Victoria.

Cynics might well argue that this was just a convenient ruse to justify the wholesale closure of private companies and the confiscation of their assets. After all, the Soviets did not investigate the specific role of these corporations but simply assumed Nazism had indelibly tainted any company doing business in Germany during the Third Reich. But our lawyers considered this useful additional information as far as our case was concerned, and so did we.

It turned out that Krausenstrasse 17/18 was not the only property where the East German bureaucrats' research found the previous owners had been Jewish. There were other examples where the "people" took over the building, but those charged with sorting out the provenance of the property honorably requested that a special note be placed in the land registry, pointing out the previous owners had been Jews.

Today, the Victoria Insurance Company is based in Düsseldorf. Its wartime record, however, remains tightly held. But not entirely hidden, as I was to discover many years later, and well after our claim had been settled.

23

BACK TO BERLIN:
THE FRUSTRATION GROWS

In March 1993, Simon and I went to Berlin for more face-to-face interviews. We met with the East German lawyers representing our Israeli relatives. The two women proved to be extremely pessimistic about our chances of success, and seemed to view Simon and me as hopelessly deluded. Living in East Germany had not made them optimistic about the prospects of citizens who challenged their government. But we did carry out a useful exchange of our findings to date.

While in Berlin, I decided to check the veracity of another of the stories Nellie had often told me. I wanted to see for myself how large and impressive the Wolff family plot had been at the famous Jewish cemetery at Weissensee, in a northern suburb of Berlin, one of the largest surviving Jewish graveyards in Europe. Dedicated in 1880, it has more than 100,000 graves, and survived the war intact.

After passing through its main entrance, we walked into an office where an elderly lady greeted us. I explained I had come to find the grave of my great-grandmother, Lucie Wolff. I gave her Lucie's date of birth and she started thumbing through a well-worn card index. To my amazement, she soon plucked out a card, which revealed not only that Lucie Wolff was buried in the cemetery, but exactly which plot she was in. She gave me a map of the site, put a mark on the grave's location, and told me which path to follow.

Weissensee Cemetery is divided into 120 sections. It was designed in a neo-Renaissance style by a notable German architect of the period, Hugo Licht. We were struck by the elaborate and overly ornate art nouveau designs of many of the tombstones. Our map took us to a large plot, up against the perimeter wall. "FAMILIE WOLFF" was emblazoned across the top of a pillared front, giving the appearance of a mausoleum.

The tomb contained not only Lucie's remains, but those of her husband, Victor, as well as his father, Heimann, and mother, Johanna. It was an impressive structure, now totally overgrown by creepers and weeds. There was an upright engraved tombstone embedded in the wall for each person buried there. Here I was, standing in front of the graves of my ancestors that had survived the ravages of war and decades of Communist neglect.

The poignancy of the moment was not lost on me. Far from it. In my mind's eye, I conjured up scenes of Herbert and Fritz standing on the very spot where I was now standing for the funerals of their parents and grandparents. What would my ancestors have made of my having found them all these years later?

It is sad that my mother's twin Marianne was not buried there.

We took photos to show the family back home in London and, in accordance with Jewish tradition, placed small stones on the graves, symbolizing a visitor had been to pay tribute to the lasting memory of the deceased.

As we left the cemetery, I reflected that yet another of Nellie's stories had proven to be true.

By the end of June 1993, my mother was profoundly frustrated at the lack of progress. She expressed her disappointment in no uncertain terms to Dr. Kühne, who patiently explained to her the difficulties he, and the other lawyers, faced. From his perspective, it had been an uphill struggle to convince the German authorities that she had any case at all.

He said that at his first meeting with Frau Mirus at the AROV she had been of the view, which she continued to hold, that the property had been sold at, or even above, market value and that alone excluded any notion of a forced sale. Herr Giese at the Finance Ministry had taken a slightly less harsh view, but nevertheless was of the opinion that our claim was, at best, borderline.

Did the officials really believe these arguments, despite our evidence to the contrary? Or were they just taking hard-line positions with an eye to future negotiations? We had no idea.

All the while, the German government was planning how and when it should relocate its various departments and offices from the West German capital of Bonn to the historic capital, Berlin. We suspected this was influencing the decisions officials made in dealing with our claim. Our building was increasingly valuable as powerful officials scrambled for prime real estate in the new, or newly restored, capital.

To our disappointment, Karsten Kühne warned that Frau Mirus "is positive that she will dismiss the claim." However, he said she would let us have a draft of her decision and he would provide a comprehensive report from our side. He urged her not to start work on her draft before she had received further information from him.

Dr. Kühne informed my mother by letter that Herr Giese was busy compiling lists about properties and purchase prices in the areas of the new capital. Herr Giese apparently believed he could prove the price the Wolff family had received in 1937 for Krausenstrasse 17/18 was higher than most other prices achieved at the time of the sale, including prices for properties that didn't have Jewish owners. We thought that extremely unlikely.

There was also more news that confirmed our worst fears. Dr. Kühne reported to my mother that Herr Giese had "indicated" that he had "new 'highest' orders." These had two parts: maintain the building Krausenstrasse 17/18 in accordance with the relocation plans of the Federal Government, and dispute the restitution claim at all costs. He did not name names, but he would later complain about obstructionism by his superiors in Bonn, which suggests political pressures rather than any focus on the facts of the case.

This report of mysterious "highest" orders was troubling. As we faced opposition from various government officials, we had no way of knowing what truly motivated them. Their views seemed to change from day to day. We didn't know if they were genuinely skeptical about our case, which seemed so strong to us, or if they were reflecting the wishes of unknown higher-ups, who simply refused to surrender a valuable building, whatever the merits of our case. It is almost always like that when you deal with government. You never know who is pulling the strings behind the curtain or what secret agenda you may be facing.

It appeared that the Transport Ministry had made a decision that at least a major part of its headquarters would move to Berlin as soon as possible. It seemed, as Dr. Kühne related it, that the government was "determined to maintain the building Krausenstrasse 17/18" and was "not interested in talks. They will wait for Frau Mirus to decide whether there is a valid claim for restitution or not."

Of course, we had already been told she did not look kindly on our case. Now, my mother felt the deck was stacked against her, not based on the merits of the claim, but because of sheer bureaucratic greed.

To round off his gloomy report, Dr. Kühne warned us "At the moment, litigation in Germany seems unavoidable. This litigation could go on for many years."

Incredibly, matters became worse.

In September 1993, we discovered that the Minister of Transport made an application to be named in the land registry as the owner of Krausenstrasse 17/18 on behalf of the German government. Could they do this? Could they make it stick? I felt as if our building was being stolen from us again, not by Nazis, but this time by an avowedly democratic government.

Dr. Kühne knew he had to move quickly. He wrote my mother:

In my discussion on the telephone with Herr Giese he admitted that your case was a "borderline case." His department, however, intends to find out where the dividing line between forced sale and unforced sale is by testing your case.

I pressed on. If we could prove that the building was sold under duress then the price achieved was going to be of paramount importance. Had it been a fair price?

We knew the history of the building next door, Krausenstrasse 19/20. According to the land registry, the Piesberger family, who were Germans from Prussia and not Jews, had owned it since the beginning of the century. Apparently, the family's fortunes had hit hard times and in 1937 the building was entered into a forced auction due to non-payment of tax and mortgage. The Allianz and Stuttgarter Life Insurance Company acquired the building at 19/20 and almost immediately sold it to the German State Railways, the *Reichsbahn.*

We needed to make the most of the fact that the almost-identical building next door was sold, on a square footage basis, for a much higher price than our building. Then, we had another surprise. German officials had complained to our lawyer about our using the media to publicize our case, but now they were using the same technique to strengthen their claim to our building.

On October 11, 1993, the *Berliner Zeitung* (*Berlin Newspaper*) published an article headlined "Not a Bad Place" and "Transport Minister Could Renovate the Building." Accompanied by a photograph of the building, the article said that the Transport Minister had instructed that the place be renovated. The newspaper reported that the former home of the East German Ministry of Transport was already flying a government flag, had newly renovated windows with thermoglass, and by the end of the year the renovations would be complete.

"The building is good and colleagues are happy here," said Ulrich Klimke, the Minister of Transport. Some 350 staff members had moved from Bonn to the building.

There was no mention of a claim of ownership of the building by the family from which it had been taken. Evidently, it did not strike anyone in authority that, given the ongoing dispute over legal ownership, it might be presumptuous to start major renovations. They acted as if they'd been there forever and intended to stay.

In January 1994, German political leaders agreed to move the nation's government and Parliament from Bonn back to Berlin. Newspaper accounts pointed out that Bonn would lose lucrative building contracts and thousands of bureaucrats, diplomats, and news correspondents. The government agreed to boost its compensation to Bonn to 2.5 billion Deutsche marks, or more than $1.5 billion.

Clearly, Krausenstrasse 17/18 was at the center of a high stakes real-estate scramble. No wonder the Transport Minister had wanted to get his agency's ownership of the building put into the land registry and written about in the newspapers. He must have had big plans for our building, and surely would have been displeased that anyone might question his claim to it.

24

THE FORMAL CLAIM

In January 1994, Dr. Kühne drafted a letter formally stating the claim, which he intended to send to Frau Mirus at the *Vermögensamt* (AROV or Assets Compensation Agency). When he submitted it to us for our thoughts, he warned that:

> I have put together all the points which I think are relevant and I have tried to deal with them in the most favourable way for you. I have taken into consideration the discussions which I had with the German authorities earlier in this matter and also the documentation which was provided by them. These discussions, although time consuming, now prove to be very valuable because the authorities have disclosed all their "ammunition." The most important issue is the financial situation of your family and the property before the time of the sale, and I have laid emphasis on this issue. We must not forget that, during my first discussion with Frau Mirus of the *Vermögensamt* in Berlin, she gave me good reasons why she would dismiss your claim for restitution. . . .

After running it past my mother—as well as Simon and me—to get corrections, additions, and clarifications, he sent it to Frau Mirus on

March 1. In essence, the claim for the restitution of the Wolff property incorporated all the research we had conducted over the previous three years and boiled down to eleven major points. (The letter sent to Frau Mirus was in German.)

1. This Jewish family had had to sell the property "willingly" after they were threatened with a forced auction. But actually the family had been the victims of Nazi persecution enacted between September 15, 1935, and May 8, 1945, which was unjust. No one can dispute that the family suffered from racial persecution. Fritz Wolff was detained in custody several times and was deported to Auschwitz in 1943 where he was murdered.

2. The Victoria Insurance Company had pressured the family to dispose of the building when they threatened them with a forced auction in November 1936. This threat had put such pressure on the Administrator of the property that he had to agree to the sale to the *Reichsbahn*. The Victoria Insurance Company, just like all big, successful companies in 1937, was closely connected to the Nazi party. Dr. Kurt Hamann, the Chief Executive, was listed by the British in "Who's Who in Nazi Germany."

3. The systematic proceedings of the Nazis with the *Reichsbahn* become obvious when we learn that the next door property, Krausenstrasse 19/20, was also taken from the owners in 1937 due to a forced auction. That property was taken first by the Allianz and Stuttgarter Life Insurance Company, who in the same year sold it on to the *Reichsbahn*.

4. The *Reichsbahn* had a concrete need for office blocks as they needed properties for the newly created *Reichsbahnbaudirektion* which was formed in July 1937. The buildings were used to house the functionaries running a new railways administration for the capital. As this was a new organization, they needed new office buildings and this is what Krausenstrasse was used for. 1937 was an especially active year as they were celebrating "100 Years of the Railways in Prussia 1837."

5. Even though the two neighboring buildings were used by the same authority, they were only linked together by making a door

opening through the dividing wall. The buildings can be easily separated by closing this door. This situation remains to date, at least when last seen internally in 1993.

6. The process of forced auction was also not legal or at any rate it was unjust. This was emphasized by the fact that on November 30, 1948, the property was taken over by the *Deutsche Treuhandstelle* and there was a note in the land registry inserted to say "the Jewish owner was forced by the prevailing political circumstances to sell the property." After 1945 the Soviet occupation government listed the Victoria as "Nazi- and war-criminals." (*Nazi- und Kriegsverbrecher*)

7. It can be seen from the detailed application by lawyer Max Michaelis on November 27, 1936, objecting to the forced auction, that the proceedings were unlawful. Already from the various reasons given to halt the forced auction by legal means, it is apparent that the family did not wish to be separated from their building. For a Jewish owner it was in every way dangerous, even heedless, in 1937 to oppose a large undertaking which was in the Nazi sphere. Only with extreme determination and good grounds would a man, a Jew, such as Michaelis, take such a step.

8. In 1928, the property was valued at RM 2,565,000. In 1929, the Victoria Insurance Company gave the family a mortgage of RM 1.2 million. There was clearly a solid cover for the mortgage. The interest rate as originally agreed on the mortgage was 8.5 percent which came to RM 102,000. This was covered by 300 percent through the total rents accruing from tenants of the building in 1931 which came in at RM 308,585. Even after the Brüning Laws in December 1931 (imposed before the Nazi-era, in order to protect tenants during the world economic crash), the financial situation was in order. The boycott of Jews, which became operative in 1933/34, threw the building into a state of crisis as for the most part the tenants were Jewish enterprises. After 1933 Aryan tenants were difficult to obtain for Jewish-owned buildings. The Jewish tenants, until their persecution, had been successful business people, and they suffered greatly and found themselves unable to pay their formerly agreed, or market value, rents. This

applied to well-known and successful Jewish enterprises which in previous times had been well able to afford to occupy one of the best and most centrally located buildings. In fact, the rental situation stabilized by January 1, 1937 and was being turned round with yearly rental income at RM 118,500.

There had been good prospects for the building to turn itself around financially at the point of the initiation of the proceedings for a forced auction. Even if only achieving minimum rental income, the *Unterdeckung* (funding gap) cover was no more than 12 percent.

The administrator, Ludwig Salomon, said in his detailed report to the *Nachlassgericht* (probate court) that, since 1936, rents had increased by 15 percent. In fact, increases of 20 percent and more could have been achieved with ease and had actually been agreed. In these circumstances, it can be seen that the rental receipts, in 1931, were three times higher than the costs of the mortgage. It is obvious, that at the time the Victoria initiated the forced sale, this was economically foolish as the mortgage was more than fully covered.

This attitude (of the Victoria) taking into account all the circumstances against a Jewish family leaves no doubt that this was a loss of property due to persecution.

9. In view of this, the price obtained was abnormally low. This can be seen because of various comparisons. The price obtained was RM 1,800,000 on a property of 2,337 square meters (25,000 square feet). This works out at a price of RM 770.22 per square meters. The neighboring property, Krausenstrasse 19/20, which was also taken from its owners, achieved a price of RM 1,400,000 and their area was 1,276 square meters (13,700 square feet). This means that a price of RM 1,097.18 per square meter was achieved, a 41 percent higher amount than the Wolff family property achieved on their "freely agreed" sale. The more friendly treatment of the neighbors is simply explained by the fact that it was a good Prussian family called Piesberger.

As explained, the nominal tax value *Einheitswert* in 1928 was RM 2,565,000. The *Wehrbeitragswert* (arms or defense tax rating) in 1936 was RM 2,700,000. Both figures were not in the remotest way achieved. In no way was a suitable price obtained. The persecuted people, in the same way as they could not obtain the correct rent, had their sale prices of property reduced. This had to be accepted by the owners, so that they only had to pay reduced ground rent and similar taxes, which were adjusted to their reduced rents received. In this way, the nominal tax value in 1931 was reduced to RM 1,882,600. This already reduced nominal tax value, because of persecution, was not obtained at the sale. It is not realistic to compare the nominal tax value of 1935, which was RM 821,400. This nominal tax value unfortunately undated for the much smaller neighboring property of 19/20 was RM 891,800. The development of the nominal tax value of the other neighboring property, Schützenstrasse 64, underlines the disproportionate relationship between the tax valuation for 1935 and the income from rents, which, in the case of the Wolff family, was reduced because of persecution. The nominal tax value for Schützenstrasse 64 in 1935 was RM 86,000. It stabilized in 1939 up to RM 189,300 and became more than double.

Through obtaining a tax valuation of RM 1,882,600 in 1931, Krausenstrasse 17/18 showed its value. A sale at this value did not show an appropriate market value price. This idea is further supported by a comparison with the statutory minimum rent of RM 190,000 following the Brüning Laws. The sale price was less than a tenth of this yearly legal minimum rent, obviously not a just market price for a prime location and well maintained business premises.

10. To make it clear, it is pointed out that the above-mentioned points are made to show the fact that the situation arose because of persecution. The final price achieved is not really the main point.

11. After the settlement by the administrator Salomon, there remained a "free" amount for the disposal of RM 57,233.33. The only member of the Wolff family was Fritz, who obtained RM 29,065.68 for "free" use. Even the choice of words shows the cynicism. Fritz Wolff was deported in 1943 and murdered in Auschwitz. He had been arrested several times since 1933. He could

certainly not, in 1937, receive money in "freedom" in the sense that law makers would understand. In 1943, when he was murdered, Fritz Wolff lost the power of free disposal.

To summarize, there is no doubt that it was a forced sale, which can be put right by the return of the property. The Victoria put the family Wolff, in the words of the administrator, into a "surprising and at short notice" situation which obliged the family to accept a forced sale, which would not, and should not, have arisen.

The forced sale in 1937 made sense in only one direction, for the Deutsche Reichsbahn, that is to say the German state.

Dr. Kühne's presentation of my mother's case ended: "*Dem begründenden Rückübertragungsantrag der Erbengemeinschaft nach Victor und Lucie Wolff ist stattzugeben*" or, in English, "The heirs of Victor and Lucie Wolff ought to have recompense."

So there it was, our case, our claim. Even given its formal language and obscure points about tax and rent, it was clear, at least to us. Dr. Kühne was making the case that Krausenstrasse 17/18 had been, in legal terms, forcibly sold. Simply put, the building had been expropriated by the Nazis from its Jewish owners.

25

GETTING THEIR OWN BACK

On March 31, 1994, my mother received another bizarre message from the German authorities. Among other things, the German officials were now arguing that because the building had been altered, they could not return it to the claimants.

This made no sense. If the Nazis hadn't taken the building in the first place it wouldn't have been altered. Various governments had occupied it for the past 60 years, without paying a day's rent to the family, and now the latest occupiers were claiming that, on account of their alterations, it could not be returned! It defied logic.

We did have one bit of good news, however. By the end of 1993, all relevant wills, birth, death, and marriage certificates had been gathered and submitted to the German Embassy in London so an inheritance certificate could be granted to my mother.

On June 8, 1994, the Embassy in London issued her certificate, official recognition that she was a legal inheritor of her grandmother, Lucie's, estate. Hans Marcus was delighted. Whether or not we won our case, at least he could now prove that his client was a legitimate claimant.

In July 1994, I told Nigel Acheson, a BBC radio documentary producer, about my mother's claim. Nigel was in charge of a series of programs entitled "Document," the basis of which was the use of original documents of historical significance. He immediately suggested making a program about the case.

Not only did he want to do a program for the BBC, but a German friend of his, Holger Jackisch, a producer with radio station MDR (*Mitteldeutscher Rundfunk*) in Berlin, wanted to do a co-production in German. This would widen the audience considerably and might put pressure on the German authorities to reconsider their position on my family's claim.

Our lawyers gave their approval, and in the last week of August my mother headed to Berlin with the BBC production team. In advance of their arrival, Nigel interviewed the eminent British historian of the Third Reich, Professor Richard Evans, who described how, from 1929 to 1933, the German economy was in a deep crisis, and when the Nazis came into power their aim was to revive production, banish unemployment, and build up the military. For several years, Hjalmar Schacht was the Reich minister for economics, and was regarded as something of a financial wizard. Ironically, he believed that attacks on Jewish businesses actually hindered economic recovery and advised against the exclusion of Jews from the German economy. Perhaps not surprisingly, this stance caused his ouster from office in September 1937.

Professor Evans went on to explain how banks and credit institutions were openly encouraged by the Nazis not to lend money to Jewish businesses and indeed to call in loans. They were hoping to force Jews to sell their businesses to Aryan buyers cheaply.

Holger, the German radio producer, had also been busy. He had contacted the Victoria Insurance Company, asking for any information they might have on their involvement with the building at Krausenstrasse 17/18. On August 24, he received a faxed response from a Herr Schmitz informing him:

> This building is not known here. It is also not the subject of an application for restitution. Unfortunately we found nothing in our archives, which sadly were decimated during the last days of the Second World War when our Berlin Head Office was destroyed. We are however happy to look into the matter further if you let us have copies of the material relating to your particular case.

If in fact this building did have a Victoria mortgage, we can at this point already point out that: As insurers, even before the Second World War, as part of the statutory investment regulations on real estate secured loans, where there were non-performing loans, we were able to act in the interest of the insured funds prudently not help as the last step to exploit the security. But let us wait and see what we can determine with the help of your documents.

What a fine response! The Victoria could only suggest that we might have had a "non-performing" loan that could have been called in because of their good management.

Holger had also sent a fax to the Federal Ministry of Transport in Bonn asking for an interview with the Minister of Transport, Matthias Wissmann, to discuss the history of the building, what plans were in place for it, and the situation concerning restitution policy and compensation issues. Not an unreasonable request because Herr Wissmann's ministry in Berlin was based in this very property. The answer from Bonn, however, was unequivocal: No interview, no statement, and no permission to enter the building.

But my mother is not so easily stopped, and she was not averse to trying her luck in gaining access. So she set out to visit her building and, naturally, the two radio producers wanted to capture her reactions as she entered—and if possible toured—her family's property for the first time in 60 years. Upon arrival, my mother fearlessly marched in and, in her impeccable German, chatted with the receptionist at the front desk. From her description of the woman's distinctively dyed red hair, she must have been the same receptionist I had myself encountered in December 1990.

Clearly unaware of the edict from Bonn that my mother was not to be allowed inside the building, this kindly woman ushered her and the two producers inside. She gave them a guided tour and answered their numerous questions—all of which were caught on tape.

The woman explained she was now an employee of the Transport Ministry but had worked in the building for 12 years. As they strolled around the first floor and through the two open-air courtyards, she exchanged pleasantries and an occasional complaint with my mother.

She was well aware that Hitler's *Reichsbahn* had used the building, and that the railways had continued to use it after the Soviets took power. The GDR (East German state) had moved in during the 1950s, she said, and 1,000 people had been employed in Krausenstrasse 17/18 and the adjoining building, 19/20.

My mother immediately noticed the black-and-white linoleum square floor tiles in the basement were the ones she remembered from her visits there as a child. The tiles were worn and tatty, but unmistakably the same. This was where she had jumped on piles of pelts as a little girl.

The receptionist took my mother to the canteen, where I had sat with Herr Münch four years earlier. She said it had an excellent menu with a choice of four meals. During the Communist era, lunch had cost as little as 80 pfennigs but now, she complained, after reunification, the price of lunch had shot up to as much as DM 6.50 (over $4)! "We've been spoiled by GDR prices," the good woman sighed.

The Federal Republic of Germany had taken over the property on October 3, 1990, and soon began renovations. My mother saw the elaborately redecorated staircase at the front entrance, the freshly painted walls, and the renovated modern windows and frames. Her tour guide shared her own thoughts about the improvements:

> What's most annoying for us are all those moves—each time the office gets refurbished all the carpets are ripped out, and we get new ones; the walls are painted and so on. . . . How much money is being wasted on this? Some rooms have been remodeled four times since reunification!

Transport Minister Wissmann's office, she said, was located on the second floor overlooking the front. He had already visited several times. The modernization process was moving at full speed, even though the authorities must have known that the building's legal status was under challenge. Perhaps their lawyers had told them that renovations strengthened their claim to the building?

My mother returned to London exhilarated by her trip, only to have Dr. Kühne report the latest nonsense from the Transport Ministry. Its officials had written to Barbara Erdmann arguing that not only were the two buildings merged, but Krausenstrasse 17/18 shared the same heating system with 19/20 and, therefore, as they could not be separated, the building could not be restituted.

Even more incredibly, the ministry alleged that this enormous building had once been the Wolff family home and had only become an office complex after its "Aryanization" by the Nazis! This argument was beyond belief. These officials seemed desperate, utterly crazed.

In exasperation, Frau Erdmann wrote to Dr. Kühne on September 21:

> I find it outrageous that the Transport Ministry now pretends that the office and business building of Victor and Lucie Wolff had previously been a residential home and it was only through the Aryanization, or even conversion by the East German Ministry of Transport, that it turned into an office building.

She added:

> Your client is very good at researching the family history. Maybe she can find some photos to show the Ministry that it was always an office building.

I was glad she thought I was good at researching. Our case might depend on it. Truly, I don't know how any claimant, without dedicated investigators, could hope to win a case for restitution or compensation. The state has all but limitless resources to set against you. Citizens get old and die.

But we had resources, too. On October 13, 1994, the BBC broadcast "Document: Getting Their Own Back" on its national Radio 4 station, taking the same title as in the *Evening Standard* magazine article published two years earlier. The German MDR station held its broadcast until four weeks later, on November 9, the anniversary of Kristallnacht, "The Night of Broken Glass."

The German program was called "Getting Her Own Back" but had the subtitle: "*Eine jüdische Hausfrau und ein deutscher Minister streiten sich um ein Grundstück in Berlin"* (translation: "A Jewish housewife and a German Minister struggle over a piece of land in Berlin"). The difference in titles, between "Getting Their Own Back" and "Getting Her Own Back," was that I appeared in the English program, whereas only my mother was interviewed for the German version.

Six radio stations broadcast the program in Germany, as did a Swiss broadcaster. Afterward, several schoolteachers contacted Holger to ask for copies for educational purposes. Just a month later, we were delighted to learn the program had won second prize among German entries for an international radio competition in Berlin.

On November 15, less than a week after the German radio broadcast, Dr. Kühne reported that he had again spoken to Frau Mirus. This woman, who had once been so skeptical of our claim, now "laughed" at the suggestion the building had ever been a residential home rather than an office block. Frau Mirus had suddenly become quite positive towards our claim and said she had written an interim finding in our favor.

Had she and her colleagues listened to the radio program?

Dr. Kühne wrote:

About this interim report, I am extremely pleased and relieved given the numerous crises we have had to endure during the processing of this matter, because I was the only party with an optimistic view at times, except of course the ever-optimistic clients.

"The ever-optimistic clients"? We tried to stay positive, but in private we had often despaired about the prospects for our case. Even now, after Frau Mirus's apparent change of heart, we remained apprehensive of what the next setback might be.

Soon, Dr. Kühne asked for documents that he could show the German authorities to prove that the property had always been a commercial, rather than residential, building. We had no difficulty providing many photographs and documents, such as lists of tenants and the copy of a 1937 letter concerning a fire insurance policy.

As if any family would live in a six-story office building!

26

LIGHT AT THE END OF THE TUNNEL

As 1995 rolled around, and we awaited the government's decision, I fretted. Dr. Kühne's colleague, Dr. Sybille Steiner, tried to reassure me everything was proceeding according to plan. I continued to worry that the Ministry of Transport's argument that the buildings were joined together—somehow incapable of being separated—meant that no claim would be honored. And what about the attempt by the Ministry to register as the owners of the property? Could they possibly get away with that?

On April 19, Dr. Steiner wrote to reassure my mother on both points:

The fact that the properties Krausenstrasse 17/18 and Krausenstrasse 19/20 are joint parcels does not constitute a problem. The decision restituting the properties will contain a decision on the separation of the two buildings.

At the moment, the Transport Ministry still has not been registered as the owner. The registration is, however, imminent. The current owner is still the *Reichseisenbahn*. Frau Mirus was concerned about to whom she should address her finding.

So far, the Finance Ministry, represented by Herr Giese, has not put any comments forward. They announced that they were going to comment on the situation, but have not done so. Frau Mirus does not want to wait any longer for their views.

On June 2, 1995, Dr. Steiner wrote with encouraging news. She had just spoken with Frau Mirus and she was:

> . . . now firmly of the opinion that this is a case for restitution. The arguments brought forward by the Federal authorities and the Finance Ministry saying that this was not a case of a forced sale and that the investments they had made on the properties and the fact that the two properties were now joined together exclude restitution are not valid in their eyes. Frau Mirus said that she would write the so-called provisional decision upon her return from holiday.

After years of such slow progress, suddenly the pace started to quicken.

By June 23, Dr. Steiner was so confident that she advised my mother to obtain a professional valuation of our building. Clearly, this would be helpful if she began negotiations on a final settlement with the German authorities. On June 27, Dr. Steiner wrote to say she had found someone to do a valuation. My mother was happy to give the go-ahead.

On July 4, Dr. Kühne met with Herr Giese, who informed him that he now had the authority to purchase the property. Herr Giese had dropped his plan to make our claim into a test case "because there are not many more cases which are similar." That was certainly true.

Herr Giese did not want to have the value of the property decided upon the capitalized value, that is, the value based on the rents, but rather on the land value—which is not as high. He claimed that the government had spent DM 10 million ($7 million) on the building and therefore had raised the capitalized value accordingly.

We disagreed, particularly after we learned that according to compensation law, claimants are only liable to repay expenses/investments in relation to the property either where they were absolutely necessary, or where they had been agreed. Obviously, we had never been consulted about any changes. Dr. Steiner's position was that these investments should not be held against the claimants. We believed the German authorities were simply trying to hold down the final purchase price.

Then, good news arrived. Thanks to a recent change in the law, if we won back the building, we would be entitled to receive rents back to July 1, 1994. This meant that the Transport Ministry could find themselves in arrears by a year or more.

Herr Giese stepped forth with a truly insulting offer. He said the government would consider settling our claim immediately for 75 percent of the building's value. This looked like an attempt to pressure an elderly woman to accept, for the sake of speed and certainty, a sale price well below the building's value. I urged my mother to reject this, and she did.

On July 12, 1995, Dr. Steiner wrote to my mother to report on our professional evaluation. The expert had done three different analyses: the value of the land, the value of the property itself, and the capitalized value. Each produced a different valuation, ranging from a low of DM (Deutsche Mark) 30 million ($21 million) to a high of DM 46 million ($33 million).

On August 30, Dr. Steiner met with Herr Giese in Berlin. He told her that he wanted to purchase both Krausenstrasse 17/18 and 19/20. He said he could offer DM 11 million ($7.9 million) to settle our claim immediately. We weren't tempted. Dr. Steiner reported that we could probably receive DM 18–20 million ($13–$14 million), so why settle now? She said she was prepared to go to Bonn to meet the officials who were delaying the settlement.

Dr. Steiner and Herr Giese continued to debate the purchase price: He argued that the building stood on land valued at DM 7,000 ($4,900) to DM 8,000 ($5,600) per square meter—suggesting a value of $14 million—but Dr. Steiner was able to demonstrate that the official figure in use for land values in that area was DM 11,000 ($7,700) per square meter—implying it was worth $19.25 million.

Herr Giese confided that he had wanted to deal with the sale of the properties two years earlier, but his bosses in Bonn had prevented him from entering negotiations. He felt that officials in Bonn had operated in a typically bureaucratic way, endlessly postponing a decision. Dr. Steiner suggested that perhaps she should go to Bonn with him to speed things up. He agreed it might be a good idea.

Perhaps my mother had been right all along, and the authorities had prevaricated in the hope that if she died, the claim would die with her. But now she knew she had a strong hand. The Finance Ministry wanted to buy the whole area, and she could endanger their plans by entering into negotiations with private property developers and investors.

27

NEGOTIATING A PRICE AND
DIVIDING THE PAYOUT

On October 27, Dr. Steiner reported that Frau Mirus was writing her finding. By November 21, 1995, matters started to move fast. Herr Giese finally made a formal offer of DM (Deutsche Mark) 19 million (about $13.47 million). The good news kept coming. We received Frau Mirus's draft decision, which was in favor of a payout.

On November 24, Dr. Steiner had another meeting with Finance Ministry officials. This time, along with Herr Giese, a representative from the Ministry of Transport was present. Dr. Steiner declared that the offer of DM 19 million was unacceptable, in part because no rents had been paid on the property since July 1, 1994. Since Frau Mirus' finding in favor of restitution had been delivered, Dr. Steiner could argue that backdated rents were now called for.

Herr Giese said that, following talks with the Justice Ministry, he now understood the law to say that owner/occupiers do not have to pay rent. But Dr. Steiner argued that whether as owners or occupiers, they had a duty to look after the property. Herr Giese estimated the rents from July 1, 1994, to December 31, 1995, as around DM 3 million

($2.1 million). The expenses they said they had invested in the building came to DM 4.6 million ($3.2 million). Dr. Steiner suggested they compromise on a final purchase price of DM 20 million ($14 million). Herr Giese said he would check with his head office.

On December 14, 1995, Dr. Steiner was back in Berlin, this time to sign the contract. The purchase price of DM 20 million had been agreed. Although the finding had not yet been rewritten to Herr Giese's satisfaction, to speed matters up, he agreed that he would be content with a brief explanation of the judgment in my mother's favor. All he insisted on was that the basis of the decision should be in line with German restitution law—the sale would not have taken place if the Nazis had not come to power. Frau Mirus agreed it was possible to proceed on this basis. We, of course, were happy to accept this obvious truth.

After six years, we had won. The contract stipulated that DM 20 million ($14 million), divided between my mother and her three siblings, would be paid by January 2, 1996.

The Jewish festival of lights, Hanukkah, started on the evening of December 17 that year. It marks the miracle of the oil in the temple in Jerusalem lasting for eight days when the Jews, who had rebelled against the Greeks, thought it would only last for one. As we took our three children to my parents' home in London to light the Hanukkah candles, there was an additional reason to celebrate. And my mother, who had been so assimilated in prewar Berlin, noted it was going to be a very good Christmas as well.

Justice had been achieved. Our family had won its legal case. The German government agreed the building belonged to us and, therefore, bought it back for its market value. But the question remained: How was the money to be divided among the surviving members of the Wolff family? There was no easy answer.

A major issue was whether Herbert's renunciation of his inheritance also applied to his possible inheritance of Fritz's half, as his brother and nearest relative, after his death in Auschwitz.

As our lawyers perceived it, Lucie Wolff had left half of her estate to her son Fritz and the other half to her daughter-in-law, Nellie, and her three children. (To be precise, she gave 4/8 to Fritz and 1/8 each to Nellie, Annemarie, Heini and Marion.) It was clear Lucie would have wanted to leave the building to her grandchildren in the event of their parents' demise.

Obviously, Lucie never knew that Herbert would divorce Nellie and remarry. The lawyers concluded that Nellie's share was one quarter and the remaining three quarters of Fritz's share of the building should go to Nellie's three children, with Micky to receive a small share because he was born in 1940, before Fritz's death.

Nellie died in 1977 and left everything (except three apartments, which she left to her grandchildren) to my mother and Heini. She did not include Marion, who had been cut off from the family for so many years. Therefore, my mother inherited part of the building not only in her own right, but also from both her mother and her Uncle Fritz.

Based on all of this, our lawyers, and the lawyers for our Israeli relatives—working together—calculated the individual shares as 11/32 parts each to Aviva and Heini, 7/32 to Marion, and 3/32 to Micky.

By this accounting, Micky and Heini, who had once expected to divide the proceeds of the building between them, now found they had to share with their sisters. They were not pleased. Soon my mother's lawyer reported that Heini and Micky were challenging the provision of 11/32 for my mother.

In other words, they might go to court to fight the lawyers' interpretation—including their own lawyers'—of German inheritance law. Were they bluffing? No one could say. But a lawsuit could tie up the money for years. Frau Erdmann and Frau Kossack, the lawyers for the Israeli side, wanted a quick solution and urged the claimants to settle out of court.

In the interest of finally resolving the issue after six years, my mother accepted 9/32. The 2/32 she surrendered probably amounted to between $300,000 and $400,000 but she had no wish to be—or appear to be—greedy. We had proved our point and were ready to get on with our lives.

The lawyers worked out the compromise and after my mother surrendered the 2/32, we were not told how it was allocated. We guessed that Micky and Heini had taken an extra 1/32 each.

On January 2, 1996, the German authorities transferred the equivalent of just under $4 million to my mother's bank account.

The money did little to change my mother's lifestyle. She was always extraordinarily frugal. She was 73 years old when the money arrived, and she'd had to scrimp and save since she left Berlin at age 11. She was not going to change. Throughout the long legal process, she always vowed that she would never let money affect her way of life, and she was true to her word.

One of the first things she did was make a donation to the Wiener Library in London for a plaque to be placed in memory of her Uncle Fritz. It hangs there today.

In the late 1980s, my parents had downsized into a small, three bedroom, one bathroom, terraced house with a tiny garden at the back in Ealing, West London. It suited them and they had no reason to move. Suddenly coming into money made not the slightest difference to their aspirations.

English tax laws are such that if you give away a sizeable amount of money, no tax has to be paid as long as you survive seven years from the date of the gift. To my mother, it made good financial sense to do just that. If she waited until she died for her children to benefit, the UK's 40 percent inheritance tax would kick in above the equivalent of approximately the first $500,000.

My mother figured she had a good few years left, and was anxious not to see her money disappear into the government coffers. Her in-laws, the Golds, had never helped my parents financially in any way. Their estate, which had been sizable, had been duly taxed at the 40 percent rate. My mother was not going to allow the same thing to happen to her.

As soon as she received the money, she called a family meeting to discuss her plans. She decided that, because no one else was going to assist Leor—who had been helpful to us and who had no relationship with his father, Micky—she would step in, and make a gift to him. She set up a trust fund for each of my three children to cover their schooling and university education and she was also very generous to me and my brother Adam. A few years later, when Adam married and had a son, she took money from her own account and established an education trust fund for her fourth grandchild.

My mother never discussed with her friends how much money she had received and no one knew she was now a wealthy woman. She had only one disappointment: "My only regret is that my parents-in-law didn't live to see this."

The Golds, she believed, would have been astonished to see the poor little refugee girl they had so scorned and patronized suddenly transformed, Cinderella-like, into a princess!

My mother had never been interested in expensive clothes, jewelry, houses, or cars. The one thing she had craved was the ability to travel. During my childhood, we went on annual camping holidays to France; we couldn't afford to stay in hotels. Now my parents could visit places they had only dreamed of. They went on vacations to China, Hong Kong, and Thailand, and took their first trip across the United States. These, as well as vacations closer to home in France, Spain, and Italy, and a cruise to Norway, were luxuries they allowed themselves.

In 2003, my father died. Soon afterward, in her 80s and in failing health, my mother accompanied my family and me to Berlin where we took our children to revisit her former home in Wannsee and to see the graves of their great-great-great grandparents (Heimann and Johanna) and great-great grandparents (Victor and Lucie) at the old Jewish cemetery in Weissensee.

My mother remained as independent-minded and feisty as ever. She did not have to do what she had always dreaded most for her old age: live in a retirement home. Instead, she was able to remain in her own house with the luxury of a caregiver staying there. For that alone, I feel all my efforts were worthwhile.

Looking back on our long battle with the German government, my mother once remarked, "Money can come and go—in this case it came back. We are lucky!"

Luck certainly played its role, but I see at least three possible reasons we won our fight for justice.

First, I like to think it was because our case was both legally and morally valid, overwhelmingly so, in fact. But that hadn't spared us several years of resistance and prevarication from German officialdom.

I also think that the powerful German language radio program "Getting Her Own Back," broadcast on the anniversary of Kristallnacht, had an impact. Some people high in government bureaucracy in Germany may finally have grasped that this Jewish housewife, my mother, wasn't going away and they were only going to look steadily worse until they awarded her the outcome she deserved.

Finally, our victory was the culmination of years of single-minded perseverance, of ignoring words of caution and of keeping relentlessly focused. My mother, my husband, and I all contributed to this, as did our lawyers.

Many Jewish families suffered much more than ours. Unable to provide legal clarity, it was very hard for survivors with buildings in Germany to achieve restitution or compensation. Even with excellent lawyers, we had to work hard to prove our case. Claimants needed money to hire attorneys and researchers, and to have the wherewithal to know where to begin to find vital documents with which to prove the validity of their claim.

Yes, luck played its part in our case, but I agree with the old saying, "You make your own luck." We worked hard to make ours.

PART THREE

28

NEW ARCHIVES, NEW ANSWERS

In 2008 our family relocated from London to Washington, D.C., as my husband was offered a job at the Washington Institute for Near East Policy. I was still too emotionally attached to the many boxes of documents, letters, and photos I had collected during the 1990s claim process to abandon them during the move. Everything, as well as transcripts of taped conversations I had made of my mother's reminiscences (and from which I have quoted extensively), crossed the Atlantic with me.

Not long after arriving in Washington, I made contact with the archivists at the United States Holocaust Memorial Museum (USHMM) and told them about the materials I had shipped across the Atlantic. Within days, the then-chief archivist, Dr. Henry Mayer, and a colleague, Stephen Mize, came to our home to examine the papers. They proposed taking my entire archive to become part of their extensive library. I appreciated the offer, but I was not ready to relinquish all the data I had gathered so that some future researcher could try to tell our story. Now, I hoped I would manage to do it myself and, with that in mind, I started to draft a few chapters

Surprisingly, I began to see how in many ways the years that had passed had served me well. The immediacy of the pursuit of our claim had gone, but history does not stand still. New archives had opened offering access to information that had been inconceivable when I first embarked on this endeavor, and the Internet enabled anyone to contact researchers and historians so much more easily than by post.

In January 2013, I met Ambassador Stuart Eizenstat, who served as Special Representative of the President and Secretary of State on Holocaust-Era Issues during the Clinton administration. He had been Special Advisor on Holocaust Issues under Secretary of State Hillary Rodham Clinton and was reappointed to that role by Secretary John Kerry in December 2013. I told him about the saga of the claim and I asked him specifically if he knew of any books about the successful restitution of a building, as opposed to works of art. He said he knew of none, and ended our conversation with the words "Don't sit here telling me about it, go home and write the story." And, he added presciently, I should focus more closely on the role of the insurance company that had foreclosed, in 1937, on the Wolff family mortgage.

A quarter of a century after the fall of the Berlin Wall, I thought it was time to try and answer the many questions I still had about my family's history and in particular the full truth of Fritz's life during his last years in Berlin.

I knew a few details already. After my mother wrote to the Red Cross in 1992 seeking information about her uncle, she eventually received confirmation that in 1938 he had been sent to Sachsenhausen concentration camp. I also knew that he had been deported to Auschwitz in 1943. But the rest was practically a total blank.

Holocaust survivors, their descendants, researchers, lawyers, academics, and all of those seeking compensation for their suffering as forced laborers, can now fill in many, but by no means all, of the missing historical narrative. It takes time, effort, commitment, stamina, and a certain degree of Internet savvy. If you are prepared to pay, there are a number of historical researchers who are able to do some of the work for you. But that is not necessary, if you have the patience to do the research yourself.

I was fortunate. I live just four miles from the USHMM, where some of the world's leading experts were able to offer me their wealth of accumulated knowledge and guide me through the information held in their digital database and microfiche library. If their museum did not hold what I was looking for, they were able to point me in the direction of the various archives and memorial institutions that might hold the key to what I wanted to unearth. Although the USHMM shares—and can access—many of the same historical documents as other institutions, researchers like me will quickly find that there is no single central database. This means that multiple e-mails, phone calls, faxes, and letters have to be sent to the assorted repositories to tap all likely sources. So it was with a degree of trepidation that I set out in summer 2014, on my quest to uncover Fritz's hidden past.

As revelations unfolded, I was impressed at how incredibly helpful younger Germans working in the field of Holocaust research are. People were unfailingly anxious to do their utmost, and many went out of their way to correspond with me and offer their assistance.

Fritz was not a man entirely without means. He came from a wealthy family and, as I already knew, he had had sufficient money to enable him to pay Dr. and Mrs. Hierl in June 1937 for his upkeep while he lived with them. I wanted to discover if any records existed that might reveal more about his life, and whether or not he had been employed anywhere. In my search for such evidence, I found out much more than I ever could have imagined.

By 1938, the Nazi police terror state was spying on everyone. At the USHMM I garnered a rich flavor of the atmosphere of the time by reading Gestapo reports, labeled "*Streng vertraulich!*" (Translation: Strictly confidential!), written during the last three months of that year.

The press, both foreign and domestic, was regarded as highly suspicious and was very closely monitored. Many editions were confiscated because the reports and cartoons were deemed critical of the Nazi regime. Lists of newspapers containing articles considered unacceptable included the *New York Times, New York Herald Tribune, Time, Life, The Times of London, Daily Mirror, Evening Standard, Daily Mail, Le Soir, Le Figaro*, and numerous German publications.

Anyone who might cause trouble was reported on—Catholic priests, Protestants, workers, national opposition parties, Jews, and even young children. One Gestapo report, for instance, written on October 7, 1938, tells of an 11-year-old boy who, along with a list of workers, was arrested because he had made treasonable comments in praise of the Communist party! A report compiled on November 9 mentions that a number of people were charged with high treason and incarcerated, including some who were collecting money for the "illegal Red Cross." Others were in trouble for daring to listen together to Radio Moscow. The report for November 11, immediately after Kristallnacht, reveals an obsession with so-called Marxist organizations, and contains several pages of named individuals taken into custody and prosecuted for expressing pro-Communist views. On November 23, the Gestapo noted some flyers were picked up, probably written by the same person, and certainly printed on the same machine on paper manufactured in Luxembourg. Their conclusion was that these must be former SA (*Sturmabteilung*) or Stormtroopers who were urging rebellion against the Nazis. One poor Jewish teacher in Berlin called Erich Bornow was hauled before a judge, charged with high treason after admitting he had written a 60-page report urging a united front under Communist leadership. Under a section of the report labeled "*Juden*" was mention of a Jewish timber merchant, Herbert Ahrens, who had been arrested on suspicion of racial defilement for having tried to have an affair with a non-Jew.

Communists were the main focus of the Gestapo's obsession—but Fritz was a Communist as well as a Jew. Where did he fit into this political maelstrom?

Heimann Wolff, founder of
H. Wolff Fur Company

Johanna Wolff, wife of
Heimann Wolff

Victor Wolff in the gardens at
Conradstrasse, 1926

Lucie Wolff, Victor's wife

Leor, Dina and Rachel
in Tel Aviv, 1990

Dina's first visit to the
building, December 1990

Dina, Aviva and Simon examine legal documents, 1992
(Photograph by David Secombe)

Cleaning the
Wolff family grave,
Weissensee, Berlin, 2003:
Simon, Daniel, Joshua,
Rachel and Aviva

Krausenstrasse 17/18 today
(Photograph by Heinrich Hermes)

Dina at back of the building on Schützenstrasse, 2016

Das Wolff Haus

Die Krausenstraße 17 wurde im Jahre 1909 als Sitz der Pelzfirma H. Wolff gebaut, eine der ältesten jüdischen Modefirmen Berlins, gegründet 1850.

Während der NS-Zeit wurde das Eigentum an diesem Grundstück zwangsweise an die Deutsche Reichsbahn übertragen.

Nach der Wiedervereinigung erwarb die Bundesrepublik Deutschland im Jahr 1996 das Grundstück von den Wolff' schen Erben.

Das Gebäude ist als Baudenkmal ausgewiesen.

The Wolff Building

Krausenstraße 17 was constructed in 1909 as the headquarters of the H. Wolff fur company, one of Berlin's oldest Jewish fashion firms.

During the Nazi era ownership was forcibly transferred to the German Railways.

In 1996, after reunification, the German Government purchased the building from the Wolff heirs.

The building is designated an historic monument.

Plaque at front of building, July 2016
(Photograph by German Federal Real Estate Agency)

29

THE EVIDENCE FROM SACHSENHAUSEN

In May 2014, I attended a conference at the United States Holocaust Memorial Museum (USHMM) entitled "The International Tracing Service Collections and Holocaust Scholarship," where I was fortunate to meet Dr. Rebecca Boehling, professor of history at the University of Maryland, Baltimore County, who at that time was director of the International Tracing Service (ITS) at Bad Arolsen. She had been appointed after the International Committee of the Red Cross withdrew from the management of the ITS to be replaced by an International Commission of the United States, Israel, and nine European nations (the German Federal Archives lending advisory support), with funding wholly from the German government.

Until November 2007, the ITS had been the largest closed archive in the world, holding records on the Holocaust, Nazi persecution, and forced laborers. But since then, it has opened up and offers access not only to tracing services, but also to other areas of scholarly research interest. Now, the ITS shares much of its data with the USHMM. During one of the conference breaks, I told Professor Boehling my story, and she immediately offered to help me.

Within days, I had a response from the staff at Bad Arolsen. They e-mailed me digital copies of the typed records in which Fritz Wolff appears listed as amongst a group of prisoners entering Sachsenhausen on November 22, 1938, and then in a group that left the camp on December 6, recorded as *Liste der Juden-Entlassungen* (literal translation: List of Jew-Releases), neatly laid out under headings of Surname, First Name, Date of Birth, Number, and assigned Block. I already knew from the 1995 Red Cross letter to my mother that Fritz had been prisoner number 13677, but now I discovered he had been in block number 61. From the list of names provided, I was even able to detect some of Fritz's fellow block 61 inhabitants. Accompanying these were scanned photocopies of the original documents, with handwritten prisoner and cell block numbers down the left hand margin.

It was upsetting, but I was just at the start of an emotional journey of discovery about how the Nazi state had treated Fritz. Much more vivid records were yet to come.

Not wanting to leave any stone unturned, I engaged Beate Schreiber, a partner in the professional historical research firm "Facts and Files" in Berlin to make inquiries on my behalf. She wrote to the Sachsenhausen Memorial and Museum in Oranienburg, north of Berlin, and soon I received the same scanned copies of the original documents as the ITS had supplied. But Dr. Astrid Ley at the Sachsenhausen Memorial and Museum also sent me printouts from her database that revealed several more insights. I learned that the records had originated from the Russian State Military archives in Moscow, having been taken by the Red Army at the end of the war. I had hoped for a head and shoulders photograph of Fritz, but Dr. Ley explained to me that although photos were taken of all the inmates on arrival at Sachsenhausen, the SS had destroyed much of the camp administrative paperwork in April 1945. However, thanks to the punctilious nature of Nazi record keeping, I was able to discern that the day after he had entered the camp, the *Geld und Effektenkammer* (money and personal effects depot) registered his personal belongings as having been deposited for storage. All inmates, Dr. Ley told me, ". . . had to hand over money, watches, etc.

when arrested and got them back when released—if the SS had not stolen the valuables in the meantime!" The SS commanding officer, whose name appears on the database connected with Fritz's release, was Karl Chmielewski, who had moved to Sachsenhausen concentration camp in 1936 where he was part of the *Schutzhaftlagerführung* (protective custody) units of the SS.

There is much information available on this hideous brute, who earned the nickname *Teufel von Gusen* (the Devil of Gusen) when he became camp commandant at the large group of camps built around the villages of Mauthausen and Gusen in Austria. Moving on later to run the Herzogenbusch concentration camp in the Netherlands, he personally stole diamonds from the inmates, scalded prisoners with boiling water, and drowned them in buckets of water. After the war, he was accused by another camp commandant of having turned prisoners' skin into wallets, and used it for bookbinding. In 1961, he was found guilty of war crimes and given a life sentence with hard labor.

I often wonder how Fritz could have dreamt this madness would blow over after his release from Sachsenhausen on December 6, 1938. Had he really been so innocent as to imagine this was a passing aberration? Had he entirely discounted the ghastly irony of the words painted on the barrack walls that read, "There is one path to freedom! Its milestones are: diligence, obedience, honesty, order, cleanliness, sobriety, truthfulness, spirit of sacrifice, and love of the Fatherland!"

At any rate, as I already knew, Fritz never left Germany. So I persevered in trying to discover more about what he did after leaving Sachsenhausen.

30

THE FATE OF
DRESDENER STRASSE 97

The experts at the United States Holocaust Memorial Museum (USHMM) pointed me in the right direction. In May 1939, the Nazis ordered a population census that included a supplementary card for each household. This card had to be filled in, as long as one occupant responded "yes" to the question of whether they had at least one Jewish grandparent. The Minority Census records have now been digitized and can be viewed in the archive collections held at the museum. I scrolled down the list of surnames beginning with "W" and there he was, "Wolff, Fritz 4.10.91" (his date of birth being October 4, 1891) under which was the name "Martin Deutsch 30.8.11." That meant his name had been included in the supplementary card filled in by the nominal head of the household—Martin Deutsch. I searched for "Deutsch M" and found a scanned copy of the May 1939 handwritten form. Seventy-five years since Fritz and the fellow occupants of his apartment at Dresdener Strasse 97 had obeyed the dictates of the Nazis to declare their racial origins, I was staring at their long-lost history. Now I knew that Fritz, like the other four inhabitants of that address, had all declared themselves to have Jewish grandparents and were all therefore, in the eyes of the racist Nazis, full Jews.

It is no surprise that everyone in the apartment was Jewish.

Two events had led to a dire shortage of living space. Earlier in the year, a report had been requested from no less than Albert Speer (whose grand plans for the redesign of central Berlin had led to the *Reichsbahn*'s seizure of Krausenstrasse 17/18 to make offices available for the railway's architects). Speer needed to free up space, which is precisely what happened. Old, established buildings in the heart of the capital were flattened, leaving many people seeking accommodation. A solution was at hand.

The "Law Concerning Jewish Tenants" of April 30, 1939—leading to what has become known as the *Entjudung des Wohnraums* (Dejudification of living space)—had withdrawn tenancy protections for Jews. The effect was to force Jews out of 30,000 dwellings in Berlin alone. All apartments and houses owned by Jews had to be registered, by law, with the Jewish community, which was then charged with implementing the new law. Jews could only rent from, and live with, fellow Jews in so-called "Jewish houses," making it easier for the authorities to track the movement of Jews and to offer Aryans access to superior living quarters after the former tenants had been forced out.

World War II began in September 1939. About 80,000 Jews were still living in Berlin. Fritz was one of them.

His fellow tenants at Dresdener Strasse 97 were Martin Deutsch, his Polish-born wife Romana, and their baby daughter, Eveline, born in Berlin on July 13, 1938. The fifth tenant was a man called Josef Rosner from Vienna, born January 12, 1908. The men, of course, all had the name "Israel" listed after their first names and the woman and her child, "Sara."

By now, I was increasingly becoming an expert at finding my way around records available online. I typed the Deutsch family names and dates of birth into the search facility on the Memorial page of the *Bundesarchiv* (German National Archives) and there appeared:

Deutsch, Martin

born 30 August 1911 in Zempelburg / Flatow / Westpreussen
wohnhaft in Berlin

Deported from Berlin 17 November 1941, Kowno (Kauen), Fort
IX

Date of death 25 November 1941, Kowno (Kauen), Fort IX[1]

Romana and Eveline were also listed—they were all deported together.

The world-renowned International Institute for Holocaust Research
at Yad Vashem in Jerusalem provided me with far greater detail. The
Deutsch family is listed, along with all the other passengers, on Transport Number 26 from Berlin to Kaunas in Lithuania on November 17,
1941. Included on the Yad Vashem website is not only a map of the
Transport's route, but also a horrifying description of what happened
to those passengers.

In September 1941, Hitler approved plans for the mass deportation
of Jews from the Greater Reich, including Berlin. Under the overall
supervision of Adolf Eichmann, Jewish community representatives in
Berlin were forced to deliver lists of people for deportation. Rounded
up and taken to the Levetzowstrasse synagogue, all the deportees had
to write a declaration of their assets, hand over all their money and
valuables, and agree that everything they owned be transferred to the
State. After they left Germany, the Gestapo sold their belongings.

The little Deutsch family was on one of over 60 trains operated by
the *Reichsbahn*, which took 35,000 Jews out of Berlin. After boarding
the train at Grunewald station, they headed to Riga but were diverted
to Kaunas. The story of what happened to these Jews is yet another
infamous event, amongst so many that occurred during the Holocaust.

1. http://www.bundesarchiv.de/gedenkbuch/de1023405.

Much has been written about it. When the train arrived at Kaunas the passengers were marched to a military facility known as Fort IX under the cover of night so the locals would not see them. Two days later, they were taken to pits and killed by Lithuanian auxiliary police and the Gestapo.[2]

The Jäger Report, written on December 1, 1941, by the commander of the *Einsatzkommando* responsible for this action, stated that on November 25 a total of 1,159 Jewish men, 1,600 women, and 175 children from Berlin, Munich, and Frankfurt were killed.[3]

Poor little three-year old Eveline, and her parents, were part of that massacre. The *Einsatzkommando* and its commander, SS Colonel Karl Jäger, were responsible for the destruction of the Jewish population of Lithuania, boasting of the murder of a total of 137,346 people, mostly Jews, in a single five-month period.

But what was the fate of the fifth resident of Dresdener Strasse 97?

I checked all the available records, archives, and memorial books but there was nothing. Then I searched the names of prisoners on the "Memorial and Museum Auschwitz Birkenau" website. My search showed *"Rösner, Josef b.1887-03-13, camp serial number: 17852."*[4]

Right name, wrong date of birth.

There are times when one should just start with the easiest option. I did an internet search on "January 12, 1908" + "Josef Rosner" and found a Joseph Rosner with the same date of birth who had died in January 1971, last known address—Miami, Florida 33134.

I ordered a copy of the death certificate from the Bureau of Vital Statistics in Florida. It revealed this Joseph Rosner was born in Austria to Oscar and Rose Rosner. He had been an artist and sculptor, had died at Abbey Hospital, Coral Gables, on January 26, 1971, and at the time of death had a surviving spouse named Sarah Rosner (née Singer). He is buried at Lakeside Memorial Park, Miami, Florida.

I telephoned the cemetery and enquired if there were any living relatives. None. The burial plot had been bought by Mrs. Sarah Rosner

2. http://db.yadvashem.org/deportation/transportDetails.html?language=en&itemId=5092826.
3. fcit.usf.edu/holocaust/resource/document/DocJager.htm.
4. http://auschwitz.org/en/museum/auschwitz-prisoners/.

(born April 1, 1910) for herself and Joseph. She had died, aged 88, on February 18, 1999, and a bank trust officer had handled her estate. I asked if the Rosners had belonged to a local synagogue—perhaps someone there might remember them. Apparently not. I had reached the end of the road.

Given the correct date of birth and country of origin on the death certificate, in all likelihood this is indeed the same Joseph Rosner who once shared an apartment with Fritz Wolff. Perhaps someone someday will contact me offering clear-cut confirmation. But in the meantime, I want to believe with all my heart that this was indeed the same man, that he escaped Nazi Germany, and enjoyed many happy years in Florida.

31

FRITZ'S LIFE DURING THE WAR

What was Fritz doing once war broke out? His life must have become increasingly intolerable. In the summer of 1940, the British Royal Air Force started bombing Berlin. Yet another indignity, this one with lethal consequences, was inflicted on the Jews. Strict racial segregation meant that Jews were prevented from taking refuge in those air raid shelters designated for the exclusive use of people deemed Aryan. This applied even if they lived in the same property. The president of the Berlin Police issued a decree on September 21, 1940: "If Jews live in the same building as non-Jews, special air-raid shelters have to be made for Jews so that they can be separated from the others living in the building."[1]

Jews either had to take refuge in "ghetto shelters" built by the Berlin Jewish community, or they huddled together as best they could inside their apartment blocks.

In his diary entry for September 24, 1940, veteran CBS correspondent William Shirer wrote: "The British really went to work on Berlin last night. They bombed heavily and with excellent aim for exactly four hours."

---

1. Nachama, Andreas, Julius H. Schoeps and Hermann Simon. *Jews in Berlin*. (Berlin, Henschel, 2002) page 220.

And he went on to describe the dire situation Jews encountered when seeking shelter.

> Where facilities permit, the Jews have their own special *Luft-schutzkeller* (air raid shelter), usually a small basement room next to the main part of the cellar, where the "Aryans" gather. But in many Berlin cellars there is only one room. It is for the "Aryans." The Jews must take refuge on the ground floor, usually in the hall leading from the door of the flat to the elevator or stairs. This is fairly safe if a bomb hits the roof, since the chances are that it will not penetrate to the ground floor. But experience so far has shown that it is the most dangerous place to be in the entire building if a bomb lands in the street outside. Here where the Jews are hovering, the force of the explosion is felt most; here in the entryway where the Jews are, you get most of the bomb splinters.[2]

Did Fritz ever regret having been such a proud and loyal German who had refused to leave the country?

After September 1941, like all Jews in Germany over age six, he would have been forced to wear the *Judenstern* (Jewish star), instantly setting him apart from every other ordinary citizen. This new decree meant that those Jews who had previously risked breaking the law by using designated Aryan air raid shelters could no longer pretend they were entitled to enter.

Fritz would have been obliged, along with his fellow Jews, to wait in line to buy food at shops during the one-hour time slot (4:00 P.M. to 5:00 P.M.) allotted to them. And he would have had a ration card with a "J" stamped on it for use in Jewish shops. Not that he would have been able to buy very much anyway. Soap, fuel for heating, shoes, and sundry other necessities were all banned for Jews. As a very modest man without dependents, it's conceivable that Fritz had sufficient private money to keep himself without the need to work. On the other

---

2. William L. Shirer, *Berlin Diary, The Journal of a Foreign Correspondent, 1934–1941* (Little Brown and Company, 1988), page 520.

hand, my mother had always assumed that in all likelihood, with the engineering qualification he had, he worked in the armaments industry and, as a useful worker, had been able to stay in Berlin longer than many others.

Oddly, the address of the Beuth-Vertrieb, the publishing house of the Association of Engineers in Germany, was also at Dresdener Strasse 97—the same building in which Fritz had been living after his release from Sachsenhausen. As an engineer, had Fritz possibly worked for this organization? After all, he lived in the same building. I e-mailed the publishing house and asked if any wartime paperwork survived. There is no record or suggestion that it ever used forced labor, but it would have made sense for Fritz to work for them. This organization exists today, but is no longer at the same address. I received a prompt reply: Their archives revealed no trace of a Fritz Wolff.

So, I next wrote to the *Landesarchiv* (State Archive) of Berlin which, according to its website, is the repository of an extraordinary cache of unique documents on the development of Berlin, its institutions, and its inhabitants. Six days after e-mailing their offices all the information I could to aid their research endeavor, I heard back from the archivist telling me, "I could identify no evidence of the activities of Fritz Wolff 1939–1943 in the collections of the State Archives in Berlin."

I tried another tack. Just over a mile from where Fritz lived in Dresdener Strasse was Fontanepromenade 15, nicknamed by Jews as *Schikanepromenade* (Bully Promenade). This was the Nazi-run office of the *Zentrale Dienststelle für Juden* (the Central Employment Office for Jews) which, from 1938–1943, organized forced labor for those Jews still remaining in Berlin. These were menial, unskilled tasks that non-Jewish Germans considered beneath them. Because Jews were excluded from working in the civil service and almost all other employment possibilities were out of the question due to the racist laws then in place, they were reduced to loading coal, cleaning the *Reichsbahn* toilets, working on production lines in factories, shoveling snow in winter, and collecting trash.

I wrote to the *Neue Synagoge* (New Synagogue) in Berlin. The Centrum Judaicum Foundation holds the pre-war records for the whole of

German Jewry, including information about individuals, associations, communities, and organizations. Did they have any records about Fritz?

I then contacted Dr. Bernhard Bremberger, an expert on forced labor in Germany during the war. Could he cast any light on what Fritz might have been doing? Dr. Bremberger promptly replied and his response depressed me. I had asked him if there were any central register of forced laborers in Berlin. He said that there was not, and there was a very simple explanation for this—the Nazi labor administration and employment offices had, for good reason, destroyed documents before the war ended. There is no compulsion for German companies to come clean about their past, no law to force them to open their archives to researchers, or to publish their dirty history on exploiting forced laborers. Even if I knew what company Fritz had been working for, and could approach the current management seeking access to their documents, it would be entirely a question of goodwill on their part were they to agree. A few companies have indeed opened up to historians, but not many. I wanted to know how many had used forced labor. It was hard to be certain, but Dr. Bremberger sent me a link to a 2001 publication entitled "*Liste der Unternehmen, die im National-sozialismus von der Zwangsarbeit profitiert haben*" (List of Companies which Benefitted from Nazi Forced Labor) containing the names of some 2,500 companies throughout Germany, many located in Berlin, that had used forced Jewish and foreign labor. But this figure is far from complete, because the list was compiled from data known in the 1950s and, as such, could not include all those businesses operating in what had been the Soviet zone.[3]

From 1941 onward, there were more than 365 camps for foreign forced workers in the Kreuzberg district of Berlin, where Dresdener Strasse was located. Several Dresdener Strasse properties are listed as having been where many of these poor souls had been housed and made to work. Fritz, of course, was not a foreigner, but I could not gain access to the records of these companies anyway, so that was a dead end.[4]

---

3. http://www.ns-in-ka.de/uploads/media/Liste_Unternehmen.pdf.
4. http://archive.today/Npg9K#selection-547.0-549.3.

Perhaps the FHXB Friedrichshain-Kreuzberg Museum might have some record of Fritz Wolff? I received a very friendly reply from archivist Erika Hausotter, telling me that the museum had no records whatsoever on him, but that she was able to give me some information on his address. At the time he was living there, the front of the building at Dresdener Strasse 97 housed a post office and some apartments. There were more businesses in the back of the premises, as contemporary address books, now available online, confirm. As Fritz is not listed in any of them, it is clear that he did not have his own apartment but was housed with others. She suggested that it was entirely possible Fritz had worked in one of the other businesses, but it was very unlikely that any records still existed to confirm this. Although the building no longer stands, Ms. Hausotter had found an old postcard with a photograph as it existed in the 1920s and had scanned and sent it to me. Now I could see for myself exactly where Fritz had lived.

Dr. Bremberger advised I should contact the Brandenburg State Archives because, prior to deportation, all Jews were required to fill out a "declaration of assets" for the tax office, including a section on their most recent employer. The reason for recording each person's last employer was because, incredibly, if there were any wages due, the authorities could proceed to collect them after the transport had left the country.

In fact, Beate Schreiber of "Facts and Files" had already mentioned to me that she had approached the Brandenburg State Archive in search of this very information.

Another course was to try and discover whether Fritz had been known at the *Reichsvereinigung der Juden in Deutschland* (the Reich Association of the Jews in Germany). A kind volunteer at the USHMM offered to help. He ushered me into his office and tapped Fritz's details into his computer, seeking any reference to his registration status. This association, established in July 1939 under the supervision of the Reich minister of the interior, was to further the emigration of Jews, to run Jewish schools, and manage welfare programs so that Jews would not be a financial burden on the state. In addition to keeping records on the remaining Jews, their addresses and personal information, it also issued

Jewish workers with "protection letters" that were to be presented to the authorities on demand.[5]

Sadly, to date, there is no trace of Fritz as having been in any way associated with the *Reichsvereinigung*. This does not mean, however, that there never will be. Perhaps one day, documents will emerge. But I very much doubt it. There was a reason why he may have been unknown to this organization . . . as I was to discover.

Clearly, Fritz had still been living in Berlin when Joseph Goebbels, the Nazi propaganda chief, made the following entry in his diary on May 11, 1942:

> We must deal again with the Jewish problem. There are still 40,000 Jews in Berlin and despite the heavy blows dealt them they are still insolent and aggressive. It is exceedingly difficult to shove them off to the East because a large part of them are at work in the munitions industry and because the Jews are to be evacuated only by families.[6]

Goebbels was to have his way before too long. Later that same year, non-Jewish labor became available as the German army moved triumphantly further east across Europe. Now, Goebbels could take a harder line, as he duly noted on September 30 in his diary:

> The Führer expressed his decision that the Jewish people under all circumstances have to be taken out of Berlin. What the industrialists say about the fine work of the Jews doesn't impress me. Now all the Jews are praised for the high quality of their work. Always arguments are raised to keep them. But the Jews are not so irreplaceable as the intellectuals say. We can get 250,000 foreign workers. The Jews can easily be replaced by foreign workers. The Jews' fine work will always be the argument of the Semitophiles.[7]

---

5. http://www.yadvashem.org/odot_pdf/Microsoft%20Word%20-%205389.pdf.
6. http://www.nizkor.org/hweb/people/g/goebbels-joseph/goebbels-1948-excerpts-02.html.
7. *The Last Jews in Berlin* (Basic Books, 1999).

One of those intellectuals referred to so sneeringly by Goebbels was without doubt Albert Speer, Hitler's architect and the man whose plans for the redesign of Berlin had led to our building on Krausenstrasse being taken by the *Reichsbahn*. Speer was not a dyed-in-the-wool ideologue on a par with his fellow Nazis.

> He [Speer] needed the skilled labor of these Jews. However much they might have prayed in secret for the English and Americans to win, in the factories most Jews worked with skill and dedication, knowing that their lives depended on it. The Berlin Jews already had been reduced to the status of virtual slaves. Speer knew that, deprived of every right and almost every material possession, they were powerless to harm the Third Reich.[8]

On February 27, 1943, the Gestapo and SS troops began what became known as the infamous *Fabrikaktion* (literally Operation Factory, but usually referred to as Factory Action).

The roundups were unspeakably traumatic, because the remaining Berlin Jews working in the armaments factories had dared to believe that they were vital contributors to Germany's war machine.

But now, all the Nazis' pretense was gone. No longer was any attempt made to mislead people into believing they were going to be resettled and therefore needed to take suitcases of clothes and provisions for their journey.

Any Jews not at work were picked up from their homes or on the streets in a citywide manhunt, staged by the Gestapo and Berlin police. Everyone wearing the obligatory yellow star was detained in full view of ordinary Germans going about their business.

The trucks took people to one of the several collection camps across Berlin: the Hermann-Göring-Kaserne (barracks) in Reinickendorf, the Clou Concert Hall at Mauerstrasse, the Grosse Hamburger Strasse camp, and the Rathenower Kaserne in Moabit.

---

8. Daniel B. Silver, *Refuge in Hell: How Berlin's Jewish Hospital Outlasted the Nazis* (First Mariner Books, 2004).

In the course of researching the claim on Krausenstrasse, I knew the end of February was when Fritz must have been rounded up, because there was no doubt he was deported on a train that left on March 1. It seemed reasonable to believe that I might manage now to find some clues as to where he had been working.

While at the USHMM conference, I met Dr. Akim Jah, an academic from Berlin who spent 13 years researching and writing a book about the deportation of Jews from Berlin, *Die Deportation der Juden aus Berlin*. I showed him the transport list for the train that had taken Fritz to Auschwitz. Dr. Jah immediately pointed to another clue—which furthered my hunch that Fritz had almost certainly been employed. Marked on the paperwork, after Fritz's address at Dresdener Strasse, were the Roman numerals "III." This had meant nothing to me—but Dr. Jah was able to explain to me that "III" denoted that Fritz had been held in the Hermann-Göring barracks in Reinickendorf. And he went on to tell me that these barracks were located not far from the *Deutsche Waffen und Munitionswerke* (German Weapons and Ammunition Plant) in Borsigwalde, a factory that employed many Jewish forced laborers. During the *Fabrikaktion*, these people had been brought directly from the factory straight to the camp. Was there a chance Fritz had been amongst them? On his return home at the end of the conference, Dr. Jah kindly sought the records of the *Deutsche Waffen und Munitionswerke* at the *Landesarchiv* Berlin for me—but there are no files left to inspect.

Dresdener Strasse is in a district of Berlin called Kreuzberg, a considerable distance from Reinickendorf. Had Fritz been picked up at home, it would not have made sense to take him all the way to the north of the city.

Dr. Jah, as well as many others, has written vividly of the horrific treatment meted out to people during the roundup and of the atrocious conditions endured by those held at the various collection points around Berlin. The Hermann-Göring barracks, where Fritz was taken, was the biggest of them all and held well over 2,000 people during the *Fabrikaktion*. Survivors' testimony collected by Dr. Jah, describes how, starting at 9:30 A.M. on February 27, black-uniformed SS men arrived at factories, ordered everyone to go outside immediately with no chance to take their coats, personal possessions or food. There, with great brutality, much swearing, and the liberal use of the butts of their guns, they shoved people down the stairs and into waiting lorries. Many, having failed to move fast enough in the eyes of the arresting SS and Gestapo officers, were simply thrown into the lorries, which resulted in broken bones.

The prisoners were brought into the collection camps and forced to stand still for several hours. No food, water, sanitary or washing facilities, beds, medicines, heating, blankets, or any other provisions were in place to care for the prisoners. The men and women were separated and everyone was forced to lie down on the bare floor for the night. The nighttime was described as an inferno of hysterical inmates, screaming small children, and moaning sick and injured people who no one could treat. So desperate were conditions that underwear was torn up into makeshift bandages. Over the next several days, Jewish community workers were allowed to supply the camp inmates with food.

German bureaucracy during the Nazi era was pedantic in the extreme. Despite all that had been done to them, the Nazi state had not quite finished plundering the assets of these distraught Jews and doing so with the pretense of legality. Before being put on the trains, each prisoner was taken to a table where they were made to complete a statement detailing their remaining assets and sign them over to the state.

Dr. Bremberger had mentioned this to me, and suggested I try to find out whether Fritz had filled in one of these statements. He had advised me that because this form apparently also asked for the name of the person's employer, it could be my last hope. Had Fritz filled in this document?

32

EXIT FROM THE REICH

On March 1, Fritz was taken, either by foot or truck, to the Güter-bahnhof Moabit freight station on Quitzowstrasse and pushed into a railway cattle car. Those who loitered were whipped to get them moving faster. SS soldiers were positioned in the control compartment to prevent attempted escapes. Far from being carried out in darkness to shield locals from the horror of it all, it was carried out in broad daylight.

Today there is a small memorial on the bridge above the tracks.

The *Fabrikaktion* removed about 6,000 Jews from Berlin. Some 1,700 Jews went underground in Berlin (5,000 in Germany as a whole). Those who remained in Berlin have been nicknamed "U-Boats," as in the German for submarines, hiding as best they could—submerged—until they were able to resurface at the end of the war. Aided by brave Germans who risked their own lives to offer these people sanctuary, ration cards, food, false papers, and escape routes, not all rescue efforts were successful. Sometimes the hidden were discovered and deported anyway.

In October 2008, a *Gedenkstätte Stille Helden* (Silent Heroes Memorial) was opened in Berlin as a tribute to these brave souls.

There is a database at the Memorial museum naming those Jews who went "illegal." Dr. Jah checked for Fritz's name, but he is not listed as having tried to disappear at any time before February 1943.

At the United States Holocaust Memorial Museum I inspected the weighty tome, *Auschwitz Chronicle 1939–1945, From the Archives of the Auschwitz Memorial and the German Federal Archives*, a remarkable work compiled by Danuta Czech, the former research head of the Auschwitz Museum. The book is a translation of original German records, mixed with eyewitness accounts. It makes devastating reading, chronicling—in excruciating detail—the events at the camp:

1943 March 2

Commandant Höss is informed at 9:40 pm that the deportation of the Jewish inhabitants of Berlin began on March 1, 1943. Again there is reference to the fact that with these transports approximately 15,000 able-bodied, healthy Jews will arrive who until now have been used in the Berlin armaments industry. It is stressed that they absolutely must be kept able-bodied.

On the same page, I found reference to the train Fritz was on. A day after leaving, the *Ost* Transport 31 arrived in Auschwitz from Berlin.

Approximately 1,500 Jewish men, women, and children arrive with an RSHA [Reich Main Security Office] transport from Berlin. After the selection, 150 men, given Nos. 104740–104889, are admitted to the camp. The other approximately 1,350 deportees are killed in the gas chambers.

Dr. Jah, who has studied the transports from Berlin in great depth, has told me that, since Danuta Czech wrote her monumental study, the numbers have been revised by others using different sources. The most up-to-date figure for the *Ost* Transport 31, and that given by Yad Vashem today, is that between 1,710 and 1,722 people were on board that train.

The USHMM has an extensive microfiche archive, including lists recovered from Auschwitz of those people who were given a number on arrival at the camp. I cross-referenced the transport number and date of the train Fritz had been on, with the names of those who had been registered to enter the camp as slave laborers. All those on the list who had survived the initial selection were much younger than he. There was no one over the age of 50. There could be little doubt that Fritz, the loyal and devoted German, had been murdered in a gas chamber shortly after arrival, even if he had made it through the train journey.

33

DEUTSCHE BANK

In May 2014, I received an e-mail from Beate Schreiber of "Facts and Files." She had written a short note that said: "Attached you will find the record on Fritz Wolff when his property was confiscated after he was deported."

With trepidation, I clicked on the attachment.

Languishing all these years in the Berlin-Brandenburg state financial authority archives were papers bearing final witness to Fritz's life. Yellowed, slightly frayed, official pages with handwritten lists of his income, assets, and price achieved at sale. It was a pitiful sight. On one page was a note beginning with the words, *Der Jude gibt an.* . . . (The Jew indicates. . . .)

There are six items recorded as revenue received, including two Deutsche Bank accounts, a repaid debt, and the sum of RM (Reichsmark) 58.50 recovered from the sale of his household furniture. Fritz's belongings amounted to the grand total of RM 13,764.18. Whoever had the duty of accounting for the last items this poor man owned was still sorting it out long after he had been murdered. The date of the final entry is as late as March 1944.

As I scrolled back and forth across the pages trying to understand them I spotted in the top right-hand corner of one of them the words

Akte Fehlt! (file missing!) underlined in red. This is a reference to Fritz's own declaration, made under duress during his final hours in the Hermann-Göring camp just prior to deportation, in which he had been made to sign over his worldly possessions to the Nazi state. At this last stage, the renowned and trusty German bureaucratic exactitude had let me down. Without the attached file, there was no way I was going to be able to learn the whereabouts of Fritz's final place of employment.

I clutched at one last hope. He had two Deutsche Bank accounts—could it be remotely possible that the bank retained records from that period and could tell me if he'd been receiving wages? I wrote to Deutsche Bank in London explaining what I was seeking and received a swift response from Kathryn Hanes, head of the press office: "I have asked our Historical Institute in Frankfurt to look in to this and they will get back to you."

Two weeks later, I received an e-mail with attachments from Dr. Martin Müller, Head of Corporate History and Archives at the Historical Institute of Deutsche Bank in Frankfurt. It would be an understatement to say I was astonished at what Dr. Müller's research revealed. As I read his e-mail, I felt chilled. For all these years, Deutsche Bank had held onto documents that portrayed the Nazis' victimization of poor Fritz. Now, a lifetime later, I was sitting in Washington, D.C., staring at it.

Dr. Müller reported that Fritz had owned both a current and a securities account with the bank at their branch at Hausvogteiplatz 11, Berlin. From the now archived paperwork, he could "reconstruct the following course of events." Both of Fritz's accounts were blocked by the tax authorities on November 17, 1938. (I recalled that this had been just after Kristallnacht and before Fritz's incarceration in Sachsenhausen.) It beggared belief that he had had the prospect of a visa to French-controlled Syria and could have fled all this horror, but he chose, instead, to stay on in his beloved Germany!

The accounts must have been unfrozen some time later because, on December 16, 1939, the office of the *Oberfinanzpräsident* (chief financial officer) Brandenburg, Berlin, wrote to him, with a copy to Deutsche Bank. Addressed to "Fritz Israel Wolff" he was informed that his monthly withdrawal limit was to be fixed at RM 120. Before me was a scanned copy of the original order. Clearly, Fritz was not without financial means and perhaps, as a very frugal man, he had been able to survive on RM 120 a month and had not needed to work. But this then begs the question: How did he manage to avoid essential war duties when all unemployed Jews were expected to register for work?

Dr. Müller sent me two more scanned documents. One was an internal letter from the Deutsche Bank's legal department dated July 3, 1943, to the deposit account checkout desk in which they refer to "*Techniker* Fritz Israel Wolff" (technician), which suggests he was known to have had some kind of work-related qualification. Fritz's date of birth is given at the top of the letter as well as his correct address at Dresdener Strasse 97, with the additional information *bei Deutsch wohnhaft gewesen* (lodging with Deutsch).

Bold, black letters at the top right-hand corner of the document announce, *Achtung! Sperr-Verfügung* (Attention! Asset freeze instruction). The legal department instruction to staff states ". . . we have found out that your above client has emigrated East as a consequence of the measures taken against Jews on 1/3/1943 [March 1, 1943]" and accordingly his assets were to be frozen and this action should be certified "if necessary through sending two copies of statements of securities (without assessment of value)."

The third piece of evidence in front of me was a letter from Deutsche Bank to the Berlin tax authorities stating that, after receipt of letters to the bank's branch office in September: ". . . the assets of the deported Jew Fritz Israel Wolff, last residence Berlin SW 68, Dresdnerstr 97, have been frozen through a directive that has been sent to him by the *Geheime Staatspolizei* [Gestapo] on 27/2/1943 in favor of the German Reich."

In accordance with your request, our branch office F 2 has settled the account which had been kept by the person in question, and has, after deduction of expenses, transferred the remaining balance of RM 530.00 to your regional tax office on the 30th of the month, under the above file reference. The account is thus balanced. The effects, which are listed in the attached itemization, are being kept suspended in the strongroom concerned at our branch office 2 where we shall be keeping them frozen in your favor.

Again—I was staring at a copy of the very document that had been written seven months after Fritz had been murdered.

In his e-mail, Dr. Müller told me that on March 13, 1944, the sum of RM 2,000 was transferred to the Berlin tax authorities following the sale of Fritz's holding of public bonds, and his deposit account was closed.

Sadly, Dr. Müller could shed no light on where, or even whether, Fritz had worked after the outbreak of the war.

For now, this is where the matter of whether or not Fritz worked as a forced laborer rests, at least until someone, somewhere, someday, comes across Fritz Wolff's name in a newly accessible archive.

34

THE VICTORIA'S HISTORY

What could I find out about the Victoria Insurance Company, which had first provided, and then withdrawn, the mortgage? At the time of writing, the company is still very much in existence. And what about the Victoria's chairman, Dr. Kurt Hamann, who had been in charge of the company when our building was seized in 1937? We had already discovered that British intelligence had listed him as a top member of the Nazi regime in 1944. But he remained the boss of the Victoria in the post-war years in West Germany, only retiring in 1976. (He died in 1981, and is buried in a suburb of Berlin.)

Strange as it may seem there is no doubt that, in the 1920s and early 1930s, the Victoria was in no way anti-Semitic. To the contrary, it actually sought business from the Jewish community in Germany.

At the Wiener Library in London, I had found a copy of a 1931–1932 Jewish business directory (*Jüdisches Adressbuch für Gross-Berlin*). All the way across the top of several pages were banner advertisements in bold black lettering for Victoria *Versicherung* (Victoria Insurance).

In placing such prominent advertisements in a directory aimed at the Jewish community, the Victoria had clearly sought to expand its business with German Jews and apparently succeeded. Many Jewish firms advertised in the directory, including Singer sewing machines, credit companies, architects, building firms, furniture companies, and even private detective agencies.

This publication not only listed a large number of Jewish-owned businesses, but also updated readers on news of what was happening across the Jewish world. There were articles on the latest events affecting Jews across Europe and the United States, news on charitable endeavors, international organizations assisting and protecting Jewish emigrants and refugees, and information on leading personalities in the Zionist Association of Germany and the Liberal Jewish community of Berlin.

In a chapter in the business directory about Jewish organizations was a detailed description of the efforts of one group funding Jewish settlements in Ukraine and the Crimea, as well as a girls' home in Bucharest. The same people had also conducted relief work in 1928–1930 in Bessarabia (now part of Ukraine and Moldova), Bulgaria, and Lithuania, and assisted international organizations helping to protect emigrants and refugees. In addition to all of these charitable projects, it had represented the interests of Jewish groups in America, England, and France, as well as in Eastern Europe.

The article ended with a list of the names of the board members and an explanation that those who served on the organization, both in Berlin and on local committees, represented "prominent personalities of all religions and political persuasions." Indeed, these people were clearly the cream of German society. One of the directors, listed as the Hamburg representative, was Max M. Warburg, the famous banker who had once advised Kaiser Wilhelm II before the First World War and who, in 1933, had served on the board of the *Reichsbank*, the German Central Bank. Immediately after the Nazis came to power, he was involved in establishing a system known by the Hebrew word for transfer—*Ha'avara*—which was a mechanism whereby German Jews going to live in Palestine could transfer some of their assets there. (In 1938, Warburg emigrated to the United States.) By advertising in this directory, the Victoria Insurance Company was clearly seeking business from the Jewish communities of Germany and beyond.

During our research on the claim, I found a 1932 report on the Victoria, which revealed its total premium income that year was RM 61.4

million (about $230 million today), of which one-third came from overseas business conducted in 19 countries all over the world. Evidently, the Victoria was highly successful. But was there any particular reason why Lucie Wolff had taken out a mortgage with it and not with some other company?

One possibility was obvious. The Wolff family had belonged to the prestigious, liberal synagogue on Fasanenstrasse, where a prominent congregant was Dr. Heinrich Stahl, who became a board member of the synagogue in 1912 and was elected to serve as president of the Berlin Jewish community in 1933–1940. Dr. Stahl had also been a director of the Victoria Insurance Company. Perhaps Lucie had sought a mortgage from the Victoria because she had known and respected Dr. Stahl (who, as noted earlier, died in 1942 at Terezín, the Nazi concentration camp in Czechoslovakia).

After the Nazis came to power, the Victoria stopped seeking business from Jews and, instead, started discriminating against them. Searching for more information, I studied the history of the Victoria. I learned that it was founded in September 1853, under a name that translates as the General Railway Insurance Company. So, right from the start, the company had been intimately connected to railways!

Railway insurance was a new concept, introduced by Otto Crelinger, a banker and member of the board of the Berlin-Potsdam Railway Company. In 1843, Crelinger applied for a royal license to start a railway transport insurance company, declaring, "it is a peculiarity of steam transport that it carries risks which in part cannot be anticipated and in part cannot be avoided, even with the greatest of care, and which are certainly of a more diverse and dangerous nature than those involved in any form of land transport up until now."

He proposed to include an insurance charge in each passenger's fare and thus to insure them automatically. King Friedrich Wilhelm IV of Prussia waited ten years to authorize the new company in 1853. The wait, at least in part, reflected initial fears that such insurance might encourage railway companies to neglect safety standards.

When approval came, Crelinger became the first managing director of the company which, in time, extended coverage for railway transport to insurance against death, accidents, and fire on the railways. Its coverage was extended to apply to land and inland waterway transport in 1858. The company began issuing life insurance in 1861 and in 1875, soon after Crelinger's death, the board changed its name to Victoria of Berlin General Insurance Company.

Why "Victoria"? Victoria was the name of the Roman goddess of victory and Germany had just triumphed in the 1870–1871 war against France. To mark that success, and other military victories, a column was erected in Berlin on top of which was placed a gold statue of the goddess. It still stands today. Also, the British Queen Victoria was a significant world figure at the time and her eldest daughter, of the same name, was the wife of the then-Crown Prince of Prussia, who later became Kaiser Friedrich III.

I had discovered that the Victoria celebrated its centenary in 1953 by publishing *Hundert Jahre Victoria Versicherung 1853–1953* (*One Hundred Years of the Victoria Insurance 1853–1953*). There was a copy for sale on the Internet. The book included a speech to mark the occasion given on September 25, 1953, by the West German Economics Minister, Dr. Ludwig Wilhelm Erhard, who, from 1963 to 1966, also served as Chancellor, the head of government. Kurt Hamann was chairman of the Victoria in 1953 and Erhard's appearance underscored both his, and the company's, continuing prestige.

The book proclaimed that, while by 1935 the Victoria could claim only 6 percent of the German life insurance market, its foreign operations accounted for 86 percent of premium income of German life insurance companies abroad. It conducted business widely—from Austria and Bulgaria to Mexico, Tunisia, and Turkey, and even the British Mandate of Palestine. The centenary book overflows with the company's self-importance and features high-minded quotations from the great German poet, Goethe. For example:

Whatever a human being clutches and handles, the individual is not enough. Society remains a brave man's greatest need. All useful human beings should respect each other, just as the builder needs the architect and the architect needs the bricklayer and the carpenter.

Was der Mensch auch ergreife und handhabe, der einzelne ist sich nicht hinreichend, Gesellschaft bleibt eines wackeren Mannes höchstes Bedürfnis. Alle brauchbaren Menschen sollen in Bezug untereinander stehen, wie sich der Bauherr nach dem Architekten und dieser nach Maurer und Zimmermann umsieht.

The introduction is written by none other than Dr. Kurt Hamann himself. A detailed chronology ensues of the history of the firm over the previous 100 years. Curiously, there is a gaping void of any information about what had gone on at the Victoria between 1939 and 1945, but it offered an explanation for this dearth of detail by Dr. Hamann himself:

Due to the bombing on 3 February 1945, we lost all our archives in the traditional Lindenstrasse, Berlin, location of the company. Therefore everything is missing of the company's paperwork. This centenary book replaces the story lost on account of the bombing.

What a fortuitous coincidence that everything was lost! I found it pretty hard to believe, especially as every other German bureaucracy I encountered appeared to have managed to salvage their prewar paperwork almost intact.

The centenary book also includes a chapter entitled *Kapitalanlageprobleme der Deutschen Lebensversicherung* (*Investment Problems of German Life Insurance*) by Ernst Teckenberg. Another fan of Goethe, he begins his chapter with a (slightly inaccurate) quote:

If we always only look at what is regulated then we think it should always be like that. However, if we realize that there are other ways round it, the rules are permanent but are also lively and changeable.

Sehen wir immerfort nur das Geregelte, so denken wir, es müsse so sein, von jeher sei es also bestimmt und deswegen stationär. Sehen wir aber die Abweichungen, so erkennen wir, dass die Regel zwar fest und ewig, aber zugleich lebendig sei.

All of this reliance on Goethe to pepper the centenary tome of the Victoria Insurance Company was deliciously ironic.

Herr Teckenberg writes about the problems of German life insurance, but also manages to weave into it his thoughts on how the Victoria Insurance Company had an obligation toward the people who took out insurance with it.

This is revisionist history to a degree, and also quite a hideous whitewash. How on earth could the company publish such a work of hypocrisy?

My research had already turned up documents that painted a far less flattering picture of the Victoria, including a list of directors naming Dr. Kurt Hamann and Ernst Teckenberg.

Both of these men had served on the Victoria's board from before the initiation of the forced auction procedure on the Wolff family's building.

In time, I was able to fill in the many missing pieces of Dr. Kurt Hamann's rise to the pinnacle of German commercial life.

In 1926, already a court assessor in the Economics Ministry, Kurt Hamann submitted a thesis entitled "Enforcement of premiums paid on shares of a distressed company" for his doctoral dissertation at the University of Marburg. (It was clearly a scholarly study as several U.S. university libraries today hold copies—including Harvard Law School, Yale Law School, and the University of California, Berkeley Law Library.) Along with his thesis, he included biographical details.

Hamann had been born on September 26, 1898, in Berlin, the son of an army doctor. He attended Mommsen Gymnasium in Charlottenburg until September 8, 1916, when he joined the army as a private. He fought on the western front and was promoted to the rank of lieutenant. In 1919, he left the army to study law in Berlin and Marburg universities and, on October 16, 1921, he passed his exams and qualified as a lawyer.

In 1925, he passed a further law exam and was made a law assessor. Early in January 1926, he was transferred from the Justice Service to the Reich Ministry. In short, he was a bright young man with good prospects.

In 2003, the Victoria published another commemorative yearbook, this time a much grander, glossy, coffee table book. Titled *Im Zug der*

Zeiten (*In the Course of the Years*), it marked the 150th anniversary of the company.

Its historical sweep is more honest about the Nazi era. It explains, even boasts, about the company's Jewish origins. The yearbook notes that senior managers were often Jews and there was a higher proportion of Jews working in the Victoria than in other parts of the insurance industry. Indeed, an anti-Semitic trade union had labeled the Victoria as being "Jewish" in 1913. But the yearbook admits that, after 1933, all Jewish employees gradually had to leave and, by March 1938, the Victoria was able to inform the German insurance supervisory authorities that, in accordance with the law, the company no longer employed Jews.

Despite the detail, the yearbook does not include everything about the Victoria Insurance Company's activities after the Nazis came to power. Having positioned itself as leading insurers to the Jewish commercial sector, the Victoria had proceeded to foreclose on many of the very people who had helped make it such a great success. I have pages and pages of addresses where the Victoria had withdrawn loans to Jews.

The Victoria Insurance Company is now part of what is known as the Victoria Group, based at the eponymous street name, Victoriaplatz, in the western German city of Düsseldorf. On its website, it describes itself as one of Germany's leading groups of full-service insurance companies. The Victoria is a wholly owned subsidiary of one of Germany's largest companies in the insurance business—the ERGO Insurance Group, which is itself part of Munich Re, one of the world's premier reinsurers.

35

THE TERRIBLE TRUTH ABOUT
DR. KURT HAMANN

I continued to pursue Hamann's record. Sometimes I was troubled: was it possible that Hamann had been a cold and ruthless business-man, but not necessarily a full-blooded Nazi? I wanted to be sure.

One afternoon, yet again putting his name into an Internet search engine, I was astonished to find a new reference to Kurt Hamann. He was listed in archives put online by an American organization called "fold3.com." This is a specialist website containing military records. I had never come across the term "fold 3" before but the group explained the meaning on its home page:

> Traditionally, the third fold in a flag-folding ceremony honors and remembers veterans for their sacrifice in defending their country and promoting peace in the world.

Much of fold3.com's website relates to American military records, going back to the War of Independence. But it also has records from the American occupation of Germany after the Second World War. In addition to being mentioned with regard to routine insurance issues, Kurt Hamann's name turned up in a 49-page file titled: "House of German Art, Munich."

There I discovered that although Hamann was able to conceal his business dealings, he had a more public record as a lover of art—Nazi art. I had known that Hitler, whose early career had been as a painter, had been obsessive about promoting his notion of pure German art. But a bit of Internet research laid bare the sordid history.

The House of German Art (Haus der Deutschen Kunst) had been a huge museum-like edifice with towering columns constructed by Hitler in the 1930s in Munich, the city where he had founded the Nazi Party. The Nazis had designated Munich the Capital of German Art and Hitler had pledged to create the "rebirth of Athens by the Isar" (the river running through the city). The Führer laid a cornerstone of the building with great fanfare on October 15, 1933, heralding the "Day of German Art." The new museum's clear propaganda purpose was to present Nazi Germany as a cultured and sophisticated nation.

When the museum opened on July 18, 1937, its first show was entitled "Great German Art Exhibition," and included huge, heroic portraits of Hitler and idealized Aryan youth as well as nudes, farmers, and German landscapes, all attesting to the glory of the Aryan race.

The following day, July 19, a very different Nazi-sponsored exhibition opened a few blocks away. It was called *Die Ausstellung "Entartete Kunst"* (Degenerate Art Exhibition), by which the Nazis meant Impressionism, Cubism, and Surrealism, all of which had won increasing popular acceptance in the first third of the 20th century.

Hitler was using his dictatorial powers to enshrine his own artistic preferences. To him, perfection was epitomized by classical Greek and Roman art, which he considered uncontaminated by the influence of Jews. To his twisted mind, modern art was a conspiracy and an act of aesthetic hostility by immoral Jews, who had debased German culture and the German spirit.

The Nazis viewed such art with contempt, associating it with the culture of the 1920s Weimar era, which they believed had undermined the true German character. The artworks in the Degenerate Art exhibition were deliberately hung in a haphazard manner. Alongside the paintings, slogans pinned on the walls used phrases such as "Revelation of the Jewish racial soul," "German farmers—a Yiddish view," and "Nature as seen by sick minds."

The art in the exhibition had been confiscated from its owners in the previous weeks by a six-man commission, appointed by Hitler's propaganda minister Josef Goebbels. The members of the commission were empowered to travel the length and breadth of Germany, seizing any art they could find in museums and private collections that might be classified as subversive or degenerate.

Over 5,000 works were seized and more than 650 paintings, books, sculptures, and prints were put on display, including works by such renowned artists as Marc Chagall, Max Ernst, George Grosz, Wassily Kandinsky, Paul Klee, Piet Mondrian, and Pablo Picasso. Not all the artists were Jewish, but all of those featured were considered to have been "contaminated" by Jewish influences.

In his speech at the opening of the exhibition, Adolf Ziegler, president of the Reich Chamber of the Visual Arts, said, "All around us you see the monstrous offspring of insanity, impudence, ineptitude and sheer degeneracy. What this exhibition offers inspires horror and disgust in us all."

The Degenerate Art exhibition ran for four months and was reportedly seen by over a million people. It was then taken on tour to 11 other cities in Germany and Austria, serving not as a cultural event, but as part of the Nazis' ever-increasing propaganda campaign against Jews. By 1941, when the exhibition ended, some three million inhabitants of Hitler's Reich had seen it.

In stark contrast, the Great German Art Exhibition was presented as the very pinnacle of what Hitler viewed as art. No one could possibly have misunderstood the message Hitler was delivering. On July 18, he spelled it out in his vitriolic speech at the opening of the exhibition. A few excerpts were enough to send shivers down my spine:

> . . . That flood of slime and ordure which the year 1918 belched forth into our lives was not a product of the lost war, but was only freed in its rush to the surface by that calamity. Through

the defeat, an already thoroughly diseased body experienced the total impact of its inner decomposition . . .

. . . On (these) cultural grounds, more than on any others, Judaism had taken possession of those means and institutions of communication which form, and thus finally rule over public opinion. Judaism was very clever indeed, especially in employing its position in the press with the help of so-called art criticism and succeeding not only in confusing the natural concepts about the nature and scope of art as well as its goals, but above all in undermining and destroying the general wholesome feeling in this domain . . .

. . . When, therefore, the cornerstone of this building was laid, it was with the intention of constructing a temple, not for a so-called modern art, but for a true and everlasting German art, that is, better still, a House for the art of the German people, and not for any international art of the year 1937, '40, '50 or '60. For art is not founded on time, but only on peoples. It is therefore imperative for the artist to erect a monument, not so much to a period, but to his people . . .

. . . I do not want anybody to have false illusions: National-Socialism has made it its primary task to rid the German Reich, and thus, the German people and its life of all those influences which are fatal and ruinous to its existence. And although this purge cannot be accomplished in one day, I do not want to leave the shadow of a doubt as to the fact that sooner or later the hour of liquidation will strike for those phenomena which have participated in this corruption. But with the opening of this exhibition the end of German art foolishness and the end of the destruction of its culture will have begun. From now on we will wage an unrelenting war of purification against the last elements of putrefaction in our culture . . .[1]

---

1. The full speech, in German, with a photo of Hitler delivering it is at: http://deutscher-freiheits kampf.com/2014/07/18/adolf-hitlers-rede-am-18-juli-1937-zur-eroffnung-der-ersten-grosen -deutschen-kunstausstellung/. The translated portions I have quoted are taken from: http:// pwad2.files.wordpress.com/2012/01/hitler.pdf extracted from the English translation by Ilse Falk published in H.B.Chipp, ed. *Theories of Modern Art* (Berkeley, CA: Univerity of California Press, 1968), pages 474–83.

As these ravings suggest, the House of German Art was a key element in the intellectual underpinnings of Nazi Germany. It sought to celebrate Nazi art and denigrate what much of the rest of the world considered the flowering of a distinct 20th-century art. Until the exhibition ended in 1944, the art on display became increasingly propagandistic with more and more images of Hitler and his henchmen, blue-eyed, blond-haired soldiers, and breast-feeding German maidens. There were also paintings of locations associated with the Führer's formative years, folk art, agricultural images, and many others that elaborated on any theme that glorified the Third Reich. The building still exists on the edge of the *Englischer Garten*, Munich's largest park. Kurt Hamann was central to this madness.

The file from fold3.com contained the 1941 Yearbook for the House of German Art. It includes a six-page text of a speech given by Josef Goebbels lauding the organization on July 26, 1941: *Wir senden Adolf Hitler unseren Gruss. Adolf Hitler Sieg Heil! Sieg Heil! Sieg Heil!* (We send Adolf Hitler our greetings. Adolf Hitler Hail victory! Hail victory! Hail victory!)

On page 23 of the yearbook is a list of the leadership of the House of German Art, which begins with Hitler, and goes on to include his propaganda chief Josef Goebbels, as well as Hermann Göring, the highest ranking member of the German military and head of the air force.

Also listed as a member of the honorary committee is: "*Hamann Kurt, Dr., Generaldirektor der Victoria zu Berlin Allgemeine-Versicherungs-Aktien-Gesellschaft.*" (Hamann Kurt, Dr., Chairman of the Victoria Insurance Company, Berlin.) Fold3.com produced another revelation. From 1941 to 1946, Kurt Hamann's effective boss, the chairman of the supervisory board of the Victoria, was Max Wessig. Like Hamann, Wessig was a member of the honorary committee of the House of German Art. Wessig is also listed in online German government archives, where his resume states that, during the Second World War, he was also on the supervisory board of *Rheinmetall Borsig*, a manufacturer of artillery, and the supervisory board of Daimler-Benz, which made engines for tanks and submarines.

Notoriously, Daimler-Benz was not only a key component in the Nazi war machine, but it also used slave labor. Kurt Hamann clearly did not keep company with decent men.

The curator of the archives in Munich confirmed that Dr. Hamann's name appears in the House of German Art annual report for 1938, where he is listed as an honorary committee member. He remained on that august body until 1944. He would, therefore, have been only too well aware of the repulsive racist and propagandistic Degenerate Art Exhibition and all it stood for.

My next discovery shocked me even more. I learned that in 2001 Professor Gerald D. Feldman of the University of California at Berkeley had published a seminal work called *Allianz and the German Insurance Business, 1933–1945*. When I obtained a copy and started reading it, I began to see why the Victoria Insurance Company would claim that there were no records of its wartime history.

Unlike the Allianz Insurance Company, which had commissioned an in-depth academic study to confront head-on the true nature of its collaboration with the Nazis, the Victoria has apparently shown no desire to reveal the truth. Professor Feldman's access to previously unavailable archives, and his rigorous research, opened my eyes further to the history of the insurance company that had foreclosed on so many Jewish businesses.

What he revealed about the true nature of the Victoria's behavior before and during the war was horrifying.

The chairman of the Victoria, just before Dr. Kurt Hamann was promoted to that position, was Dr. Emil Herzfelder, a Jew. He led the company from 1932 to 1935, and tried to mitigate the virulent anti-Semitic campaign the Nazis launched in 1933. These began with a nationwide boycott of Jewish businesses, and then proceeded with new laws that stripped away the rights of Jews.

The Law for the Restoration of the Professional Civil Service of April 7 mandated that all non-Aryans—defined as those who had one parent or grandparent who was Jewish—be excluded from the civil service. Another law of April 11 excluded Jews from the legal profession. In both cases, however, exemptions were made for Jews who had done military service or had been in the civil service or had been practicing [law] before 1914. Legislation was also passed on April 22 limiting the institutions in which Jewish physicians could practice, and restrictions were imposed on

April 25 limiting the number of Jews who could attend universities . . . No less portentous than the aforementioned organized
boycott and legal measures, however, were the "spontaneous"
efforts to drive Jews from employment by putting pressures on
businesses to eliminate their Jewish employees and to designate
as 'non-German' those companies with Jewish directors, supervisory board members, or personnel.[2]

Professor Feldman wrote that, in an effort to counter this all-out
attack on Jews, prominent Jewish businessmen, including the Victoria's Dr. Emil Herzfelder, Rudolf Loeb of Mendelssohn & Co. bankers,
and Hamburg bankers Max Warburg and Carl Melchior, "launched an
effort to fight economic exclusion while trying to meet the Nazis half-
way by encouraging young Jews to shift out of urban and professional
activities and move into agriculture and other forms of manual labor."
     These leaders hoped they could put a stop to the economic boycott,
promote the retention of Jewish employees, and eliminate the clauses
in public contracts which discriminated against, and enabled the firing
of, Jews. They had, of course, underestimated—as many decent people did—the full evil of the Nazi plan to rid Germany of hundreds of
thousands of its law-abiding, productive citizens. Feldman wrote that
the insurance industry came under strong pressure to fire its Jewish
employees, especially those in key positions. Kurt Daluege, a Nazi party
member since 1922 and a member of the SS, who was to take over the
Prussian Police in April and become head of Himmler's Order Police in
1936, forwarded to the Reich Supervisory Office of Insurance a denunciation that the Victoria was "Jewified" and corrupt.
     As Professor Feldman noted, in an understatement, insurance
companies that rid themselves of Jews "could thus gain a competitive
advantage."
     Despite the best efforts of Dr. Herzfelder and his fellow Jewish insur-
ance company executives, they could not stem the tide of racial hatred.
Dr. Herzfelder left Germany in 1935. When war broke out in 1939, he
was living and working in Britain where, as a German national, he was
categorized as an "Enemy Alien" and liable for internment. A record at

---

2. Feldman, Gerald. *Allianz and the German Insurance Business, 1933–1945*, page 67.

the British National Archives in Kew reveals that, in 1940, a tribunal released him from this onerous fate, designating him as a "Refugee" working as an insurance adviser for the National & Colonial Insurance Company.[3] In 1946, Dr. Herzfelder became a British citizen, and died in London in 1970.

After Dr. Herzfelder departed, Kurt Hamann became the Victoria's new chairman. One year later, in 1936, the Victoria started foreclosure proceedings against our building. One sentence in Professor Feldman's book leapt off the page at me. He wrote these words about the insurance of the workshops at Auschwitz:

> By October 1942, the plants were valued at RM 1,535,100, [$614,040 or nearly $8.8m in 2013] and Allianz now gathered a consortium to insure them; it took 25 percent of the risk, with consortium members Aachener und Münchener (20 percent), Magdeburger (20 percent), Schlesische Feuer (15 percent), Victoria (10 percent), and Silesia/Bielitz (10 percent) taking the rest.

These policies were treated as a "State Secret." The insurance companies were not going to advertise their involvement in death camps.

It is beyond revolting. The Victoria Insurance Company insured parts of Auschwitz—where my mother's uncle, Fritz, and a million other Jews were killed. It was a vicious circle: The Victoria seized our family's building and transferred it to the German Railways; Fritz had been deported to Auschwitz courtesy of those same railways and the Victoria was insuring the buildings at the death camp where he was exterminated.

The consortium was not a one-off group. It continued operating and wrote its last policy for Auschwitz on October 15, 1944, to cover 1944–1945. Auschwitz was eventually liberated by Soviet forces on January 27, 1945.

———

One night I was again perusing the Internet. I must have searched "victoria insurance" and "kurt hamann" a hundred times, but on this

---

3. British National Archives, HO 396/178 page 72.

occasion I happened upon an entry for the former chairman of the Victoria Insurance Company that I had never seen before.

Perhaps the item had been only recently posted. Or maybe it was mere luck that led me to this new information. But what came up astounded me.

Mannheim University (Germany) Rector's report of 2009–2010:

Dr. Kurt-Hamann-Stiftung [Stiftung = Foundation.]

Das Stiftungskapital der 1979 errichteten Dr. Kurt-Hamann-Stiftung beträgt 173.500,00 Euro. Aus dem Ertrag ist die Förderung von Forschungsvorhaben auf dem Gebiet der gesamten Versicherungswissenschaft an der Universität sowie die Vergabe eines Dr. Kurt-Hamann-Preises für hervorragende Dissertationen und Diplomarbeiten aus diesem Bereich vorgesehen. Außerdem besteht die Möglichkeit bei der Victoria Lebensversicherungs-AG ein 3-monatiges Praktikum zu absolvieren.

I copied and pasted into an online translator and pressed return:

The endowment established in 1979, in memory of Dr. Kurt Hamann has capital of 173,500 Euro. The endowment's income funds academic research in the field of insurance science at the University as well as a Kurt Hamann prize for the most outstanding dissertations and diploma theses. There is also the possibility of a three-month internship at the Victoria Life Insurance Company.

It was incredible! Here is one of Germany's finest academic institutions, the University of Mannheim, boasting a foundation named for Kurt Hamann.

Knowing that the Victoria Insurance Company is now part of the world-renowned Munich Re, I went to the latter's website. On its Corporate Responsibility page, the Munich Re boasts of its commitment to education:

> Some talented young people lack the means to make the most
> of their potential. For this reason, in cooperation with the Dr.
> Kurt Hamann Foundation, the ERGO Insurance Group supports
> diploma candidates at the University of Mannheim.

The saga only became more extraordinary. The website went on to
explain about the annual Kurt Hamann prize, no doubt a prestigious
award. One recipient, who received the prize for his dissertation at the
University of Mannheim, was Stefan Lippe, who became chief executive officer of the giant insurer Swiss Re in 2009.

How much did the University of Mannheim know about Dr. Kurt
Hamann and his leadership of the Victoria Insurance Company from
1935 through the Second World War? Did they know he was a leading
member of the Nazi regime? Did they know that, under his direction,
the Victoria Insurance Company foreclosed on scores of Jewish businesses and sometimes directly turned them over to the Third Reich?
Did they know that the Victoria Insurance Company helped insure
workshops at Auschwitz?

If they didn't know, should they have known? Do the students who
win the annual prize know it honors a man many of us might consider
to have been a war criminal? Did the University of Mannheim care
about these issues?

I found these questions deeply disturbing. Finally I resolved to contact
the University and the Victoria Insurance Company to see if I could get
answers from them. In early August 2013 I had e-mailed them with my
questions.

I quickly received a response from the University telling me that the
Rector, Professor von Thadden, was away but would be informed of my
inquiries after his return. In the meantime, an immediate investigation into my allegations would be launched. But I received no further
feedback.

I hoped the university would consider renaming its Stiftung.

The response from the Victoria, or rather its holding company,
ERGO, arrived in August 2013. The company spokeswoman wrote:

> In recent decades, Victoria has invested considerable time and
> energy into researching its own history, and has also investi-

gated whether any members of the Board of Management were members of the National Socialist party between 1933 and 1945. As a result of this research, we can confidently confirm that Dr. Hamann was not a member of the National Socialist party.

I found this a curious statement because in my e-mailed inquiry, I had never alleged that Dr. Hamann had been a Nazi. She continued:

With this information in mind, we are unable to comprehend your claims about Dr. Hamann regarding this issue. The Victoria Insurance companies played only a subordinate role as part of the Nazi-controlled economy between 1933 and 1945.

Effectively claiming that having a 10 percent insurance stake in slave labor workshops at Auschwitz was merely a "subordinate role" in the Nazi-controlled economy is a curious formulation. I, for one, beg to differ, as I suspect the court of public opinion would do as well.

I had asked whether the company had made any public comment on Professor Feldman's discovery that the Victoria had insured Auschwitz. The spokeswoman's response was:

We supported him in every aspect of his research and are not in possession of any further knowledge on this matter.

I took this to mean no, the company had never made any public comment.

Despite all my research, I found no evidence that, after the collapse of Nazi Germany in 1945, Dr. Hamann was ever put through a formal denazification process about his wartime role.

And what of the Victoria Insurance building today? The former address of the Victoria in Berlin was Lindenstrasse 20-25, Berlin SW 68. That building still stands. It is exactly the same address at the top of all the correspondence between the Victoria and the Wolff family representatives and the courts during the 1930s. From photographs, it remains stunningly beautiful and imposing with carved figures and wreaths adorning the outside. And right above the front entrance, above an arch with two pillars on either side, surrounded by small angels, are the words *VICTORIA VERSICHERUNG* engraved in large capital letters.

These days it is just an ordinary address housing numerous businesses, charities, and educational foundations. There is even a Victoria Restaurant. I was particularly struck by two of the institutions that, according to the Internet, are located inside. They could not have chosen a more apt and poignant address.

One is the Permanent Office of the International Holocaust Remembrance Alliance whose website informs the reader that this organization, with 31 member countries, ". . . is an intergovernmental body whose purpose is to place political and social leaders' support behind the need for Holocaust education, remembrance and research both nationally and internationally."

The other is the *Stiftung EVZ* (*Erinnerung, Verantwortung, Zukunft*) (Foundation for Remembrance, Responsibility, and Future). Established in 2000, the foundation's primary purpose was to make payments to former forced laborers. The payments programs were completed in 2007. The German government and German industry provided the foundation's capital of 5.2 billion Euro ($6.7 billion). A total of 358 million Euro ($463 million) was set aside as foundation capital to fund project support. The foundation finances its long-term funding activities out of the income generated by this capital.

The website is in both English and German. It states under the section titled "A Critical Examination of History":

> The foundation of EVZ aims to anchor the history of forced labour under National Socialism in the German and European culture of remembrance. The victims are given a voice and their experiences of National Socialism are preserved for future generations.[4]

Auseinandersetzung mit der Geschichte

---

4. http://www.stiftung-evz.de/eng/funding/critical-examination-of-history.html.

Die Stiftung EVZ will die Geschichte der NS-Zwangsarbeit in der deutschen und europäischen Erinnerungskultur verankern. Dabei kommen die Opfer zu Wort, die ihre Erfahrungen im Nationalsozialismus nachkommenden Generationen vermitteln.[5]

Under the heading "Commitment to the Victims of National Socialism" is the statement:

The surviving victims of National Socialism are now very elderly. Many suffer extreme material hardship and are socially isolated. In Central and Eastern Europe and in Israel, the foundation supports initiatives that strengthen local and international efforts to help victims of forced labour and other National Socialist injustice. It funds model projects that offer a decent standard of social and medical care and which support intergenerational dialogue.[6]

Engagement für Opfer des Nationalsozialismus

Die Opfer des Nationalsozialismus sind hochbetagt. Ihre Lebenssituation ist oft prekär und gekennzeichnet durch einen Mangel an gesellschaftlicher Teilhabe. Die Stiftung EVZ unterstützt in Mittel- und Osteuropa sowie in Israel Initiativen, die die Hilfsbereitschaft für Opfer von Zwangsarbeit und anderem NS-Unrecht lokal und international stärken. Sie fördert Modellprojekte für eine würdige soziale und medizinische Betreuung und für den generationenübergreifenden Dialog.[7]

The foundation has a lengthy list of publications including *Hitler's Slaves: Life Stories of Forced Laborers in Nazi-Occupied Europe*; *Impulses for Europe: Tradition and Modernity of East European Jewry*; and *A Mutual Responsibility and a Moral Obligation: Final Report*

---

5. http://www.stiftung-evz.de/handlungsfelder/auseinandersetzung-mit-der-geschichte.html.
6. http://www.stiftung-evz.de/eng/funding/commitment-to-the-victims-of-national-socialism.html.
7. http://www.stiftung-evz.de/handlungsfelder/engagement-fuer-ns-opfer.html.

on Compensations Programs of the Remembrance, Responsibility and Future Foundation.

And the foundation has developed an international travelling exhibition entitled *Zwangsarbeit. Die Deutschen, die Zwangsarbeiter und der Krieg* (Forced Labor. The Germans, the Forced Laborers and the War) with accompanying literature that commemorates how, "During World War II, more than twenty million persons from all over Europe were forced to perform labor in the German Reich and the occupied countries." The website points out that between 2001–2007, the foundation, which was established especially for this purpose, ". . . joined seven international partner organizations in overseeing individual compensation payments to 1.66 million former forced laborers."[8]

The former site of the Victoria Insurance Company strikes me as a most fitting home for such a foundation—but are its occupants aware of what went on inside all those years ago?

---

8. http://www.stiftung-evz.de/fileadmin/user_upload/EVZ_Uploads/Stiftung/Geschichte/NS
-Zwangsarbeit_englisch/120313-en-broschuere-ausstellung-f.-leihnehmer-final.pdf.

36

SWISS BANKS AND
OTHER MATTERS

In 1998, I read newspaper reports that the Swiss banks had, more than half a century after the end of the war, reversed years of obstinacy and announced they would negotiate a global settlement to compensate Holocaust victims, and their heirs, who had once held accounts in Switzerland. Their ignominious position for more than 50 years had been to agree only to compensate those claimants who could demonstrate legitimate claims on long dormant accounts. Of course, most people had no paperwork to prove their case. The banks had spent years denying that dormant accounts still existed, and simply refused to search their archives or proactively assist in resolving claims. But under pressure from U.S. officials threatening sanctions, the Swiss banks capitulated and set up a fund for compensation.

We knew that the Wolff family had bank accounts in Switzerland. They had been able to take advantage of German tax rules and, by spending several months each year outside the country, had reduced their tax obligation. We had no idea if any accounts for the family still existed, but we advised my mother to lodge a claim.

In June 2003, my mother received notice that an award had been granted by the Claims Resolution Tribunal under its Holocaust Victim Assets Litigation process for an account in the name of Fritz Heinrich Wolff. The bank's records revealed that the account owner was indeed Fritz Heinrich Wolff, that he had lived in Berlin-Hermsdorf in 1933, and that no evidence existed that either he or his heirs closed the account and received the proceeds. The Claims Resolution Tribunal wrote:

> Given that in 1933 the Nazis embarked on a campaign to seize the domestic and foreign assets of its Jewish nationals through the enforcement of flight taxes and other confiscatory measures including the confiscation of assets held in Swiss banks; that the Account Owner was arrested by the Nazis four times between 1933–1943, exposing him to the coerced disclosure and confiscation of his assets including those located abroad; that the Account Owner remained in Germany until his deportation to and murder at Auschwitz, such that he would not have been able to repatriate his account to Germany during this period without its confiscation. . . .

An award of 156,000 Swiss francs (then worth around $126,000) was made. Herbert had long ago established that he was Fritz's heir on everything other than the Krausenstrasse property and, accordingly, all the money went to Herbert's appointed beneficiaries, his sons, Heini and Micky. They did not offer to share the proceeds with their sisters.

A year later, a very different scenario emerged with regard to two accounts discovered in Lucie Wolff's name—a demand deposit and a custody account. Although she had died in 1932, a year before Hitler came to power, the account had remained open for some reason after her death.

In its 2004 award, the Claims Resolution Tribunal considered the notion that the accounts had been emptied under duress ". . . that while the Account Owner was not a Victim of Nazi Persecution, the Account Owner's two sons [redacted in the online document but identifiable as Herbert and Fritz] were both Victims of Nazi Persecution." Recognizing that Herbert had fled Germany "due to Nazi persecution" and that

Fritz had "eventually perished in Auschwitz" the Swiss Claims Resolution Tribunal found ". . . that either heir may therefore have yielded to Nazi pressure to turn over the accounts in an attempt to ensure their safety." In conclusion, ". . . there is sufficient probability that the account proceeds were not paid to the Account Owner's heirs."

The Tribunal determined that compensation should be paid on both accounts, which amounted to a total of 189,250 Swiss francs (at the time, around $153,000).

The Court, having examined the line of inheritance, decreed that my mother and her brother, Heini, were each entitled to 11/32 each, Marion to 7/32, and Micky to 3/32. The calculation was precisely as our lawyers had worked out and what my mother had been denied, in 1995, by her brothers in Israel. So, by threatening to go to court to stop her inheriting her now demonstrably rightful 11/32 share of Krausenstrasse, she had accepted just 9/32 and had effectively been short-changed by her brothers. It was far too late to do anything about the wrongful allocation in relationship to the building, but it was good to know we had been right all along.

It really is a miracle that I found out so much about the forced sale of Krausenstrasse 17/18, and I often wonder how much more there might be to unearth, if only I could locate the right archive. In the process of compiling the necessary documents to launch the restitution claim, I had the great good fortune to discover so much about my family history. For that alone I am profoundly grateful. For me, the process was partly hard work and partly serendipity.

While researching and writing, I came across a 193-page list on the Internet of properties once owned by Jews in former East Germany for which the Claims Conference, formerly known as the Conference on Material Claims Against Germany, had been paid monies by the German government.

The New York-based Claims Conference is the organization that, initially in regard to West Germany, sought compensation for unclaimed Jewish property and firms that had been forced out of business by the Nazis. The money was then used to set up medical treatment, social services, and retirement facilities for Holocaust survivors, as well as offer support for Holocaust education, documentation, and research.

In the preamble to the list is an explanation that each entry represents "years of legal struggle by the Claims Conference to recover formerly Jewish properties lost in the Holocaust."

It went on to say, "Had the Claims Conference not taken these steps, Jewish assets that remained unclaimed after the filing deadline would have remained with the owners at the time (including in many cases the original 'aryanizers') or reverted to the German government."

The list stated, ". . . includes proceeds arising from the sales of restituted assets, settlements, compensation paid by the authorities for assets that could not be restituted, and bulk settlements, and covers both private and communal property."

Having discovered the list, I searched it for a mention of Krausenstrasse 17/18. To my astonishment, on page 171, there it was. The Claims Conference listed the building as one of the addresses for which it has received monies from the German government.

Berlin Krausenstr. 17/18 €827,214.64

A separate document gave the names of eight companies that had rented offices in the building from the Wolff family. But no information was attached to the individual company names as to how much compensation had been awarded for each. In March 2013, I wrote to the chief executive of the Claims Conference, Greg Schneider, as well as the chairman, Julius Berman, asking for an explanation. At the end of November I heard from the press office with a one-sentence note:

In response to your query, the Claims Conference recovered proceeds for other businesses that were located at the same address.

I contacted our lawyers and asked them why the Claims Conference could have received this money—more than $1 million. Dr. Sybille Steiner suggested a likely reason:

Owners of a business that had been expropriated/sold etc. due to persecution were entitled to receive compensation for the loss of the business irrespective of whether they owned the property from which the business had been run. The Claims Conference will have received compensation with regard to those businesses which had been located in Krausenstrasse 17/18 and which [would] have been lost due to persecution.

What happened to the former business owners who rented office space in Krausenstrasse and who had a legitimate right to compensation for their losses? Were any of them or their heirs still alive?

Type "Krausenstrasse 17/18" into any Internet search engine and it should reveal a Wikimedia page with a photograph of the building.[1]

The website explains "It was built from 1908 to 1909 to a design by the architect Friedrich Kristeller" and continues by explaining that it had once been owned by Victor Wolff and in 1996 the German government paid reparations to his descendants. Today the building has been designated an "historic landmark."

Further digging revealed that the Berlin City government had granted it this landmark status and its website confirms many of the details I had labored hard to discover in the 1990s. To my surprise, it refers to Victor Wolff having owned "one of the largest fur stores in Germany" and it is refreshingly honest in confronting the tragic history of the building, stating that, in 1937–1938, the interior was remodeled by the *Reichsbahn* after its "expropriation from the Jewish owners." The "very elegant main staircase" is all that remains of the original interior from the H. Wolff golden age.[2]

Having got this far, I felt that a more formal recognition of the building's history needed to be made. Rather than a mere mention on a website, I much preferred that a plaque be put at the front entrance. To this end, in November 2013, I wrote to Dr. Peter Ramsauer, the then Minister of Transport, Building and Urban Development. Six weeks later, I received a reply from one of Dr. Ramsauer's officials. To my surprise and delight, Karl-Heinz Collmeier, on behalf of the minister, agreed that it is necessary "to document the historical background outside for all visitors

---

1. http://commons.wikimedia.org/wiki/File:Berlin,_Mitte,_Krausenstrasse_17-18,_Dienst gebaeude_Bundesverkehrsministerium.jpg.
2. http://www.stadtentwicklung.berlin.de/denkmal/liste_karte_datenbank/de/denkmaldaten-bank/daobj.php?obj_dok_nr=09080296.

and pedestrians" by affixing a plaque to the building. He assured me that he would arrange for such a plaque to be made. I wrote back to thank him and asked him to contact me once it was ready to be put in place. Despite many more e-mails, nothing happened. I like to believe that this was due to bureaucratic muddle rather than any attempt to bury the building's past. In January 2012, the Federal Agency for Real Estate (*Bundesanstalt für Immobilienaufgaben*) took ownership of the building, but the Ministry of Transport had continued to manage it. But in July 2014, technical and infrastructural facility management passed to the Federal Agency for Real Estate as well.

So in July 2014, I wrote to this agency asking for an update on the planned plaque. On August 21, 2014, I received an e-mail from Herr Lutz Lange telling me, "We will review your request and inform you as soon as we have new information available." While the Ministry of Transport still has a handful of offices located there, today Krausen-strasse 17/18 is the location of the Federal Ministry of the Environment, Nature Conservation, Building and Nuclear Safety.

I recently learned that my mother's childhood home at Conrad-strasse 1, Wannsee, has also been listed by the Berlin City government as being of historical architectural importance. An Internet link has a photo of the house, a lengthy description of its history, and information about its former owners—who included Rudolf and Paula Pringsheim, the grandparents of Katia Mann, who married the famous German novelist and Nobel laureate Thomas Mann. Readers are told the grounds included "a carriage house, farm buildings, sheds and greenhouse," and that it is an important representative of a picturesque residential house with "half-timbered architecture of the 16th century." Curiously, no mention is made of the Wolff family whatsoever—merely a passing reference to the fact that in 1936 the property was converted into apartments. I wonder if anyone stops to ponder the date and what might have led to this change in design and use! The park which once surrounded the house complete with Grecian statues, where my mother and her siblings used to run around, is long gone. More than a dozen modern houses have been built on the grounds.[3]

---

3. http://www.stadtentwicklung.berlin.de/denkmal/liste_karte_datenbank/de/denkmaldaten-bank/daobj.php?obj_dok_nr=09075535.

Germany has, to a great extent, come to terms with its appalling past. There is a private, voluntary organization that places a small, 4 inch square, slightly raised concrete block on top of which is a brass memorial plaque, known as a Stolperstein (literally, a stumbling stone or block), on the sidewalk at the address where a victim of Nazi persecution last lived voluntarily. The majority of these stones are in memory of Jewish victims of the Holocaust who were deported and murdered. But many commemorate those who emigrated to escape persecution or who committed suicide. Stolpersteine (the German spelling of the plural for Stolperstein) are also laid for non-Jews—those who suffered under the Nazis because of their race, religion, sexual orientation, Communist sympathies, or mental and physical disabilities.

There are several explanations for the use of the term *"stumbling stone." One is that pedestrians do exactly that, when they chance upon them. They then see the inscription at their feet, stop to read it, and are forced to remember that someone once lived there. The aim is to ensure the past is never forgotten.* Another is that before the Holocaust, if a German tripped over a protruding stone, he would say "There must be a Jew buried here."

German artist Gunter Demnig founded the Stolpersteine project in 1996, and it is now the world's largest memorial initiative. To date almost 60,000 plaques have been placed in over 1,400 locations across Europe. More than 7,000 are in Berlin alone.[4]

I wrote to the organization asking for a *Stolperstein* to be laid outside Fritz's last address at Dresdener Strasse 97 Berlin. I felt that this was the least he deserved as a suitable coda to his life and dreadful last few years.

---

4. https://www.stolpersteine-berlin.de/en

37

AN UNWANTED DISCOVERY

At the close of 2014, I received an e-mail from Barbara Welker, archivist at the *Neue Synagoge* (New Synagogue) in Berlin, which houses the Centrum Judaicum Foundation—the archives of German Jewry before 1945.[1]

Nothing could have prepared me for this last piece of information in the incredible jigsaw puzzle that had been the life of Fritz Wolff.

In March 1926, Fritz had apparently gone to his local district court and formally renounced Judaism. This official resignation was, Ms. Welker explained to me, merely a bureaucratic procedure that was notified by the court to the Jewish community, which duly recorded this, in handwriting, on index cards. Ms. Welker attached a scan of the record, known as an *Austrittskarte* (exit card).

I did not want to know this. That Fritz had willingly walked away from his heritage was shattering news to both my mother and me. If anyone else in the Wolff family had ever had the merest hint of this, not a word of it had ever been mentioned. Perhaps Fritz's devotion to Communist ideology had led him to believe in the dream of universal humanity? God alone knows! But it did not protect him one iota from

---

1. http://www.centrumjudaicum.de/en/cj-archiv.

the bestiality of the Nazis. As Ms. Welker said to me in her e-mail, since the Nazis defined Jews as a race, it made not the slightest difference whether Fritz was a member of the Jewish community or not. Fritz's ancestors were Jewish; therefore, so was he.

The tragedy is that while Fritz had lived his life as an atheist and a Communist, he suffered and died as a Jew.

38

A STOLPERSTEIN FOR FRITZ

June 25, 2015, was a bright sunny day in Berlin. My husband, younger son Joshua and I walked from the Courtyard Marriott hotel at the end of Krausenstrasse to Fritz's former address at Dresdener Strasse 97, about fifteen minutes away. The location is nothing like that depicted in the 1920s photograph I had been sent by the local Kreutzberg Museum. This had revealed an ornately carved five-story building, and clearly visible was the post office at street level (dating back apparently to 1915). The image was one I had carried in my mind's eye of where Fritz had last lived. But it no longer even faintly resembled the last dwelling he had known before deportation. Today the address is the site of the huge Berolina housing co-operative, constructed during the Soviet era of East Berlin.

We were in for more surprises. The previous day, we had met Mary Bianchi, a volunteer with the Stolpersteine project, who had told us about how the ceremony would be conducted. She had had to gain approval and permission from the Berolina management committee for the laying of the Stolperstein and informed us this had been enthusiastically welcomed and considerable interest expressed. Indeed, a small article had been published in the local newspaper informing everyone of the time and date of the forthcoming event. Mary had found a local oboist who would play as onlookers arrived and she told us that after the stone itself was put in the ground, a cantor would say kaddish—the Jewish prayer for the dead. Whether Fritz, the committed Communist who had turned his back on Judaism, would have approved of this I didn't wish to hazard a guess! But it seemed fitting to me. Mary said I would then address whoever was there and explain the history of what had happened and she would translate into German. We were all set.

As we waited for the famed Gunter Demnig to arrive and the oboist played, from all directions crowds of Berolina residents started to gather. We knew none of them, but there they were—young and old alike, even women pushing strollers. It was absolutely fascinating.

Mr. Demnig's arrival was not dissimilar to a celebrity event. I had not appreciated the extent of his fame and people were genuinely excited to see the man himself clutching his buckets and trowels with which he digs up part of the existing paving stone to replace it with a Stolperstein and its inscribed bronze plaque. All Stolpersteine begin with the words "Hier wohnte" ("Here lived") and each has one name and a brief description of that individual's fate. Fritz's stone gives his full name, date of birth, imprisonment in Sachsenhausen in 1938, deportation on March 1, 1943, and murder in Auschwitz.

HIER WOHNTE
FRITZ HEINRICH WOLFF
JG. 1891
SACHSENHAUSEN 1938
DEPORTIERT 01.03.1943
ERMORDET IN
AUSCHWITZ

After kaddish and my little speech, we each laid a white rose around the Stolperstein. I was touched that several local people had openly wept while kaddish was recited and I was also quite amazed that some had arrived with flowers. The event seemed to affect them deeply.

By a quirk of fate Joshua, who was able to be at the ceremony, was born on January 27, the same birthday as his great great grandmother

Henrietta Danziger (Nellie's mother). His middle name is Frederick, the anglicization of Fritz. More poignantly, January 27 is also the day when Auschwitz was liberated, in 1945, by the Soviet army. It is the date now commemorated as International Holocaust Remembrance Day and in Britain as Holocaust Memorial Day.

There is a Stolperstein at Mommsenstrasse 60 in Charlottenburg in memory of general practitioner and paediatrician Dr. Walter Rudolf Kristeller, son of Friedrich Kristeller, the architect of the 'Wolff Building' in Krausenstrasse. Walter and his wife Ellen were deported on November 29, 1942 to Auschwitz where they were murdered.

I hope one day to be able to honor the memory of the four fellow residents of the apartment on Dresdener Strasse who once lived with Fritz. I have no idea if the Deutsch family has any living descendants and I have so far failed to find any relatives of Josef Rosner.

PART
FOUR

39

DECLARATIONS

After this book was first published in hardback in August 2015, it didn't take long for there to be a reaction! A mere six weeks after publication and over two years since I had first contacted Mannheim University, I received an e-mail from Prof. Dr. Ernst-Ludwig von Thadden, the Rector. He informed me that he had read the book and, as a consequence, two weeks earlier, had written to his two Mannheim University fellow board members of the Dr. Kurt Hamann Foundation (which consists also of two representatives from ERGO insurance group—the legal successor of the Victoria) and told them of my findings. A meeting had been scheduled with them for the end of that very week. Prof. von Thadden told me that he had found the book's contents "very interesting and touching" and that he had learnt a lot from it. He regretted what had happened to my family. "Those were evil times, populated by evil people." I was surprised to read his words: "I do not think that renaming the foundation will be adequate. We must do more." He concluded by thanking me for my work which constituted ". . . one more piece of evidence about an evil time in Germany's history we have the duty to deal with." He assured me that this matter had his "fullest attention" and he would get back to me after the entire board had met.

He was back in touch on November 8. He wanted me to know that he had been invited to inspect the Victoria Insurance archives in Düsseldorf, an important step before reaching a decision on the future of the foundation, since ". . . there seems to be evidence that Kurt Hamann was largely exculpated in the hearings of the OMGUS [Office of Military Government, United States] and that he received support from Emil Herzfelder, his Jewish predecessor at the helm of the Victoria, who was driven out of office in 1935 and emigrated to London." He suggested: "One possible way forward may be to use the foundation money to commission a professional study of the life and times of Kurt Hamann."

I responded by proposing "it is the role of the Victoria Insurance Company as a whole, under Dr. Hamann's leadership during the Third Reich, which might be the more illuminating. A study such as that conducted on the Allianz, by Professor Gerald Feldman, should be seriously considered."

The next missive from Professor von Thadden arrived on December 23 informing me that the members of the Board had all met and ". . . we agreed that something has to be done with the Hamann foundation and discussed a range of possible measures. . . . We have agreed to examine the different possible options further in the next few months, and to seek legal advice when necessary. These options range from a change of name to the winding up of the foundation."

He reported that I was welcome to visit the archives myself, adding that "To me, it seems worth while to investigate the personality of Kurt Hamann, who seems to have been one of the many people in the grey area between 'good' and 'bad' in the German economy of the Nazi time. Since the foundation is named after Hamann and not after the company I would be glad if we had the opportunity to do so."

I felt quite sympathetic to the poor man's plight—burdened with a foundation in the name of Kurt Hamann. He concluded: "Be assured that I am most indebted to you to bring this piece of history to the fore that touches the history of Mannheim University in this unexpected way. Please keep going."

He wasn't going to have to ask me twice! This was a challenge and I was ready to face it!

Just how deserving was Dr. Hamann of the honor the University of Mannheim had accorded him?

I already knew he had once worked as a lawyer at the Justice Ministry. I again contacted Beate Schreiber of the Berlin historical research firm "Facts and Files" and asked her what details might exist about Dr. Hamann's earlier career in the 1920s and early 1930s. Her enquiries at the *Bundesarchiv* (German National Archives) led to my receiving 123 scanned pages of Dr. Hamann's Justice Ministry personnel file.[1]

It was something of an eye opener. Clearly Dr. Hamann had been a very clever man. He had passed his PhD thesis "cum laude," and joined the Ministry of Justice in 1926, employed as a judge in the Berlin State court. But within a matter of months, he went on attachment to the Ministry of Economics. Curiously, he continued to be a civil servant even after joining the Board of the Victoria Insurance Company in 1932, despite his salary being paid by his new employer. After a year at the insurance company, he requested the Ministry of Justice renew his attachment and this was granted. In 1935, having been asked to take over as chairman from Emil Herzfelder, who had fled the country, Dr. Hamann formally requested, and was granted, official release as a staff member of the ministry. It was all there, in black and white in front of me. I was coming face to face with history.

Of course, I knew all about the speed at which the Nazis had enacted laws to severely limit the rights of Jews. As early as April 7, 1933, the "Law for the Restoration of the Professional Civil Service" had been enacted. Anyone deemed non-Aryan or "politically unreliable" was ineligible for employment in the civil service. And everyone working in the public sector had to prove Aryan ancestry. On June 10, 1933, Dr. Hamann had done exactly that, declaring and signing the following statement:

I hereby officially declare: despite careful examination I have found no circumstances that could justify the assumption that I am not of Aryan descent; in particular none of my parents or grandparents belonged to the Jewish faith at any time.

---

1. BArch Berlin R 3001/58789.

I am aware that I will be officially prosecuted with the object of dismissal, if these claims are not truthful.

Ich versichere hiermit dienstlich: Mir sind trotz sorgfältiger Prü-fung keine Umstände bekannt, die die Annahme rechtfertigen könnten, dass ich nicht arischer Abstammung sei; insbesondere hat keiner meiner Eltern—oder Grosselternteile zu irgendeiner Zeit der jüdischen Religion angehört.

Ich bin mir bewusst, dass ich mich dienststrafrechtlicher Ver-folgung mit dem Ziele auf Dienstentlassung aussetze, wenn diese Erklärung nicht der Wahrheit entspricht.

I fully recognize that if Dr. Hamann wished to remain a lawyer, he had no option but to do it. Nevertheless, it was unsettling.

Three months later, on September 15, 1933, he made another dec-laration. This time he was answering the requirements of the April 11, 1933, "First Regulation for the Implementation of the Law for the Restoration of the Professional Civil Service." All officials had to attest to the history of their political activity, dating back to November 1918.

Dr. Hamann had handwritten on the form that, after his return from the war in 1919, he had been involved in establishing the German National Student Fraternity (*deutschnationale Studentenschaft*) at the University of Berlin and had risen to be Federal president of this organization (*Vorsitzender im Reich*). He had resigned from that office in 1920 when he took up an internship. Since then, he had not been politically active and was not a member of any political party.

The Nazis were particularly keen to know who was, or had ever been, a member of particular organizations. The form everyone had to fill in named them as follows: Black, Red, Gold Banner of the Reich (*Reichsbanner Schwarz-Rot-Gold*), which believed in defending par-liamentary democracy, the Republican Association of Judges (*der Republikanische Richterbund*) and Civil Service Association (*Beam-tenbund*), which both stood for an independent judiciary, the League for Human Rights (*die Liga für Menschenrechte*) or the Iron Front (*die Eiserne Front*), an anti-fascist, anti-Communist, anti-monarchist, pro-democracy paramilitary organization founded by the Social Democratic Party in 1931. Dr. Hamann signed his official declaration that he had never belonged to any of them.

His credentials to move in the slipstream of the Third Reich seemed impeccable. This man of such upright standing, I already knew, had been on the honorary committee of the House of German Art from 1938 (and not merely from 1941 as my earlier discovery had revealed). Curiously that fact does not appear on the official Bundesarchiv internet page about Dr. Hamann.[2]

But on rechecking his entry I saw that Dr. Hamann was listed as having been a member, in 1941, of the Committee for Insurance Law of the Academy for German Law (*Akademie für Deutsches Recht*). Hitler's lawyer, Hans Frank, founded the organization in 1933 and was its first president until 1942. (He also served as Governor-General of occupied Poland from October 1939. Tried at Nuremberg, he was hanged as a war criminal.) Frank intended the Academy should have some influence on Nazi legislation, though this never actually came to full fruition. It was a prestigious organization with members coming from the highest echelons of German public life—including Joseph Goebbels and Hermann Göring. Various committees were formed, aimed at developing the foundation for a National Socialist legal system. In September 1941, there were six Berlin members of the Committee dealing with mortgage law. These included two directors of the Allianz insurance company and two from the Victoria—Dr. Kurt Hamann and Ernst Teckenberg, whose early membership of the Nazi Party I had already uncovered. The Academy for German Law was not viewed favorably by the Allies at the end of the war.

---

2. http://www.bundesarchiv.de/aktenreichskanzlei/1919-1933/01a/adr/adrhl/kap1_1/para2_43.html

40

THE VICTORIA'S WAR

The relationship between those at the helm of the Victoria with their counterparts at the Allianz struck me as intriguing. I thought back to Professor Feldman's book on the history of the Allianz and spotted a connection. Since neither ERGO nor the University of Mannheim showed any appetite to investigate further the wartime activities of the Victoria Insurance Company, I thought I should at least try to do it myself. After all, this is the company that ruined the Wolff family's financial security (and that of countless other Jewish families), and by their actions altered a very large part of my personal family history.

Ambassador Stuart E. Eizenstat had long ago advised me to focus on the role of the insurance company involved in the seizure of the Wolff building. Perhaps I had paid insufficient attention to this particular angle of the story. To that end, I asked Beate Schreiber if she could search in the *Bundesarchiv* for the documents referred to by Professor Feldman in a footnote in his book on the history of the Allianz, which mentioned the consortium insuring workshops at Auschwitz. What exactly was being insured?

Within a couple of days, scanned copies of the paperwork arrived. The Victoria Insurance Company had argued to me in 2013 that it "played only a subordinate role as part of the Nazi-controlled economy between 1933 and 1945." But even a 10 percent share in a consortium was stomach churning.

I was staring at the Allianz-issued policy itself with the first page boldly stating that the insurance was for the factory of the *Deutsche Ausrüstungswerke GmbH* (DAW), a company owned by the SS (*Schutzstaffel*), Hitler's elite military unit.[1]

Translated as "German Equipment Works," DAW operated factories using forced labor in a number of concentration camps. The factory at Auschwitz, where 700 forced laborers were expected to work, was in the area of the main camp, known as Auschwitz I, although several hundred yards from the main barrack buildings. (The main extermination camp, Auschwitz-Birkenau, also known as Auschwitz II, lies to the northwest. A third camp to the east, Monowitz, also known as Auschwitz III, was the giant SS-run factory of I. G. Farben.)

The DAW factory location at Auschwitz was described on the insurance policy as *"Gelände des K.Z."* which translates as in "the grounds of the concentration camp." The policy was organized through the SS office in Kattowitz, a nearby Polish city. Although dated and signed on August 20, 1943, it was backdated to cover the period October 15, 1942, until October 15, 1943 but was renewable "jährlich"—on a yearly basis. The policy was for fire and explosions with coverage on the buildings, equipment, and materials in the carpentry workshop.

One section stood out:

Special security patrols are not taking place, because the workshop is located in the grounds of the concentration camp, which is under permanent military guard.

Eine besondere Bewachung findet nicht statt, da sich der Betrieb auf dem Gelände des Konzentrationslagers befindet, welches ständig militärisch bewacht wird.

The most astonishing part was the utterly mundane nature of the correspondence conducted between the Allianz, as lead insurer, and

---

1. BArch, Berlin NS 3/217 pages 052-057.

the SS bureaucrats. Two letters preceded the issuance of the formal insurance contract. The first, dated October 27, 1942, mentioned how the director of the Allianz's Kattowitz office would like to revisit the plant at Auschwitz, as he wanted to revalue the buildings before expanding the insurance coverage there![2]

As if insuring a perfectly ordinary workshop or factory, not one using forced laborers under appalling conditions, a letter, dated December 22, 1942, discussed quite nonchalantly how a reevaluation had now taken place.[3]

The sum to be insured had been raised from RM 1,535,100, as quoted in October, to a total of RM 2,136,150 made up as follows:

Buildings to new value of RM 1,000,000
Technical and commercial factory equipment actual cash value
   of RM 215,000
Resources, materials finished and unfinished, to maximum
   amount of RM 900,000
Cleanup costs of 1 percent at RM 21,150

And listed below that was the percentage each consortium member would be responsible for—the Victoria is listed at 10 percent.

Eight months later, on August 20, 1943, the full policy document revealed that the sum insured had risen once more and was now RM 3,217,000 with the annual premium set at RM 14,758.15. The Allianz received an income of RM 3,704.00 per annum, and the Victoria RM 1,481.65.

What exactly was going on in these buildings? An eyewitness report gives a horrifying portrait of what the forced laborers working in the DAW factory at Auschwitz endured. Rudolf Vrba, a Slovak inmate who had arrived at Auschwitz in June 1942, managed to escape from the camp in April 1944. Vrba had actually worked at the DAW factory in Auschwitz I. He later gave a detailed report of what was happening there.

---

2. BArch, Berlin NS 3/217 Pages 103-4.
3. BArch, Berlin NS 3/217 Pages 098-099.

My job was painting ski boards. We had to finish a minimum of 110 pieces per day; anyone who could not complete that amount was flogged in the evening. We had to work very hard to avoid the evening punishment. Another group manufactured boxes for shells. On one occasion 15,000 such boxes when finished were found to be a few centimeters shorter than ordered. Thereupon several Jewish prisoners, among them one Erdelyi (who was said to have relatives in Trencin-Ban), were shot for sabotage.[4]

Although the Victoria offered a highly sanitized version of its wartime activities in its 100th anniversary book published in 1953, its 150th anniversary volume, published in 2003, has a photo on page 81 of a group of Auschwitz prisoners staring from behind barbed wire. The accompanying caption explains that the photo is of inmates at the Auschwitz concentration camp after liberation by Soviet troops on January 27, 1945. It goes on to say that the camp was built in 1940 by the SS and in 1941 turned into a death camp, where a million people were killed. It came as no surprise to me that there is not the slightest hint of the Victoria's role at that camp.

The Victoria's 10 percent share in the Allianz-led consortium was not its sole involvement in the business of concentration camp insurance. Someone in Germany, aware of *Stolen Legacy*, e-mailed me with some very intriguing news. This is the dream scenario for a journalist—a source offering fresh information. I was told that there was another insurance policy relating to a different SS-owned factory. My informant said that papers in the *Bundesarchiv* would show this. I responded, asking for the reference numbers, and a message came back with the precise details. And sure enough, this person was as good as their word. In 1942, the Victoria had a 5 percent share in a consortium, put together by Allianz, issuing fire insurance for DAW workshops at the infamous Buchenwald concentration camp, near the city of Weimar in Germany. That facility, also using forced labor, produced wood and metal products for the SS.[5]

---

4. http://germanhistorydocs.ghi-dc.org/pdf/eng/English45.pdf.
5. BArch, Berlin NS3/279, page 199.

ALLIANZ UND STUTTGARTER VEREIN
VERSICHERUNGS · AKTIEN · GESELLSCHAFT

098

Vorsitzer des Aufsichtsrats: August von Finck · Vorstand: Dr. Hans Heß, Vorsitzer:
Edward Hilgard, Dr. Rudolf Schloßmann, Wilhelm Arendts, Dr. Carl Berthinger, Gustav Kaufmann, Georg Kögin, Dr. Paul Lux, Rudolf Märbin,
Dr. Clemens Malhoiss, Ludwig Neumßier, Dr. Alfred Wiedemann, Dr. Franz Noll, Dr. Walter Cyprian, Dr. Hans Goudefroy, Alfred Haase,
Dr. Friedrich-Carl Netsch, Dr. Johannes Nühlhauer, Ernst Rausche, Ludwig Simms.

Herrn
Reichsführer-SS

Amt W IV

Berlin-Lichterfelde-West
Unter den Eichen 127

		Stw. B.	Amt W IV / ___
Eing.: 2 8. DEZ. 1942	Abt.:
Akt. Nr.:	

| Ihre Zeichen | Ihr Schreiben vom | Unsere Zeichen | Berlin W8, Taubenstraße 1-2 |
| | | H/W/R.3) | 22.Dezember 1942 |

Feuer-Abteilung

Betrifft: S.A. 24 911a
Deutsche Ausrüstungswerke GmbH., Berlin-Lichterfelde-West,
Unter den Eichen 127
Wagnis: Auschwitz Krs. Bielitz   -   Vs. 908 506

Wir nehmen Bezug auf die Ende November ds. Js. mit Ihrem sehr
geehrten Herrn Dr. H o r n gehabte telefonische Besprechung,
wonach aufgrund des Ersatzantrages, den Sie uns inzwischen über
Herrn Subdirektor Max B e i e r zukommen ließen, ein neuer
Versicherungsschein ab 15. Oktober 1942 auf die Dauer eines
Jahres bei Außerkraftsetzung des bisherigen Versicherungsscheines
Nr. 908 506 ausgestellt werden soll. Der Ersatzantrag sieht eine
Gesamtsumme von 2.136.150 RM vor, die sich wie folgt verteilt:

Gruppe 1 - Gebäude zum Neuwert		1.000.000 RM
" 2 - technische und kaufmännische Betriebseinrichtung zum Zeitwert		215.000 RM
" 5 - Rohstoffe, unfertige und fertige Erzeugnisse pp. Höchstsumme Grundsumme 450.000 RM		900.000 RM
		2.115.000 RM
" 10 - Aufräumungskosten 1% (gegen bisher 2%)		21.150 RM
	zus.	2.136.150 RM.

Wir bestätigen Ihnen, dass das Werk Auschwitz nunmehr in Gesamthöhe von 2.136.150 RM verbindlich gedeckt worden ist. Von der
genannten Gesamthöhe haben übernommen:

die Aachener und Münchener	20 %
" Magdeburger	20 %
" Schlesische Feuer	15 %
" Victoria	10 %
" Silesia / Bielitz	10 %
" Allianz	25 %.

Durch Beschluß der Hauptversammlung vom 18. 0. 40 wurde unsere Firma
in Allianz Versicherungs-Aktiengesellschaft geändert.

December 22, 1942 letter
BArch, Berlin NS3/217 page 098

41

THE CURIOUS CASE OF
DR. EMIL HERZFELDER

The more I unearthed, the greater my skepticism about what I had been told. Did Dr. Emil Herzfelder really help to exonerate his successor, Dr. Hamann? Why would Dr. Herzfelder, a Jew hounded from his prestigious position in Germany to exile as a refugee in London, act as a referee for Dr. Hamann?

I felt I needed answers so, on February 28, 2016, I contacted Dr. Alexander Becker, Head of Special Tasks Communications at ERGO, the Victoria's parent company, asking to visit the archives to read and take copies of the documentary evidence. I explained that I was updating my book for a paperback edition and so "I therefore need to be able to complete writing within the next three months."

A few days later, I received an e-mail asking me to sign a form agreeing to submit any text to ERGO resulting from the use of the archives in order to avoid miscommunication and possible legal disputes. This was a first! Not one archive, institution, or library had ever stipulated such conditions. Had I been approaching a family and asking for access to personal letters, then I might have expected such a request.

ERGO is one of the largest insurance companies in Europe. I was not minded to sign such a document, since it could tie me up in arguments about whose interpretation of historical context was the more accurate.

Dr. Becker's e-mail contained the intriguing information that "Hamann was one of the very few CEOs of large insurance companies who was allowed to keep his post after 1945. We *assumed* (my emphasis) that the assessment of his predecessor, Emil Herzfelder, played a role in that."

What did this mean? That an assumption of integrity was made based on an assessment by one man, Dr. Herzfelder? Was there anything else? Surely ERGO had looked a bit deeper than that.

So what exactly was the status of Dr. Hamann?

The ERGO archives, Dr. Becker informed me, contain "extensive and cordial correspondence between Hamann and Herzfelder until the latter died in 1970 as well as documents dealing with the difficulties for Victoria management to ensure Herzfelder's remuneration from 1935 under the governmental foreign exchange controls."

Dr. Herzfelder had indeed given his views on Dr. Hamann. But this hardly amounted to a thorough vetting of his past.

The Finance Division of the Office of Military Government, United States (OMGUS), in readiness for the imminent defeat of Germany and the necessity of reconstituting a viable insurance system in the country, had sent a Captain Norbert A. Bogdan to interview Dr. Herzfelder in London.[1]

Capt. Bogdan's one-and-a-half-page report, dated April 11, 1945, included reference to Dr. Herzfelder's recommendations for three men as being "both politically reliable and outstanding in their field." One of the three was Dr. Hamann. I have the report. That is, apparently, the sum total of what Dr. Herzfelder had to say on the matter. This was before the end of the war. Did Dr. Herzfelder know that, under Dr. Hamann's leadership, the Victoria had been part of a consortium insuring buildings where forced laborers had worked for the SS at Auschwitz? I doubted it!

---

1. BArch, Koblenz OMGUS files (Office of Military Government for Germany (U.S.) Z 45 F 2/110/1.

I put this to Dr. Becker (at that point I was not yet aware of the Buchenwald connection). His response was not at all what I had expected and might offer a glimpse into why Prof. Dr. von Thadden suggested Dr. Hamann fell into some kind of moral "grey area" during the Nazi era. But, as I now discovered, Dr. Herzfelder was not an altogether objective referee for his successor.

Dr. Becker informed me that Emil Herzfelder had left Germany in 1935 on a business trip on behalf of the Victoria and, rather than return to Nazi Berlin, it was agreed that he would take on responsibility for its international business based first in Paris and later in London. His contract "ended in 1938 and it was not possible then to extend it." So, while the Victoria was foreclosing on multiple Jewish premises all over Berlin, including in 1937 the Wolff family building on Krausenstrasse, Dr. Herzfelder remained on the payroll of the company.

And, extraordinary as it may be, while Dr. Hamann was on the Honorary Committee of the House of German Art (alongside men who would emerge as the most notorious war criminals of the Third Reich), the Victoria maintained contact with, and indeed paid, the former Jewish chairman.

In the 1950s, according to Dr. Becker, Dr. Herzfelder's claims for his Victoria shares, life insurance, and pension benefits were all "amicably settled." He even brokered some more business for the Victoria from London! Dr. Hamann and Dr. Herzfelder "maintained a long-standing personal and business friendship" with Dr. Hamann making repeated visits to London to see his old friend until the latter's death in 1970.

Dr. Becker admitted that he was unable to confirm whether or not Dr. Herzfelder knew about the consortium insuring workshops at Auschwitz.

I managed to obtain a copy of Dr. Herzfelder's will from the British National Archives. His wife had predeceased him and there were no children. Dr. Herzfelder died on March 6, 1970, leaving his estate to a number of relatives and employees, including £50 (worth $125 at the time) to his gardener and £25 ($62) to his barber. Dr. Hamann is mentioned in the will, but not as a beneficiary. It transpires that Dr. Herzfelder owned two pieces of art that he wanted valued after his death and offered to Dr. Hamann, or his successor at the Victoria, if they were prepared to buy them. One was a portrait of the late Otto Gerstenberg, chairman of the Victoria Insurance Company from 1888 to 1913 and the other was an etching by Max Liebermann with Mr. Gerstenberg's signature. The proceeds of this sale were to be handed over to the trusts he had established for the benefit of his heirs. He left no personal memento to his former colleague, who was referred to in the will simply as "Dr. Hamann."

All this suggested to me that Dr. Herzfelder had never been a disinterested party to the fate and continuing employment of Dr. Hamann.

42

DIRECTIVE 38

The more I looked, the more I uncovered—that is the joy of successful research. In February 2016, I decided it was time to revisit the British National Archives in Kew where, twenty-three years previously, Simon had found the 1944 British War Office copy of "Who's Who in Nazi Germany" listing Kurt Hamann. Now I wanted to know whether the postwar Allied Control Authority, also known as the Allied Control Council (*Alliierter Kontrollrat*), had been aware of the existence of Dr. Hamann.

By mid-1944, it had become obvious that Germany was going to lose the war, and the Allies started preparations for dealing with the predicted collapse of the country. The Allied Control Council, formally constituted on August 30, 1945, comprised the United States, United Kingdom, and the Soviet Union. (France joined later and had a vote, but no duties). The remit of the Control Council was to issue laws, orders, proclamations, and directives that would enable the country to function by abolishing Nazi laws and organizations and returning Germany to structured civilian rule.

I wondered if there were files on any of these activities held in Kew that may be relevant to my story. I was in luck.

The Allied Control Authority had established a Coordinating Committee to consider the need for what was termed the Union of Berlin Insurance Companies (*Arbeitsgemeinschaft Berliner Versicherungsbetriebe*). Essentially, the Allies needed to know whether a central organization was required to help reestablish a nationwide German insurance industry. All four Allied powers were represented on the Committee and on March 15, 1947, their respective opinions were submitted for consideration (the US and UK delegations submitted jointly).

The Americans and British viewed the group as a medium for unofficial meetings of representatives of Berlin insurance companies. The Soviet delegation begged to differ.

They were vehemently opposed to what they viewed as an attempt to establish an insurance cartel, in direct violation of the tripartite decision made at the Potsdam Conference (held July 17–August 2, 1945), at which the US, UK, and Soviets had determined post-war European policy. Under a section headed "Economic Principles" was protocol IIIB, paragraph 12, to the effect that at the earliest practicable date, the German economy should be decentralized for the purpose of eliminating the present excessive concentration of economic power as exemplified in particular by cartels, syndicates, trust, and other monopolistic arrangements.[1]

Along with other complaints about the ambitions and membership of the Insurance Association, the Soviets pointed to the fact that it ". . . is headed by former directors of large Insurance Companies which formed part of the largest concern in Nazi-Germany and which were active throughout the country." Four individuals were named as being unacceptable—Dr. Hamann was one of them.

The Soviet delegation singled out Dr. Hamann as "one of the leaders of the [Insurance] Union" and complained that on March 8, 1946, he had defined the aim of the group as ". . . to organize in Berlin a powerful Island which will hold its position after the failure of an Eastern plan."

The reason they took particular exception to the Union was that ". . . the organizing principles of this Association are in agreement with the organizing principles of the largest German concerns which existed in Germany under Hitler. The Professional Association com-

---

1. http://www.ibiblio.org/pha/policy/1945/1945-08-02a.html.

prises at present 263 Insurance Companies, 83 of which are nation-wide, with branches throughout Germany. The role played by these companies in financing the war is well-known. For instance, in 1942 the Hitler Government was provided the sum of 9 billion Marks for military purposes, without compensation, by them."

In concluding their opinion on the future of the association, the Soviet delegation demanded that it be "dissolved immediately," that authority should be given to the Berlin Magistrate to hold special meetings with the heads of private insurance companies to discuss individual questions in regard to insurance undertakings of the City, and finally: "In view of the doubtful political past of the members of the Association it is necessary that they should be investigated in accordance with Directive no. 38 of the Allied Control Authority."[2]

What was Directive 38?

I searched for a copy on the Internet. Published in October 1946, its full title is: "The Arrest and Punishment of War Criminals, Nazis and Militarists and the Internment, Control and Surveillance of Potentially Dangerous Germans."[3]

The object of the Allies was to establish a common policy for Germany in punishing "war criminals, Nazis, Militarists, and industrialists who encouraged and supported the Nazi Regime." In order to carry out the principles established at the Potsdam Conference, it was deemed necessary ". . . to classify war criminals and potentially dangerous persons into five main categories and to establish punishments and sanctions appropriate to each category." Zone Commanders had "full discretion" as regards application of the principles set out in Directive 38. They and their local tribunals had the authority to upgrade or downgrade individuals between the five categories defining persons of concern:

1. Major offenders;
2. Offenders (activists, militarists, and profiteers);

---

2. British National Archives, FO 371/64566, 1947 Germany, File No. 3916. Minute dated 15 March 1947, Allied Control Authority Coordinating Committee, *Arbeitsgemeinschaft Berliner Versicherungsbetriebe* (Union of Berlin Insurance Companies). Appendix A, Opinion of the Soviet Delegation.

3. http://images.library.wisc.edu/History/EFacs/GerRecon/Denazi/reference/history.denazi.i0015.pdf.

3. Lesser offenders (probationers);
4. Followers;
5. Persons exonerated (those included in the above categories who can prove themselves not guilty before a tribunal).

I was curious why the Soviets might have thought Dr. Hamann worthy of investigation under the rubric of Directive 38. I examined the document in detail. Perhaps it was on account of Part II, Article 3 A:II:1 which stipulated that those people who fell into the second worst category of "Offenders" were "Activists" who had used "[p]ersonal reputation or his position of power in political, economic or cultural life . . ."

And then there was also Article 3 A:II, point 6:

Anyone who in the service of national socialism ridiculed, damaged or destroyed values of art or science . . .

Wasn't that the case of Dr. Hamann, as chairman of the Victoria, being on the honorary committee of the House of German Art?

Or how about Part II, Article 3, C:II, point 3 on "Offenders" being "Profiteers," which stated:

Anyone who obtained or strove for advantages for himself or others at the expense of those who were persecuted on political, religious or racial grounds, directly or indirectly, especially in connection with appropriations, forced sales, or similar transactions.

The terms "appropriations" and "forced sales" certainly struck me as apt, not only for what happened to my own family's building at Krausenstrasse 17/18, but also to the many other Jewish-owned properties foreclosed on.

Directive 38 contained a number of appendices. My attention was drawn to Appendix A, Part II which deals with people:

[w]ho, because of the character of the crimes allegedly committed by them . . . will be carefully investigated and, if the results of the investigation necessitate a trial, must be brought to trial as offenders and punished if found guilty.

There were two sections that were particularly pertinent. Section M on Private Business and Professions, point 10:

Private enterprises in industry, trade, commerce, handicraft, agriculture and forestry, banking, insurance, transportation, etc.—Enterprises which because of capital invested, the number of their employees, the kind of production, or for any other reason are, of themselves, important and essential.

And Section N on Jurists, point 1:

Managers and Treasurers of the *Akademie für Deutsches Recht* (Academy for German Law).

Finally, Appendix A, Part III, dealt with those persons who might be charged as "lesser offenders." The Allies believed this group should be "carefully investigated" and if there is evidence of guilt ". . . charged as lesser offenders and punished if found guilty."
Point 7:

Persons who have profited by acceptance or transfer of property incidental to the spoilation of formerly occupied territories, "Aryanizing" or confiscation of property on political, religious or racial grounds.

Point 18:

Employees of important enterprises in trade, industry, agriculture or finance with the title Generaldirektor, Direktor, President, Vicepresident . . . and all members of the Board of Directors, the chairmen and deputy chairmen of the Board of Supervision . . . in so far as they were policy-making technical personnel, and all persons with power to hire and fire employees.

Was it possible that the Soviets considered Dr. Hamann, as chairman (or, in German, *Generaldirektor*) of a major insurance company, was a certain candidate for scrutiny? So what happened? I knew that

Dr. Hamann, in his capacity as chairman of the Victoria, had been listed by the British War Office in 1944 as a member of the leadership of Nazi Germany. Did he not fit into the definition of someone who, at the very least, should be investigated? If not, why not?

I can only surmise.

The Victoria's head office on Lindenstrasse, Berlin, suffered major damage when, in February 1945, American bombers attacked the city in a daylight raid. Some 1,000 employees took shelter in the basement, and two were killed. Three months later, the war ended and the building was in the Soviet sector. The Victoria needed to find new premises.

It is not clear exactly where Dr. Hamann was living, but a letter, dated July 22, 1947 which I found in the US National Archives and Records Administration (NARA), College Park, Maryland, revealed that there was some confusion as to his whereabouts by at least two of the Allied Powers—the US and the UK. In a letter sent to a Col. J. R. Kellam in the Finance Division of British headquarters in Berlin, a Mr. H. L Gage, apparently an American based in Düsseldorf on detachment to the British Control Commission there, expressed frustration with Dr. Hamann. Two of Col. Kellam's colleagues had visited him making enquiries about Dr. Hamann, "who they thought spent much time in Düsseldorf." He went on: "They appeared to be interested in the exact nature of Hamann's powers to blind the Victoria company, both prior to and after occupation."[4]

If Dr. Hamann had decided to relocate his activities to Düsseldorf, in the British Zone, he might have made a wise decision. One insight into why can be gleaned from a letter I found, in a file at the British National Archives in Kew, dated March 9, 1949, from the Information Services Division in the British Zone of Hamburg to the HQ in Berlin. The subject line of the letter, written by a Mr. H. L. Ormond, was "Result of Denazification in the British Zone."

It is generally accepted that denazification in the British Zone has become a pure farce.[5]

---

4. U.S. National Archives and Records Administration, College Park, MD, Record Group 260, Records of U.S. Occupation Headquarters, World War II, M1922, roll 60, 00796.
5. British National Archives, FO 1049/1892, Denazification 1949. Letter dated 9 March 1949, Subject: Result of Denazification in the British Zone.

A mere four years after the end of the war, there was little appetite to pursue war criminals, Nazi collaborators, and those who had turned a blind eye. The world had had enough of all that.

It could be immensely irritating to Dr. Hamann's successors that I have raised the issue of the Victoria Insurance Company's wartime activities. But I really wanted to try to understand it all. So, on April 12, I e-mailed Dr. Becker with a list of questions about the results of my research. Just over two weeks later, on April 29, I received a response from him. He said he was sorry I was not coming to visit the archives, which are not usually open to the public. He explained that the user rules were derived from a 1998 "manual for business archives" and that no one has ever objected to them before. He told me that I did not have to seek approval or cede editorial control, merely allow for "clarification" of whatever I might write.

However, he was prepared to scan and send me any documents deemed relevant, although this could take some time due to "capacity constraints." Dr. Becker reminded me that the ". . . Victoria's headquarters in Berlin [had] been largely destroyed in February 1945, which resulted in the loss of a large part of business records and documents."

Curiously, he wrote: "Up to now, I did not come across documents pertaining to the topics raised in your mail. Therefore, we would be happy if you felt like sharing your findings with us." He concluded by asking me to provide him with a copy of Dr. Herzfelder's will.

This all seemed at odds with the official ERGO response I had received in August 2013 when I had been told that in recent decades the Victoria had invested considerable time and energy into researching its own history.

43

MANNHEIM AND HAMANN: THE MISSING YEARS

All my historical research led me constantly to wonder how Dr. Hamann had been able to hide his past so efficiently after the war. Not only had he been awarded Germany's highest civilian honor, the Federal Cross of Merit, in 1953, but he even had a foundation named after him. I needed to understand how this had come to be.

Surely a man who had been at the very pinnacle of a major insurance company all through the war years would have triggered some kind of investigation before such honors were bestowed upon him?

The history of the foundation, I discovered, was that in September 1978, a Professor Dr. Rudolf Wildenmann, former Director of Mannheim University, wrote to Dr. Hamann saying he was thinking of recommending him to the university's senate as an Honorary Senator. If Dr. Hamann agreed to such a proposal, the procedure could begin. Not surprisingly, a month later, Dr. Hamann accepted the offer. The resume submitted to the committee considering his appointment was four pages in length but was oddly lacking in detail about his wartime activities!

There was mention of his service for the Kaiser during World War I, his bar exams in 1925, his judicial activities working at *Amtsgericht Charlottenburg* which was followed by employment at the Federal Ministry of Economics. Shortly thereafter, in 1928, he was seconded as a consultant to the German Foreign Ministry and sent to work on economic issues, first in the German Consulate in Chicago and then at the embassy in Washington, D.C. On return to Germany, he had worked on matters concerning German World War I reparations payments. In 1932, he had joined the board of the Victoria Insurance Company in Berlin, becoming chairman in 1935. Naturally there is mention of his award of the Federal Cross of Merit in 1953 as well as a curious recommendation that "he has a pronounced sense of justice and his constant effort. . . ." ("*Sein ausgeprägtes Gerechtigkeitsempfinden und sein stetes Bemühen. . . .*").

The missing years don't seem to have troubled anyone at the University of Mannheim! Why was that? Could it have been that in early 1979, a mere four months after being invited to join the Senate, Dr. Hamann and Dr. Heinz Schmöle, his successor as chairman of the Victoria, offered DM 100,000 (about $55,000) towards a university foundation? On April 25, 1979, the Regional Council of Mannheim approved the establishment of the Dr. Kurt Hamann Foundation.

44

THE ENIGMA OF
DR. KURT HAMANN

On our 2015 trip to Berlin, Simon and I took a train from the Mitte district and headed southwest to the outer suburb of Dahlem. Our destination, 45 minutes away, was the quaint fourteenth-century St. Anne's Church (*Sankt-Annen-Kirche*), one-time parish of no less a figure than Martin Niemöller, who had been appointed junior pastor there in 1931.

Today he is widely known for the quotation, of which there are multiple renditions along the lines of:

> *First they came for the Socialists, and I did not speak out because I was not a Socialist* (sometimes "Socialists" is rendered "Communists").
>
> *Then they came for the Trade Unionists, and I did not speak out because I was not a Trade Unionist.*
>
> *Then they came for the Jews, and I did not speak out because I was not a Jew. Then they came for me—and there was no one left to speak for me.*

Yet the Lutheran Niemöller held pronounced anti-Semitic views, was devoutly anti-Communist, and welcomed Hitler's rise to power. Only when the Nazis attempted to apply their racial laws to church membership (and thereby exclude anyone classified as Jewish), did he object and take a stand. But this was because Niemöller felt that people who had converted to Christianity should not be discriminated against.

In May 1934, Niemöller had been a founding member of what came to be known as the Confessing Church, which declared open opposition to the Nazis' interference in church governance. He was arrested time and again from then on until 1937 when he was sentenced to seven months in prison. Not long after his release he was rearrested and spent over seven years in concentration camps, first in Sachsenhausen and then Dachau.

Niemöller recognized the German people's complicity with the Nazi regime (especially that of the Protestant church leadership) and believed they had to accept responsibility for the Holocaust. He admitted his own guilt at not having done enough to protect the victims of the Third Reich. Nevertheless, he disapproved of the way the denazification proceedings were conducted by the Allies, calling them a "witch hunt."

We quickly found Dr. Hamann's grave. It is in a prime position, close to the church itself. It had freshly delivered flowering plants around it.

Dr. Hamann's personal history is not so very hard to uncover, as I have proved. Despite my best endeavors, I have found no evidence to date that Dr. Hamann ever went through a denazification process. I have located no records to this effect in the *Bundesarchiv* offices based in Berlin, Lichterfelde, Koblenz, or Duisburg (which covers North-Rhine-Westphalia and thus Düsseldorf).

Some might argue that his role during the Nazi era was comparatively insignificant. I would beg to differ.

In the words of political philosopher John Stuart Mill: "A person may cause evil to others not only by his actions but by his inaction, and in either case he is justly accountable to them for the injury." Dr. Hamann is not with us today to explain himself. His memory, however, lives on.

Dr. Hamann was a luminary of German post-war society. Should he have been? I leave it to readers to form their own judgment.

As for the wartime history of the Victoria Insurance Company, I found enough to trouble me greatly. Is it not high time ERGO confronted the past of its subsidiary the Victoria and published a study along the lines of that conducted by the Allianz?

45

UNFINISHED BUSINESS

A few months after the hardback edition of *Stolen Legacy* was published, I received an e-mail from a total stranger in London. Lucy Hooberman wrote to tell me she had been searching for books that might describe the cultural life of Berlin Jews during the 1920s and 1930s and had chanced upon mine. Imagine her astonishment when she discovered mention of Dick & Goldschmidt, one of the companies renting office space in Krausenstrasse 17/18. Her maternal grandfather, Fritz Leopold Rosenthal, had once worked for the company. As a young man he had done an apprenticeship in the city of Bradford, in the north of England, in the wool textile industry. Just as my grandfather Herbert had done, Fritz Rosenthal had served in the German army during World War I. He had married in Budapest in 1924 and moved to Berlin, where Lucy's mother and uncle were born, and joined the firm of Dick & Goldschmidt. And, just like my grandfather, he had left Berlin in 1933. But instead of heading to the British Mandate of Palestine, he had gone to England. Dick & Goldschmidt had registered its business operations in Britain but had continued paying rent on office space in the Wolff building up to 1937 when the Victoria Insurance Company foreclosed on the mortgage.

When war broke out, Lucy's grandparents were evacuated to York-shire. By then Mr. Rosenthal had risen to be a director of Dick & Goldschmidt.

On a recent trip from Washington to London, Lucy and I met. We soon realized that we had more in common than merely our shared ancestral history in Berlin. We had, incredibly, both worked concurrently at the BBC for many years! The world truly is a small place!

This entire saga was never primarily about the money—although that was, of course, a great help to my mother and her siblings. It was about a principle—achieving a moral victory. In the process of recovering the building, mere bricks and mortar, I unearthed details and insights into my family history that would have been lost for all time had I not embarked on this enterprise.

I am not naïve enough to think that it would have been easy for the Victoria Insurance Company, and Dr. Kurt Hamann as chairman, to stand firm against the Nazi project. Nor do I allege the company was a major collaborator on a par with, say, the *Reichsbahn* or I.G. Farben. Nevertheless, it strikes me that Dr. Hamann's, albeit comparatively limited, role was sufficient to have given pause for thought. Even his low-key involvement in the Nazi economic and cultural endeavor, to my mind, raises questions about whether he really was a suitable recipient of a German federal honor and worthy of having an institution named for him. If I could discover so much, so easily about his past, surely others could have done the same.

My deadline—the end of May—to complete the updates for the paperback edition passed. But there remained a few loose ends.

I contacted Dr. Becker on June 1, 2016, and asked him if he was aware that the Victoria had been part of a consortium insuring Buchenwald. On June 6 he replied saying his archives revealed that, in 1997, the Victoria had received information about the Auschwitz and Buchenwald policies covering the workshops owned by the SS-affiliated DAW on the grounds of the two concentration camps. He gave me the *Bundesarchiv* reference for the consortium's annual insurance policy for the Buchen-wald factories, dated May 1943-May 1944. Thanks to Beate Schreiber at "Facts and Files" in Berlin, within days I had the documents themselves.[1]

---

1. BArch, Berlin, NS3/768 pages 052-055.

Dr. Becker also had some startling new information. He told me that in 1997 the company's then-archivist had visited the *Bundesarchiv* in Berlin ". . . and uncovered one more contract, also for a DAW enterprise, situated in Stutthof. In all three cases, the contracts were acquired by Allianz Sub-Director Max Beier (beginning in 1942), and the risk was then spread by building consortia."

Dr. Becker sent me a scanned copy of a one-month preliminary insurance policy, covering November 1—December 1, 1944, sent by Allianz to an SS office in Berlin. The documentation showed that Allianz had put together a consortium of six insurers—the Victoria's share had been 10 percent—insuring ten wood-processing workshops at the concentration camp at Stutthof.[2]

The United States Holocaust Memorial Museum has a great deal of information on this concentration and extermination camp. Built in September 1939, Stutthof is 22 miles east of Danzig (now Gdansk) in an area that today is part of Poland. The camp, where tens of thousands were incarcerated, was an especially brutal place. Many were killed in the gas chamber with Zyklon B or given lethal injections by the camp doctors. Others perished in typhus epidemics. Yet more were starved or simply worked to death.[3]

There are vivid first-hand testimonials from former prisoners on the USHMM website.[4]

Before the Soviet army liberated it on May 9, 1945, over 100,000 people had been incarcerated at Stutthof and more than 60,000 killed.

The DAW factory's supply of forced laborers came from the prisoners at the camp.

Dr. Becker went on to say he hoped his archivist would be able to send me copies of the correspondence between Dr. Hamann and Dr. Herzfelder by the end of June. I explained that my editor had extended the deadline to June 17 in order to accommodate him, but after that it would be too late.

On June 10, I received an e-mail from Prof. Dr. von Thadden, Rector of Mannheim University, who had been copied into the e-mail from

---

2. BArch, Berlin NS 3/269 pages 041-044.
3. https://www.ushmm.org/wlc/en/article.php?ModuleId=10005197.
4. https://www.ushmm.org/wlc/en/gallery.php?ModuleId=10005197&MediaType=OI.

Dr. Becker. He told me that a meeting of the Dr. Kurt Hamann Foundation board was likely to be held in early July.

> We need to have a board meeting in order to implement any change we may consider. Most changes further require the approval of the *"Regierungspräsidium"* in Karlsruhe (county administration). As in the U.S. there are strict laws governing the administration of foundations.
>
> I shall propose to the foundation board to dissolve the Hamann Foundation and to use the foundation capital to commission an extensive scientific study of Kurt Hamann's life, transferring any residual funds to the university foundation for charitable use according to the university foundation's bylaws. I expect ERGO to cooperate in this study, in particular to put its archive at the disposal of the historian undertaking the study. When I visited the ERGO last year for our first foundation board meeting, I found a lot of good will on the side of ERGO and a very professional and cooperative archive. I am therefore confident that things will develop as wished, but it is too early now to be more concrete.

Eleven months after *Stolen Legacy* was published, the future of the Dr. Kurt Hamann Foundation was finally coming under more serious scrutiny.

46

1943: DR. HAMANN
IS DENOUNCED

In the last week of June, my manuscript was finished and duly sent off to my editor, Jon Malysiak. He read it, made a few suggestions, and then forwarded it to the copy editor and design department.

On Sunday, July 3, the weekend of the U.S. Independence Day, Dr. Becker at ERGO, the parent company of the Victoria, sent me the first installment in a deluge of e-mails that continued over the following week—a total of 113 pages—just under 200MB of material. The documents, he said, were a "representative collection" he had chosen to give me a picture of Dr. Hamann.

The e-mailed papers were a disparate compilation. There was a curious single-page instruction written by Dr. Herzfelder on October 7, 1934, detailing notifications the Victoria might issue on his death and who should attend his funeral—he wanted to keep it small. Also included was material relating to Dr. Herzfelder's appointment in 1935 as head of the international division of the Victoria and the company's formal notification of this change to the various Nazi authorities.

Six pages of scanned documents contained the denazification form of the Victoria's chief actuary, Dr. Carl Wolfgang Sachs, a board member from 1932–1965. Dr. Sachs declared himself to be a Protestant, though his father had been born a Jew. Under the Nazis, this meant he was classified as only a *"Halbjude"* (half-Jew), thus able to remain in his job. In January 1945, the Gestapo had sent poor Dr. Sachs to a forced labor camp near Dresden, from which he had been liberated in April by Allied troops. Dr. Sachs had filled in the post-war Military Government of Germany's *Fragebogen* (questionnaire).

Dr. Becker wrote that he could find no denazification papers relating to Dr. Hamann.

A collection of letters from Dr. Herzfelder, written after the war, revealed how he had sought information and evidence from the Victoria about his former contracts of employment, annuity, pension, and shares, to which Dr. Hamann had responded personally. And there was copious correspondence about a 1950s court case brought by a former Jewish manager of the Victoria, Kurt Jachmann, who by then was living in New York and suing for compensation. (He lost the case after both Dr. Hamann and Dr. Herzfelder disputed his claim.) Some very dull post-war documents dealing with the re-establishment of the Victoria's supervisory boards was included, along with several exchanges of friendly personal letters between Dr. Hamann and Dr. Herzfelder from the late 1940s to the latter's death in 1970.

It is clear that the two men wrote to one another often, with courteous birthday greetings, news of holidays, congratulations on the Victoria's centenary celebrations, and even mention of Dr. Hamann visiting his friend in London, as well as discussion of business matters between the Victoria and National & Colonial Insurance in London—Dr. Herzfelder's new employer.

Although Jon, my editor, had put the manuscript into production, I asked if he would allow me to write an extra chapter to cover this additional material. The June 17 deadline had passed, but he said he would see what could be done.

Dr. Becker wrote that he would have far preferred me to visit the archive in Düsseldorf "to prevent any later discussion about the selection of the documents." Helpfully, he had written an explanatory note guiding me through the scanned papers. At the very top of his list of numbered points, he drew my attention to the contents of one tranche of documents he was sending.[1] These concerned an anonymous denunciation in 1943 of Dr. Hamann "for helping his Jewish friend Herzfelder." It had been sent to the Reich Supervisory Agency for Insurance, the Nazi organization that regulated the Victoria insurance company.

This sounded intriguing, and so I turned my attention first to the vicious denunciation of Dr. Hamann, dated June 26, 1943. In essence, the main allegations made were:

- In the summer of 1932, Dr. Herzfelder was elected chairman of the Victoria insurance company and soon afterwards brought in his friend, Dr. Kurt Hamann. After the Nazis came to power in 1933, Dr. Hamann (who, the accuser noted, was not a member of the party) was appointed operations manager.
- In 1934, Dr. Herzfelder recognized that he would not be able to keep his position and started to prepare for his emigration—assisted by Dr. Kurt Hamann.
- "In retrospect one can recognize that the friends had a well thought out plan." Dr. Herzfelder ensured that Dr. Hamann became his successor, and in return, Dr. Hamann ensured Dr. Herzfelder's economic future abroad.
- In the summer of 1935, Dr. Herzfelder did not return from a business trip. He stayed in London. After the *Nürnberger Judengesetze* (the anti-Jewish Nuremberg Laws) were passed, it became clear that Dr. Herzfelder would not return to Germany.
- Dr. Hamann knew of Dr. Herzfelder's emigration plans. Instead of firing him, Dr. Hamann commissioned him to manage the international businesses of the Victoria Insurance Company (to the great surprise of the overall management of the international business department).

---

1. ERGO Archive, A0503-00002 Bd. 03.

- Dr. Herzfelder's contract was renewed, even though he had emigrated abroad—which should have rendered him ineligible for employment.
- It is incomprehensible how someone could conclude a five-year-contract with a Jew, despite clear orders from the government to eliminate Jews from the economy. This indicates Dr. Hamann's malicious intent from the start.
- Dr. Hamann wanted to tie himself to the Jew for the long term in order to force the Victoria to pay Dr. Herzfelder for as long as possible.
- Although Dr. Hamann did not officially contribute to the contract—while unofficially, he surely did—he should have annulled it and dismissed Dr. Herzfelder without compensation, although they were friends and Dr. Hamann owed Dr. Herzfelder his job.
- It was a mockery, and not in the interests of the Victoria Insurance Company, that Dr. Hamann appointed an emigrant as the head of the department for international business.
- Dr. Herzfelder was well paid and also reimbursed for his business trips. If this is the case, then it could only have been possible through false information, since all payments should have been approved by the authorities.
- The contention that they [the Victoria] had to commission Herzfelder into the international business department because no one else was available is so ridiculous that it is not worth commenting on. (*Der Einwand, das Auslandsgeschäft hätte Herzfelder übergeben werden müssen, da niemand anderes zur Verfügung gestanden hätte, ist so lächerlich, dass es sich nicht lohnt dazu Stellung zu nehmen.*)
- Dr. Hamann awarded Dr. Herzfelder a lifelong pension, payable in Germany. Someone who does this for an emigrated Jew, a declared enemy of the Reich, gives him the hope of returning to Germany.
- It basically means that this German business leader [Hamann] is hoping for the fall of the Reich. (*. . . es beudetet im Grunde, dass dieser deutsche Wirtschaftsführer auf den Untergang des Reiches hofft.*)

- In summary, it has to be said that Dr. Hamann bought his position from his friend Dr. Herzfelder, and he violated his duties and paid Dr. Herzfelder with money and foreign exchange from the Victoria. Due to his previous behavior, it is entirely possible that Dr. Hamann will continue to support Dr. Herzfelder with payments as soon as he finds an opportunity.

Dr. Hamann was informed of this denunciation shortly after it was made and, on July 14, submitted a ten-page response, with attachments. As a study in how a man at the pinnacle of his profession, occupying a leading position in the business world during the Third Reich, rebutted the accusation of being friendly to Jews, Dr. Hamann's response is most illuminating.

He stated that he had been appointed to the Victoria board on September 1, 1932. Before that he had been an advisor at the Economic Ministry. He had met Dr. Herzfelder in 1926 while dealing with export credit insurance, but after that he had been assigned to a different field and had not seen Dr. Herzfelder again until 1932. It was, therefore, inappropriate to say that he and Dr. Herzfelder were friends. In fact, he owed his recruitment to the Victoria to the influential former chairman, Dr. Otto Gerstenberg, whom he had known for many years.

Dr. Hamann asserted that it was false to allege he had helped Dr. Herzfelder prepare to emigrate. Dr. Herzfelder had indeed been on a business trip when the Nuremberg Laws were passed. Given the content of the new legislation, it had become clear to both Dr. Herzfelder and the Victoria's supervisory board that he could no longer remain as chairman. Dr. Herzfelder went to London and the former chairman of the supervisory board, Dr. Scharf, traveled there to negotiate personally with him. Dr. Herzfelder had resigned as chairman of the Victoria and was commissioned to lead the international business department.

In a revealing and insulting comment, Dr. Hamann wrote that the legal situation did not allow the Victoria to fire Dr. Herzfelder immediately.

In contrast with other Jews, apart from his belonging to the Jewish race there was nothing incriminating against Herzfelder.

*Gegen Herzfelder lag im Gegensatz zu zahlreichen anderen Juden
abseits seiner Zugehörigkeit zur jüdischen Rasse nichts Belas-
tendes vor.*

Dr. Hamann continued that it had been out of the question, in the
view of the Victoria's supervisory board, to transfer Dr. Herzfelder to
other work in Germany. But on the other hand, it was also not acceptable to continue paying him without his working for the company, as
this would free Dr. Herzfelder to seek employment in another country.
He feared that if Dr. Herzfelder had decided to sue the Victoria in a foreign court, this would surely have been used for propaganda purposes
against the interests of Germany.

Dr. Hamann explained that he was unable to take on the responsibilities of Dr. Herzfelder and there was no other suitable person available.

Dr. Hamann revealed that the Victoria's supervisory board had
something else in mind. The insurance sector in most of the countries
the Victoria operated in was strongly influenced by Jews. And he gave
an example of the Balkan nations, where the Victoria's subsidiaries had
mostly Jewish directors.

The procedure against these Jewish employees who should
have been dismissed quickly and efficiently in accordance with
National-Socialist [Nazi] principles encountered massive criticism and complete incomprehension with the relevant authorities in the countries concerned. Every time I was going to dismiss
a Jewish director in accordance with the Berlin party orders, the
countries emphasized that their general public would see this as
a hostile political action for which the Victoria would be held
responsible.

*Das Vorgehen gegen diese jüdischen Kräfte, die dem national-
sozialistischen Grundsätzen entsprechend möglichst schnell und
wirksam abzubauen waren, stiess damals in diesen Ländern an
den maasgebenden Stellen noch auf starke Ablehnung und völlige
Verständnislosigkeit, und jedes Mal, wenn ich im Einvernehmen*

mit Berliner Parteistellen zu dem Abbau eines jüdischen Leiters schritt, wurde mir aus den betreffenden Ländern bedeutet, dass dies in der dortigen Öffentlichkeit als eine feindliche politische Aktion angesehen werde, für die man die Victoria im ganzen verantwortlich machen würde.

And so it seems, according to Dr. Hamann, that the Victoria's supervisory board came up with an ingenious but vile plan.

The board decided that it was useful to continue employing Dr. Herzfelder, because he was able to fire a number of Jewish directors and they could not accuse him of being antisemitic.

As a result, by 1939, the Victoria Insurance Company succeeded in Aryanizing its entire extensive foreign branches, which would not have been possible without serious damage if we had tried to execute the orders out of pure political interests and in a rush.

Im Ergebnis wurde erreicht, dass die Victoria bis zum Jahre 1939 ihre gesamte umfangreiche Auslandsorganisation ohne schwere Schädigung der deutschen Belange und der Interesen des Unternehmens arisiert hatte, was nicht möglich gewesen wäre, wenn man diese Massnahmen unter rein politischen Vorzeichen durchgeführt und zeitlich überstürzt hätte.

The work of Herzfelder was, from the start, set in this context.

Die Tätigkeit Herzfelders wurde daher von vornherein unter diesen Gesichtspunkt gestellt.

Dr. Hamann explained that Dr. Herzfelder only ever traveled once, or not at all, to countries where the *Judenproblem* (Jewish problem) did not exist, such as Portugal, Spain, Denmark, and Sweden.

Dr. Herzfelder had started in Austria and, by the end of 1937, finished working in Romania and Hungary. By March 1938, he had completed his work in Czechoslovakia, Greece, and Bulgaria.

Continuing his defense, Dr. Hamann set out in detail the basis of his predecessor's remuneration and his own role in depriving Dr. Herzfelder of it. As chairman of the Victoria, Dr. Herzfelder had received a substantial salary with bonus. From 1936 on, he had been paid considerably less but only received a fractional amount to use outside of Germany—as an emigrant, the rest had all been transferred into a mandatory blocked account. When Dr. Herzfelder's contract of employment expired in 1939, he was entitled to a pension. However, Dr. Hamann wrote that he had refused him a payout, as Dr. Herzfelder was a hostile Jew who had emigrated to an enemy country (meaning Britain).

In his statement, Dr. Hamann wrote that the Victoria had kept the Nazi authorities informed throughout Dr. Herzfelder's employment with the company since he stepped down as chairman. On November 4, 1935, Dr. Hamann and fellow board member Ernst Teckenberg had written to the Economics Minister, informing him they had commissioned Dr. Hamann to work for the Victoria's international department. They asked that Dr. Herzfelder be released from the limitations of dual residency, stating that it was yet to be decided where he would live abroad, and requested permission to pay him RM 3,000 a month overseas. They attached a declaration of all Dr. Herzfelder's assets in Germany—his stocks, insurance policies, and even his house at Bismarckstrasse 18/20. Ironically, this was just across the Kleine Wannsee lake from my mother's former home at Conradstrasse 1. The Wolff family and Dr. Herzfelder had been practically neighbors!

On June 7, 1938, Dr. Hamann and Ernst Teckenberg wrote together to Herr Schulz, a Gestapo officer based at the infamous Prinz Albrechtstrasse headquarters of the Nazi secret police, informing him about monies paid by the Victoria during 1937 to Dr. Herzfelder and itemizing precisely how it was used. Various taxes and debt repayments consumed the entire amount. And on the same day, Dr. Hamann wrote another letter to Herr Schulz, telling him that in the period from January 1937 to March 1938, Dr. Herzfelder had been to Austria, Czechoslovakia, Hungary, Bulgaria, and Romania. However, his work commitments were now being reduced.

The paperwork was in front of me. This is how the Nazis came to take all of Dr. Herzfelder's possessions. Dr. Hamann concluded his defense to the anonymous denunciation by stating that, after the order about handling enemy property was issued, the Victoria had been obliged to report on insurance contracts it held. In August 1940, the Gestapo confiscated the policies belonging to people, such as Dr. Herzfelder, who had left Germany. Then, in late 1941, the 11th Amendment to the Reich Citizen Law was passed, legalizing the confiscation of the remaining assets belonging to Jews who had emigrated.

Therefore, Herzfelder never received a penny of his pension nor his invalidity pension.

Herzfelder hat daher niemals einen Pfenning Pension oder Invaliditätsrente erhalten.

These documents left me with further questions. How can one judge Dr. Kurt Hamann? And how should we judge Dr. Herzfelder, if Dr. Hamann's assertions were accurate that he was used by the Victoria to fire fellow Jews? How was Dr. Hamann able to revive his friendship so swiftly with Dr. Herzfelder after the war? Did Dr. Herzfelder ever know what his friend had written about him? Was Dr. Hamann's self-defense a true picture of what really happened or was it just posturing to save his own position?

I ask myself over and over: Was Dr. Hamann an evil enabler of Nazi goals—leading a company that foreclosed on Jewish properties, sacked Jewish employees, participated in consortiums insuring SS-owned slave labor workshops in death camps? Or was he just an insurance professional living in troubled times, looking after himself but being generous, as far as he was able, to his Jewish predecessor?

The case for being forgiving of Dr. Hamann is undermined by the facts that beyond his responsibilities at the Victoria Insurance Company, he also joined the Nazi cultural institution, the House of German Art, and was involved at the Academy of German Law, attempting to redraft insurance law along Nazi lines. He was also sufficiently prominent a personality to have attracted the attention of the Allies, who named him in the 1944 edition of the British War Office publication *"Who's Who in Nazi Germany."* He was, therefore, an active participant in Hitler's dream for Germany. He escaped censure, but I believe it is not too late to pass judgment.

I am acutely aware that millions of people perished during the war. Communities were wiped out. The long, rich, history of European Jewish culture across the continent was, by and large, destroyed. The Wolff family's plight does not compare with what so many others went through. Mass murder is obviously the incomparably greater crime than the injustice of a stolen building.

But in telling my family's story I believe I have shown that, with perseverance and a just legal system, it is possible to right a wrong. More importantly, I have fulfilled a fundamental, indeed priceless, human desire—to discover one's own link to the past.

Nowadays I frequently meet people who desperately want to tell me their own tragic tales—of insurance policies unpaid, pensions not honored, buildings lost, art works plundered and inheritances vanished. It is heartbreaking. They, just like me, want to reclaim their own legacies and recover what was stolen from them. I wish them well.

I can only agree with Ambassador Stuart E. Eizenstat, who wrote in the foreword, that there is still so much unfinished business from the Nazi era.

POSTSCRIPT

A Plaque at Last

In August 2014, after I heard from Lutz Lange at the Federal Agency for Real Estate that he would inform me about progress on a plaque to be affixed to the wall at the entrance to Krausenstrasse 17/18, I sat back and waited . . . and waited!

Nothing happened.

Almost two years and several e-mail exchanges later, there was still no progress. In spring 2016, I was contacted by the BBC and asked if I would fly to Berlin to take part in a short film about my quest to recover the building and discover my family history. The BBC contacted the German authorities, asking for permission to film there and informed them that plans were in place for a cameraman and production team to fly to Berlin. Within days, I received an e-mail that my request for a plaque had now been approved and I was asked to submit my desired wording.

Perhaps it would have happened in due course, though the lack of response to my e-mails suggests to me that it would not. In my opinion, the news that the BBC would be arriving focused the bureaucrats' minds! Indeed, when I turned up with the crew at the entrance to the building, not only was Herr Lange there to greet me, but he was accompanied by a colleague who showed me an example of what the plaque would look like.

In July 2016, a plaque was duly affixed to the outside wall at the entrance to Krausenstrasse 17 (in summer 2013, the Wolff building, formerly known as 17/18 was renumbered as simply 17 and its neighbor, the former 19/20 is now plain number 18). It reads, in German and English, as follows:

Das Wolff Haus

Die Krausenstraße 17 wurde im Jahre 1909 als Sitz der Pelzfirma H. Wolff gebaut, eine der ältesten jüdischen Modefirmen Berlins, gegründet 1850.

Während der NS-Zeit wurde das Eigentum an diesem Grundstück zwangsweise an die Deutsche Reichsbahn übertragen. Nach der Wiedervereinigung erwarb die Bundesrepublik Deutschland im Jahr 1996 das Grundstück von den Wolff' schen Erben.

Das Gebäude ist als Baudenkmal ausgewiesen.

The Wolff Building

Krausenstraße 17 was constructed in 1909 as the headquarters of the H. Wolff fur company, one of Berlin's oldest Jewish fashion firms.

During the Nazi era ownership was forcibly transferred to the German Railways. In 1996, after reunification, the German Government purchased the building from the Wolff heirs.

The building is designated an historic monument.

SELECT BIBLIOGRAPHY

IN ENGLISH:

Authers, John, and Richard Wolffe. *The Victim's Fortune: Inside the Epic Battle over the Debts of the Holocaust.* New York: HarperCollins, 2002.

Barkai, Avraham. *From Boycott to Annihilation—The Economic Struggle of German Jews 1933–1943.* Hanover, NH: University Press of New England, 1989.

Bazyler, Michael J. *Holocaust Justice: The Battle for Restitution in America's Courts.* New York: New York University Press, 2003.

Czech, Danuta. *Auschwitz Chronicle 1939–1945.* From the Archives of the Auschwitz Memorial and the German Federal Archives.

Dean, Martin, Constantin Goschler, and Philipp Ther, eds. *Robbery and Restitution: The Conflict over Jewish Property in Europe.* New York, Oxford: Berghahn Books, 2007.

Dean, Martin. *Robbing the Jews: The Confiscation of Jewish Property in the Holocaust, 1933–1945.* New York: Cambridge University Press, 2008.

Dwork, Deborah, and Robert Jan van Pelt. *Flight from the Reich: Refugee Jews, 1933–1946.* New York: W.W. Norton, 2009.

Eizenstat, Stuart E. *Imperfect Justice—Looted Assets, Slave Labor, and the Unfinished Business of World War II.* New York: Public Affairs, 2003.

Feldman, Gerald D. *Allianz and the German Insurance Business, 1933–1945.* New York: Cambridge University Press, 2001.

Freeman, Simon. *Getting Their Own Back*. London: ES: The Evening Standard Magazine, 1992.

Gilbert, Martin. *The Holocaust—The Jewish Tragedy*. London: Collins, 1986.

Gross, Leonard. *The Last Jews in Berlin*. New York: Simon and Schuster, 1982.

Kreutzmüller, Christoph, *Final Sale in Berlin: The Destruction of Jewish Commercial Activity 1930-1945*. Berghahn Books, English language edition, 2015. Translated by Jane Paulick and Jefferson Chase.

Larson, Erik. *In the Garden of Beasts: Love, Terror, and an American Family in Hitler's Berlin*. New York: Crown, 2011.

Le Tissier, Tony. *Berlin Then and Now*. London: Battle of Britain Prints International, 1992.

Levin, Itamar. *The Last Chapter of the Holocaust: The Struggle over the Restitution of Jewish Property in Europe*. Jerusalem: Jewish Agency for Israel, 1998.

Megargee, Geoffrey P. *Encyclopedia of Camps and Ghettos 1933–1945 Vol I*. Bloomington: Indiana University Press, 2009.

Meyer, Beate, Harmann Simon, and Chana Schutz. *Jews in Nazi Berlin: From Kristallnacht to Liberation*. Chicago: University of Chicago Press, 2009.

Miller, Douglas. *Via Diplomatic Pouch*. New York: Didier, 1944.

Miller, Douglas. *You Can't Do Business with Hitler: What a Nazi Victory Would Mean to Every American*. Boston: Little, Brown, 1941.

O'Connor, Anne-Marie. *The Lady in Gold: The Extraordinary Tale of Gustav Klimt's Masterpiece, Portrait of Adele Bloch-Bauer*. New York: Alfred A. Knopf, 2012.

Rürup, Reinhard, ed. *Topography of Terror: Gestapo, SS and Reichsicherheitshauptamt on the Prinze-Albrecht-Terrain. A Documentation*. Berlin: Arenhovel, 1991.

Segel, Harold B., and Egon Erwin Kisch. *The Raging Reporter: A Bio-Anthology*. West Lafayette, IN: Purdue University Press, 1997.

Shirer, William L. *Berlin Diary: The Journal of a Foreign Correspondent 1934–1941*. Boston: Little, Brown, 1941.

Silver, Daniel B. *Refuge in Hell: How Berlin's Jewish Hospital Outlasted the Nazis*. New York: Houghton Mifflin, 2003.

Snyder, Louis L. *Encyclopedia of the Third Reich*. New York: Paragon House, 1989.

Stoltzfus, Nathan. *Resistance of the Heart: Intermarriage and the Rosenstrasse Protest in Nazi Germany*. New York: W.W. Norton, 1996.

de Waal, Edmund. *The Hare with Amber Eyes: A Hidden Inheritance*. London: Chatto and Windus, 2010.

IN GERMAN:

Gottwaldt, Alfred, und Diana Schulle. *Die Judendeportationen aus dem Deutschen Reich 1941–1945*. Wiesbaden: Marix Verlag, 2005.

Gottwaldt, Alfred, und Diana Schulle. *Juden ist die Benutzung von Speisewagen untersagt—Die antijüdische Politik des Reichsverkehrsministeriums zwischen 1933 und 1945*. Teetz: Hentrich & Hentrich, 2007.

Gottwaldt, Alfred. *Die Reichsbahn und die Juden 1933–1939—Antisemitismus bei der Eisenbahn in der Vorkriegszeit*. Wiesbaden: Marix Verlag, 2011.

Hundert Jahre: Victoria Versicherung 1853 to 1953. West Berlin: Victoria-Feuer-Verischerungs AG, 1953.

Im Zug der Zeiten—150 Jahre Victoria. Düsseldorf: Victoria Versicherungs-Gesellschaften, 2003.

Jah, Akim. *Die Deportation der Juden aus Berlin: Die nationalsozialistische Vernichtungspolitik und das Sammellager Grosse Hamburger Strasse*. Berlin: be.bra Wissenschaft Verlag, 2013.

Westphal, Uwe. *Berliner Konfektion und Mode: die Zerstörung einer Tradition, 1836–1939*. Berlin: Edition Hentrich, 1986.

ACKNOWLEDGMENTS

I am indebted to many people for their help and encouragement while researching and writing this book.

My mother was invaluable from the start. She spent many hours answering my questions, reminiscing into my tape recorder, translating countless documents from German into English and, stoically, even agreed to being interviewed for three days on camera. She proofread my drafts and held the manuscript galleys, which I was editing while visiting her in London. She died on January 30, 2015, a week after she turned 93 and, sadly, never held the finished book which she had so eagerly anticipated. I was in London with her. She would have been gratified to know that her beloved uncle Fritz is not forgotten.

I am grateful to my cousin Leor Wolff in Tel Aviv for helping me find the address of the building and for his efforts in tracking down Israeli death certificates and wills. I was thrilled when, in January 2016, he became a father and named his son Hillel. We now have a revival in the family of the illustrious "H.Wolff" name. My aunt Marion kindly gave me her many memories of growing up in Palestine. People who helped me with photographic research and illustrations include my cousin Danny Wolff (son of Heini), Israeli tour guide Yoav Avneyon as well as Kibbutz Sde Boker archivist Aviva Popper. Tamar Merose graciously agreed to my use of the photo of her cousin Barbara Propper.

In Berlin, Josef-Thomas Göller played a more important part than he could possibly know at the time by finding the pre-war German business directory that confirmed the address of the Wolff family building. Dr. Christoph Kreutzmüller, then working in the Department of Modern History at Humboldt-University, now a curator at the

Jewish Museum in Berlin, mined his database in search of records for the company H. Wolff.

Manolya Ezgimen in Berlin embraced the story wholeheartedly. The photographs she found brought to life the fashionable fur coats my great grandfather once produced and the business headquarters he built. Author and broadcaster Uwe Westphal enlightened me with his detailed knowledge of the pre-war Jewish fashion world. His guidance and friendship in the process of updating the book for the paperback edition has been extraordinary.

Beate Schreiber, at historical research firm "Facts and Files," employed her expertise on German archives enabling me to gain deeper insights into my family's past.

Prof. Dr. Rebecca Boehling's former colleagues at the International Tracing Service (ITS) in Bad Arolsen, Ute Peters and Verena Neusüs, diligently searched their records for me.

Dr. Ulrich Baumann, deputy director of the Foundation Memorial to the Murdered Jews of Europe, offered me advice on where to search and also managed to decipher the faded 1944 document listing Fritz's residual assets.

Dr. Astrid Ley at the Sachsenhausen Memorial and Museum supplied me with documents giving details of Fritz's detention at that camp.

Juliane Grossmann and Uta Fröhlich at the Nazi Forced Labor Documentation Center of the Topography of Terror Foundation made many suggestions of where I might find information.

I appreciate the efforts of Erika Hausotter at the FHXB Friedrichshain-Kreuzberg Museum who sent me an old photograph of the building at Dresdener Strasse 97, now demolished.

Gisela Erler at the Landesarchiv, Berlin, Diana Finke archivist at the Geheimes Staatsarchiv Preussischer Kulturbesitz (Secret State Archives of Prussian Heritage), Marianne Schmal at the Bundesarchiv Berlin-Lichterfelde and Dr. Martin Müller head of Corporate History and Archives at Deutsche Bank AG, were all immensely helpful. At ERGO Insurance, my thanks to Markus Holmer, historian and archivist, who provided me with the photograph of Dr. Kurt Hamann as well as to Dr. Alexander Becker for answering my queries and supplying me with scanned documents and a photograph of Dr. Emil Herzfelder.

Dr. Akim Jah offered me his expertise on the deportations of Berlin's Jews during the infamous 1943 Fabrikaktion. Dr. Bernhard Bremberger, an expert on forced labor during the Nazi era, made many recommendations on where I should look for more material.

I am profoundly grateful to Mary Bianchi at the Stolpersteine-Berlin project, for her assistance in organizing a "stumbling stone" and to Gunter Demnig for placing it in the sidewalk where Dresdener Strasse 97 was once located.

Without the help of Barbara Welker, archivist at the *Neue Synagoge* Berlin—Centrum Judaicum Foundation, I would never have uncovered the one, last, incredible detail of Fritz's history.

At the United States Holocaust Memorial Museum, librarians Megan Lewis, Ronald Coleman and Vincent Slatt went out of their way to guide me through the immense amount of material in the archives. Others at the museum who gave me their time include Peter Landé, Judith Cohen, William Connelly and Bashi Packer. I was also fortunate to tap the expert knowledge of Dr. Robert M. Ehrenreich (Director, University Programs).

This book is substantially enriched by the research of the producers of the two radio programs: Holger Jackisch of Mittel Deutsche Rundfunk who tragically died of cancer at the age of only 42 in 2001 and my former BBC colleague Nigel Acheson who died also of cancer in 2008 aged 57. I remember them both fondly.

I will always be indebted to Hans Marcus, Dr. Sybille Steiner, Dr. Karsten Kühne and Inge Bahlmann, my mother's legal team in Britain. The law firm to which they belonged was Pritchard Englefield & Tobin which, in September 1992, changed its name to Pannone & Partners. Since May 1, 2013 the firm has been known as Thomas Eggar LLP.

Dr. Sandie Byrne and her colleagues at Oxford University's Department of Continuing Education encouraged me to write this book during my three-week study stay at the university's Exeter College in the summer of 2012.

Susanne Jünger, a former BBC colleague, helped organize and translate many of the assorted German language letters and legal papers I had gathered over the course of the claim.

In Washington D.C., the editor of *Moment* magazine, Nadine Epstein, and my colleagues there all tolerated my absence from the office while I finished this book. Thanks to Gritt Wehnelt and Michael Czogalla for proofreading the hardback edition. I was fortunate that Thomas Siurkus was in Washington at *Moment* as a visiting fellow from Germany on the "Action Reconciliation Service for Peace" program and able to help research and translate the new archival material for the paperback edition.

My appreciation goes to Richard Yates of Hybrid Studios for designing and developing the book's online presence at www.stolenlegacy.com and to my publicist in Washington D.C., Jill Bernstein.

Patrick Anderson worked on the first draft of the hardback edition, turning a complicated tale into a more comprehensible narrative.

My friend and literary agent, Robbie Anna Hare, saw the potential for this story from when I first gave her the outline. She made many suggestions on how to improve its telling and steered it through to completion. Any writer lucky enough to secure her talent and persistence will indeed be fortunate. Robbie and her colleague at Goldfarb & Associates, Ronald Goldfarb, supported by Gerrie Sturman, are a force to be reckoned with.

Ambassador Stuart E. Eizenstat's advice that the story was worth telling was greatly appreciated. His wisdom was the impetus I needed to complete the manuscript I had started writing. Additionally, his foreword puts the saga of Krausenstrasse 17/18 in its wider historical context.

My editor at Ankerwycke, Jon Malysiak, was a perfect delight to work with. I am truly thankful that this book was in his experienced hands. Thanks to Tahiti Spears who did a splendid job in capturing the mood of the story in her cover, also to Betsy Kulak for all the work she did on the interior design and the photo insert, and to Marisa L'Heureux who shepherded it through the production process from copyedited manuscript to the finished book.

Of course my children, Daniel, Rachel and Joshua have lived this story almost their entire lives. I thank them for their patience and interest and hope they feel, as I do, that I have rescued from oblivion a large part of their family history and legacy.

Only one person always believed in me. My husband, Simon, enthusiastically threw himself into the project from the outset. Without his steadfast assistance and encouragement, the case would not have been pursued as vigorously as it was. And without his support, this book would never have been written.

Dina Gold
August 2016
Washington, D.C.

INDEX

BOOK CLUB DISCUSSION QUESTIONS

1. This book focuses on three strong female characters. Which do you think is the strongest? Nellie, who left Germany with her children? Annemarie/Aviva, who grew up far away from her family? Or the author, who reclaimed her family's stolen property?
2. Many Holocaust survivors do not want to talk about the past and what they went through. The author writes about her mother having the same feeling. Was the author's mother right to tell her to forget about reclaiming the building? What made her feel this way and why do you think the author chose to ignore her and pursue the case?
3. The book's title is *Stolen Legacy*. Apart from the building, what else was stolen from the Wolff family?
4. Were the human weaknesses and conflicts between members of the family, as related in the book, a necessary part of the story?
5. Who is your favorite character and why?
6. Why do you think the author shows so little emotion?
7. In the book's foreword, Ambassador Stuart E. Eizenstat writes that "there are several important lessons we discover from this impressive book" including how difficult it has been to get property returned to original owners and how people are still able to find, more than 70 years after the end of the war, evidence that enables them to seek belated justice. Are there any other lessons that can be learned?
8. Fritz Wolff felt more German than Jewish. He was incarcerated in Spandau prison in 1933 and Sachsenhausen concentration camp in 1938. On May 31, 1939, Fritz wrote a letter to his sister-in-law Nellie

in which he said, "I maintain that this whole quarrel is a love quarrel between nations. . . . If there is ever any question about which nation I belong to, the only answer is Germany."

Can you imagine what made him think this way after all he had been through? Can you empathize with him for not leaving Germany when he had the chance?

9. Dr. Kurt Hamann, chairman of the Victoria Insurance Company, which foreclosed on the Jewish-owned building at Krausenstrasse 17/18, had a foundation named in his honor. How do you think the University of Mannheim and ERGO—the current owner of the Victoria—should have responded to the author's revelations?

10. If you had been in Dr. Kurt Hamann's position between 1933 and 1945, what would you have done?

11. How do you judge Dr. Emil Herzfelder?

12. Is *Stolen Legacy* merely a Jewish story or does it have greater universality?

13. What was the most surprising part of this book to you?

14. Can you think of a different way of telling this story?

15. How important is this book to the teaching of Holocaust history?

STOLEN LEGACY BERLIN TOUR

Visitors to Berlin may be interested in going to the following locations related to *Stolen Legacy*:

- **Krausenstrasse 17/18.** (Near Checkpoint Charlie.) The Wolff building, now a federal government ministry, and renumbered as Krausenstrasse 17. Read the commemorative plaque on the front, placed there in 2016. Go to the back of the building on Schützenstrasse, now numbered 64, where the entry archway retains its original features. Note the carvings, unchanged since 1910 when the building's construction was completed.
- **Lindenstrasse 20-25.** (Ten minutes' walk to the east.) This was the headquarters of the Victoria Insurance Company in the 1930s and 1940s. Heavily damaged by bombing in 1945 it contains offices of various organizations but the edifice survives, bearing the words VICTORIA VERSICHERUNG in large letters.
- **Dresdener Strasse 97.** (Another ten minutes' walk further east.) This is the last address of Fritz Wolff before he was deported to Auschwitz in March 1943 and murdered. The actual building no longer exists but a *Stolperstein* (memorial stone) in honor of Fritz was placed in the nearby sidewalk in summer 2015.
- **Weissensee Jewish Cemetery.** (A cab ride to north-east Berlin.) The graves of the author's great-great and great grandparents are in section G4, on the southern wall of the cemetery, the closest to Jerusalem.
- **Fasanenstrasse Synagogue.** (A cab ride to west Berlin.) The synagogue attended by the Wolff family in the 1930s. It was

destroyed by a Nazi mob on Kristallnacht in November 1938. A Jewish community center has been built on the site.

- **Conradstrasse 1, Wannsee.** (A cab ride to the suburbs, about 10 miles west of the city center.) This is the childhood home of the author's mother. The original house still stands, as do the large wrought iron gates to the drive. Several houses have been built on what was once a park-like garden.
- **Am Grossen Wannsee 56-58.** (A ten minute walk to the north.) The House of the Wannsee Conference. Now a museum, this lakeside villa is where, in January 1942, senior Nazis planned the annihilation of Europe's Jews.
- **Sachsenhausen concentration camp.** (More than 20 miles north of Berlin.) Fritz Wolff was held here for two weeks after Kristallnacht in 1938.
- **The Memorial to the Murdered Jews of Europe (central Berlin).** The stark monument, located just south of the Reichstag and Brandenburg Gate, close to the location of Hitler's bunker.